Thought and Language

Lev Vygotsky

translation newly revised and edited by Alex Kozulin

The MIT Press
Cambridge, Massachusetts
London, England

This book was set in Baskerville by Achorn Graphic Services, and printed and bound in the United States of America.

Library of Congress Cataloging-in-Publication Data

Vygotskiĭ, L. S. (Lev Semenovich), 1896–1934.
 Thought and language.

 Translation of: Myshlenie i rech'.
 Bibliography: p.
 Includes index.
 1. Psycholinguistics.   2. Thought and thinking.
3. Language acquisition.   4. Child psychology.
I. Kozulin, Alex.   II. Title.
P37.V94 1986   401'.9   85-24040
ISBN 0-262-22029-6
ISBN 0-262-72010-8 (pbk.)

20 19 18 17 16

Frontispiece of Lev Vygotsky and facing title page from the original
Russian edition (1934) of *Thought and Language*

Л. С. ВЫГОТСКИЙ

МЫШЛЕНИЕ и РЕЧЬ

ПСИХОЛОГИЧЕСКИЕ ИССЛЕДОВАНИЯ

Под редакцией
и со вступительной статьей
В. КОЛБАНОВСКОГО

ГОСУДАРСТВЕННОЕ
СОЦИАЛЬНО-ЭКОНОМИЧЕСКОЕ ИЗДАТЕЛЬСТВО
МОСКВА 1934 ЛЕНИНГРАД

Contents

Vygotsky in Context

The bits and pieces of information we have been able to gather about Vygotsky's life portray him as a strange transplant from the era of encyclopedists and romantics to the age of commissars and conditional reflexes. A student of literature, philosophy, and esthetics, Vygotsky plunged into psychology at the age of twenty-eight, and died of tuberculosis ten years later. A prodigal reader, he felt equally at home with commentaries on Shakespeare's tragedies, the philosophy of Hegel, and clinical studies of the mentally retarded. A profound theoretician, he was also a man of practice who founded and directed a number of research laboratories, including the first Russian Institute for the Study of Handicapped Children. As Stephen Toulmin so aptly remarked, Vygotsky carried an aura of almost Mozartian giftedness. And yet he lived in times that were hardly favorable to Mozarts.

I

We do not know much about Vygotsky's life. He left no memoirs, and his biography has yet to be written. That leaves us with the task of putting together the scattered reminiscences of Vygotsky's friends and coworkers.

Lev Semenovich Vygotsky was born in 1896 in the town of Orscha in Belorussia to a middle-class Jewish family. His father, a manager with the United Bank of Gomel, was obviously an educated person and even a kind of philanthropist—he actively supported the local public library. His son's education was unconventional; Lev studied with a private tutor for many years, and enrolled in a Jewish gymnasium only at the junior high school level. By the age of eighteen Vygotsky already had become an accomplished intellectual—his essay on *Hamlet,* which later became an integral part of *The Psychology of Art* (1925), was written at that time.

According to Semyon Dobkin, Vygotsky's school friend, Vygotsky was particularly interested in the philosophy of history and was a recognized leader of a small circle of high school students concerned with the problems of Jewish culture and history. "Vygotsky was at that time very enthusiastic about the Hegelian view of history. His mind was then engaged by the Hegelian formula 'thesis, antithesis, synthesis. . . .' "[1]

Although Vygotsky's interests clearly belonged to the humanities and social sciences, at the insistence of his parents he applied to the Medical School of Moscow University. Since he had graduated from the gymnasium with honors and a gold medal, Vygotsky's chances for admission were good, even though the university's quota for Jews was only three percent. But a new executive order of the minister of education, issued in 1913, jeopardized these hopes, for while preserving the quota, it required Jewish applicants to be enrolled by casting lots, making admission not a matter of mental attainment but of blind luck. Vygotsky was, naturally, pessimistic about his chances. But then it happened—a cable came from Moscow informing him that he had been enrolled by the draw. One well may wonder whether it was this episode that later was to prompt Vygotsky to consider a role for the casting of lots in the organization of individual behavior.[2]

The years spent in Moscow, 1913–1917, became a period of intensive study and the acquisition of ideas from seemingly disparate fields. By his first semester at Moscow University, Vygotsky had already transferred from the Medical School to the Law School, apparently as a kind of compromise between his own wishes to draw closer to humanities and the practical wishes of his parents. But Vygotsky was not satisfied with the humanities courses at Moscow University. Many of Moscow University's leading professors had left to protest the repressive actions of the minister of education; some of these professors subsequently taught at private Shaniavsky University, which for a short while became a center of academic liberalism and innovation. Without dropping out of Moscow University, Vygotsky enrolled at Shaniavsky as well, majoring in history and philosophy.

Moscow in the 1910s was quite an exciting place for a young intellectual. Unorthodox and innovative trends in science, the humanities, and the arts were emerging, and it seems that Vygotsky pursued them all. Theater, among other things, became a focus of his interests. He admired Stanislavsky's Art Theater, and later used Stanislavsky's notes for actors in his *Myshlenie i rech,* translated into English as *Thought and Language.* Vygotsky was also fascinated by the innovative interpretation of *Hamlet* produced in Moscow by Gordon Craig.

As an aspiring literary critic, Vygotsky showed a keen interest in the "structuralist revolution" being carried out in linguistics and literary theory. Most probably it was his cousin, David, a member of the Petrograd Formalist School, who acquainted Vygotsky with the works of Roman Jakobson, Lev Jakubinsky, and Viktor Shklovsky. These names were soon to appear on the pages of Vygotsky's works dedicated to the problems of the psychology of art and the psychology of language.

Being a connoisseur of poetry, both classical and modern, Vygotsky did not hesitate to put poetic images in his psychological works. He was particularly interested in the poetic treatment of the agony endured when thought seeks, but cannot find expression in, words. It is in the context of that problem that the lines of the poets Tiutchev, Gumilev, and Mandelstam appear in *Myshlenie i rech.*

Philosophy was among Vygotsky's favorite subjects. His lifelong interest in Spinoza was possibly prompted by his sister Zinaida, who, while studying at Moscow Women's University College, chose Spinoza as the topic of her graduate paper. Vygotsky sought in Spinoza an alternative to Cartesian dualism, which, by splitting the human being into machinelike body and spiritual mind, established for centuries to come the conflict between materialistic, scientific psychology and idealistic, philosophical psychology. In his works Vygotsky reveals a penetrating knowledge of philosophers as diverse as Descartes, Hegel, Marx, the neo-Kantians, Husserl, and James.

Upon graduating from Moscow University in 1917, Vygotsky went to Gomel, where his parents were then living, and where the October Revolution of 1917 was to find him. The years in Gomel, 1918–1924, were to be a germinating period for Vygotsky's psychological thought. On the surface, life was hardly cheerful. Vygotsky's health started deteriorating: "He was unwell, it was difficult to get food, and there was tuberculosis in their family."[3] Teaching literature in a provincial school also hardly fit Vygotsky's aspirations. However, he soon left the school for a position at a local teachers' college. It was at this college that Vygotsky delivered his first lectures in psychology, and for the first time encountered the problem of the education of the physically handicapped, the problem to which he was to return more than once.

The titles of the books he was reading from those years

in Gomel give some idea of the direction in which Vygotsky's thought was moving. According to Dobkin, Vygotsky had a keen interest in James's *The Varieties of Religious Experience,* Freud's *Psychopathology of Everyday Life,* and *Thought and Language,* the book of the nineteenth-century Russian linguist and follower of Humboldt, Alexander Potebnja. The impact of these studies on his views of the unconscious, religious experience, and language is seen in Vygotsky's first large research project, *The Psychology of Art.* Vygotsky finished the manuscript in 1925 and presented it as a Ph.D. thesis at the Moscow Institute of Psychology. *The Psychology of Art* was first published, in Russian, only in 1965 (the English translation appeared in 1971[4]).

Although it is very tempting to venture into an extensive analysis of this masterpiece of the young Vygotsky, I shall limit myself to a couple of comments. First, the very title of Vygotsky's book suggests that to him psychology was a method of uncovering the origins of higher forms of human consciousness and emotional life rather than of elementary behavioral acts. This preoccupation with specifically *human* functions, in opposition to merely *natural* or *biological* ones, was to become a trademark of Vygotsky's lifework. Moreover, it suggests that Vygotsky never believed that psychological inquiry should be considered as a goal in itself. For him, culture and consciousness constituted the actual *subject* of inquiry, while psychology remained a conceptual tool, important but hardly universal.

Second, in the very beginning of *The Psychology of Art* Vygotsky argued that psychology cannot limit itself to direct evidence, be it observable behavior or accounts of introspection. Psychological inquiry is *investigation,* and like the criminal investigator, the psychologist must take into account indirect evidence and circumstantial clues—

which in practice means that works of art, philosophical arguments, and anthropological data are no less important for psychology than direct evidence.

In the case of *The Psychology of Art,* certain structuralist literary approaches together with the psychoanalytic concept of catharsis supplied him with the method of inquiry into the perception of works of art. In later works Vygotsky turned to other concepts and different methods, but he never ceased to uphold the principle of reconstructing psychological phenomena from data seemingly belonging to other disciplines. Although Vygotsky was to modify the ideas to be found in *The Psychology of Art,* the work bears clear signs of intellectual maturity. With this work, Vygotsky, still in his late twenties and never to receive formal psychological training, emerged as an original thinker, with his own ideas on what constitutes the subject and the method of psychological study.

II

Vygotsky entered professional psychology impetuously, one may say in an onslaught. On 6 January 1924 the Second Psychoneurological Congress was held in Leningrad. Vygotsky delivered a talk on "The Methodology of Reflexological and Psychological Studies." His thesis was simple: Scientific psychology cannot ignore the facts of consciousness. Taking aim at the reflexologists, Vygotsky argued that while reflexes provide the foundation of behavior, we can learn nothing from them about the "construction" erected on this foundation—which means that neither the category of consciousness nor that of the unconscious can be ignored. Studies of the Würzburg School, as well as those of the Gestaltists, should be incorporated into scientific psychology. This statement must be considered in the context of the times. It challenged the position of leading Soviet behavioral scientists, from

Pavlovians to Bekhterev and Blonsky, who either viewed consciousness as an idealist superstition or limited its sphere of applicability to descriptive, nonscientific psychology. But there was at least one receptive listener in that audience, Alexander Luria. In Luria's account, "Instead of choosing a minor theme, as might benefit a young man of twenty-eight speaking for the first time to a gathering of the graybeards of his profession, Vygotsky chose the difficult theme of the relation between conditioned reflexes and man's conscious behavior. . . . Although he failed to convince everyone of the correctness of his view, it was clear that this man from the small provincial town in western Russia was an intellectual force who would have to be listened to."[5]

Luria's enthusiastic recognition of Vygotsky had very practical consequences. Although only twenty-six years old at that time, Luria already held the position of academic secretary at the Moscow Institute of Psychology, and he managed to persuade its director, Konstantin Kornilov, to invite Vygotsky as a research fellow. In the fall of 1924, Vygotsky and his wife Roza (née Smekhova) moved to Moscow.

In its initial stage, Vygotsky's program for the new, nonreflexological scientific psychology contained the following directions: It had to be developmental; it had to resolve the problem of interrelation between higher mental functions and the lower, elementary psychological functions; and it had to take socially meaningful activity (*Tätigkeit*) as an explanatory principle. But before turning this sketch into an articulated research program, Vygotsky felt obliged to take on the theoretical crisis in psychology, the result of which was *The Historical Meaning of the Crisis in Psychology*, finished in 1926, but published only half a century later, in 1982.[6] (Vygotsky's *Crisis* does not stand alone as a critique of psychology as practiced in the 1920s. *Die Krise der Psychologie* of Karl Bühler ap-

peared only a few months after Vygotsky finished his
work, and the writings of the Swiss psychoanalyst Ludwig
Binswanger and the German-American Hugo Münsterberg antedated Vygotsky's concern with the *method* of
psychology.)

From the outset of his book, Vygotsky claimed that his
intention was to bring forth a "methodological," that is,
metapsychological, analysis of the crisis in psychology.
His position, therefore, was that of a theoretician who
assesses the crisis from the "outside," rather than that of a
professional psychologist tied to some partisan point of
view. Psychological scholarship in the 1920s fell into a
number of schools—behaviorism, reflexology, psychoanalysis, Gestalt psychology, and so on—which challenged each other on theoretical or methodological
grounds. Vygotsky went beyond affirming this state of
affairs to showing that not only their theoretical and
methodological approaches but their very facts were incompatible. In doing so he introduced, with great effec-
tiveness, a notion that much later was to become popular
in the philosophy of science as "theoretically laden facts":
"Any fact, being expressed in terms of these systems
[introspectionism, behaviorism, and psychoanalysis]
would acquire three entirely different meanings, which
indicate three different aspects of this fact, or more precisely, three different facts."[7] A group of facts existent in
one system sometimes simply disappears in the other. To
Pavlovians, the idea that a dog *remembers* food in the instant the bell rings sounds fantastic. To psychoanalysts,
the Oedipus complex is an empirical fact; to behaviorists,
it is a fiction.

Vygotsky arrived at the conclusion that the divisions
among the systems of psychology were so serious and
their basic theoretical premises so liable to various interpretations that we should speak here of different sciences
rather than of a number of schools within one science.

More than that, some of these systems of psychology were so closely connected with philosophy and the humanities that there was no reason to squeeze them into the conceptual framework of science.

It is of interest that more than fifty years after Vygotsky, Sigmund Koch came to a somewhat similar conclusion in a work marking the hundredth year since psychology had taken to itself a place among the sciences.[8] Almost repeating Vygotsky, Koch claimed that the nineteenth-century myth of psychology as a unified science did not and could not sustain the test of time; psychology is, rather, a collection of studies having absolutely different theoretical foundations and methodologies.

Vygotsky, however, was not content with asserting the divergences within psychological scholarship. Tracing the evolution of psychoanalysis, reflexology, Gestaltism, and personalism, he revealed a uniform pattern to their development, an aggressive expansion in a desperate attempt to attain methodological hegemony. The first stage in the development of each of these systems is an empirical discovery that proves to be important for the revision of the existing views concerning some specific behavioral or mental phenomena. In the second stage of its development, the initial discovery acquires a conceptual form, which expands so as to come to bear on related problems of psychology. Even at this stage the ties between conceptual form and the underlying empirical discovery are eroded; the former becomes an abstraction almost unrelated to the latter, existing, however, because of the reputation built upon the latter. The third stage is marked by the transformation of the conceptual form into an abstract explanatory principle applicable to any problem within the given discipline. The discipline is captured by this expanding explanatory principle—all behavior turns out to be a sum of conditional reflexes, or unconscious

motifs, or gestalts. At this moment the explanatory principle loses its power, since nothing is left outside it, but
the inertia of expansion pushes it until the whole domain
of psychology is absorbed by it. At the fourth stage the
explanatory principle disengages itself from the subject
matter of psychology and becomes a general methodology applicable to all fields of knowledge, at which point—
Vygotsky observed—it usually collapses under the
weight of its enormous explanatory claims. It ceases to
exist as an independent intellectual principle and merges
with one of the dominant philosophies or worldviews.
Vygotsky suggested that upon becoming a worldview the
"psychological idea reveals its social origin, which earlier
was concealed under the guise of a fact of knowledge."[9]

The uniform character of the development of the
schools of psychology indicated to Vygotsky the necessity
for some "general psychology" that would provide a
methodological guide for all the psychological disciplines. On the one hand, the enormous and illegitimate
methodological claims of particular psychological systems
were nothing but the symptoms of crisis; on the other
hand, however, these symptoms could be understood as
the genuine and legitimate desire to have a general
methodology of psychological research. Vygotsky made it
clear that only epistemologically competent metapsychological analysis of the current state of psychological
knowledge could provide a genuine general methodology—what he called "general psychology." To the question, Where may the resolution of the crisis come from?,
Vygotsky gave a dialectically sharpened answer: From
the crisis itself! For this purpose, however, the crisis
should be reconsidered as a positive, rather than as a
negative, phenomenon. To comprehend the crisis as a
positive phenomenon—that is, to see it through the
Hegelian concept of "contradiction"—means to discover
those forces that stand behind the apparent dispute over

the "need" to become a general methodology. The basic contradictions underlying all symptoms of crisis should therefore be considered as the moving force in the development of psychology at any given historical moment.

Following the theoretical analysis undertaken by Hugo Münsterberg in his *Grundzüge der Psychotechnik* of 1914, Vygotsky applied epistemological analysis to distinguish two major poles of attraction dividing all psychological systems: the naturalist and idealist worldviews. The crisis brought about naturalistic scientific psychology and philosophical descriptive psychology. Objective historical development of the contrasting worldviews turned out to be a hidden source of the crisis.

Another source was practical psychology. Vygotsky observed a major difference between so-called applied psychology, which is secondary to that particular system from which it has sprung, and a genuine practical psychology, which elaborated its methods in the context of its own practice. For example, the applied psychology of Münsterberg, which started from idealist premises, was "forced" to arrive at naturalistic conclusions. Approaching practical problems, psychologists change their a priori conceptual schemas along the lines dictated by practice itself. Practice, therefore, joins philosophy as a force pushing psychological systems toward the opposite poles of naturalism and idealism.

Vygotsky almost prophetically foresaw the concentration of psychological systems at the opposite centers of behaviorism and phenomenology. Modern developments show that Vygotsky was not mistaken in his diagnosis. Behaviorism and the theory of conditional reflexes have become the ultimate manifestation of naturalistic experimentalism, while philosophic and humanistic studies have grouped around the phenomenological paradigm. But the label "science," according to Vygotsky, had to be reserved for the naturalistic studies; phenomenology had to break ranks with the scientific paradigm and openly approach its subject with the help of the methods developed in philosophy and the humanities. This lobbying on behalf of behaviorism and other naturalistic approaches might seem inconsistent with his concern with the higher mental functions. Vygotsky, however, clearly indicated that his diagnosis of the crisis did not imply satisfaction with the existing systems of naturalistic psychology. He emphasized that "the question still remains open, whether we have a right to call psychology precisely a naturalistic science. Only because West European psychology had never known social psychology, it identified its subject as that of naturalistic science."[10]

The last section of the *Crisis* is devoted to discouraging attempts to find a "third way" other than that of scientific or philosophical psychology. In Vygotsky's view, three major attempts of this kind had been made: by Gestalt psychology, by the personalism of William Stern, and by so-called Marxist psychology. In the case of Gestalt-psychology, Vygotsky asserted that objectively, and sometimes even against the will of its own masters, this discipline had gradually become a part of the naturalistic tradition and lost its image as a "third way." As to Stern's personalistic psychology, Vygotsky held that the development took the opposite course. Starting with the concrete scientific problems of differential psychology, Stern had arrived at an avowedly idealistic, teleological theory of the psyche, and proceeding in this direction, had failed to establish an independent "third way" for psychology, merging instead with the philosophical tradition.

Vygotsky directed his strongest criticisms, however, against those of his colleagues who ventured to establish Marxist psychology as an alternative to naturalism and idealism. Vygotsky's refutation of the Marxist psychology of Konstantin Kornilov and others was threefold: these scholars sought Marxist support "in the wrong places"; they assimilated "the wrong material"; and they used this material "in a wrong way."[11] Vygotsky strongly opposed the method of casually picking and choosing quotations from the classics of Marxism. He also emphasized that the dialectical method is quite different in biology, history, and psychology, and that therefore there are no Marxist magic formulas for solving the problems of psychology. "Immediate application of the theory of dialectical materialism to the problems of science, and particularly to biology and psychology, is impossible, as it is impossible to apply it instantly to history and sociology."[12] No one philosophical system, including Marxism, would be able to help psychology until it had established an intermediate link in the form of methodology. The only legitimate way for Marxism to become useful for psychology was in its possible contribution to general methodology. "Any other 'contributions' . . . would inevitably lead to mere scholastic verbiage."[13]

For the rest of his life Vygotsky desperately sought this new methodology that would make psychology scientific, but not at the cost of the naturalization of cultural phenomena, and that would make use of the Marxist method without degenerating into "Marxist psychology."

Vygotsky's research program started taking shape in his early paper "Consciousness as a Problem of Psychology of Behavior" (1925). The major goal of that paper was to restore the legitimacy of the concept of consciousness, but not at the expense of the return to introspective mentalistic psychology. The major objection Vygotsky had to the mentalistic tradition was that it confined itself to a vicious circle in which states of consciousness are "explained" by the concept of consciousness. Vygotsky argued that if one is to take consciousness as a *subject* of study, then the *explanatory principle* must be sought in some other layer of reality. Vygotsky suggested that socially meaningful activity (*Tätigkeit*) may play this role and serve as a generator of consciousness.

Vygotsky's first step toward concretization of this principle was the suggestion that individual consciousness is built from outside through relations with others: "The mechanism of social behavior and the mechanism of consciousness are the same. . . . We are aware of ourselves, for we are aware of others, and in the same way as we know others; and this is as it is because in relation to ourselves we are in the same [position] as others are to us."[14]

One cannot but find a striking similarity between this statement and the concept of significant symbol developed by George H. Mead: "As we shall see, the same procedure which is responsible for the genesis and existence of mind or consciousness—namely, the taking of the attitude of the other toward one's self, or toward one's own behavior—also necessarily involves the genesis and existence at the same time of significant symbols, or significant gestures."[15] It seems that Mead's revision of behaviorism and Vygotsky's struggle for consciousness had much in common—both authors pointed to the same phenomena and followed similar methodological paths.

According to Vygotsky, human higher mental functions must be viewed as products of *mediated* activity. The role of mediator is played by *psychological tools* and means of interpersonal communication. The concept of a psychological tool first appeared in Vygotsky's thought by loose analogy with the material tool, which serves as a mediator between the human hand and the object upon which the tool acts. Vygotsky obviously was under the influence of the Hegelian notion of "cunning of reason": reason's mediating activity, which, by causing objects to act and react on each other in accordance with their own nature, in this way, and without any direct interference in the process, carries out reason's intentions. Like material tools, psychological tools are artificial formations. Both are naturally social but while material tools are aimed at the control over processes in nature, psychological tools master natural forms of individual behavior and cognition. Although sensory-motor schemas connected with practical actions also may become psychological tools, the latter usually have a *semiotic* nature. Psychological tools are internally oriented, transforming the natural human abilities and skills into higher mental functions (Vygotsky noted such psychological tools as gestures, language and sign systems, mnemonic techniques, and decision-making systems—for example, casting dice). For example, if an elementary effort at memorization connects event A with event B through the natural ability of the human brain, then in mnemonics this relation is replaced by A to X and X to B, where X is an artificial psychological tool—a knot in a handkerchief, perhaps, or a written note.

Vygotsky thus made a principal distinction between "lower," natural mental functions, such as elementary perception, memory, attention, and will, and the "higher," or cultural, functions, which are specifically human and appear gradually in a course of radical transformation of the lower functions. The lower functions do not disappear in a mature psyche, but they are structured and organized according to specifically human social goals and means of conduct. Vygotsky used the Hegelian term "superseded" (*aufgehoben*) to designate the transformation of natural functions into cultural ones.

If one decomposes a higher mental function into its constituent parts, one finds nothing but the natural, lower skills. This fact, argued Vygotsky, secures the scientific status of his method, which needs no speculative metaphysical categories in order to approach the higher forms of behavior. All the "building blocks" of higher behavior seem absolutely materialistic and can be apprehended by ordinary empirical methods. The latter assumption does not imply, however, that a higher function can be reduced to lower ones. Decomposition shows us only the material with which the higher functions are built, but says nothing about their construction.

The constructive principle of the higher functions lies outside the individual—in psychological tools and interpersonal relations. Referring to psychological tools as instruments for the construction of higher functions, Vygotsky wrote, "In the instrumental act, humans master themselves from the outside—through psychological tools."[15] As to the structural role of interpersonal relations, Vygotsky followed Pierre Janet, who claimed that intrapersonal processes are just transformed interpersonal relations: "Each function in the child's cultural development appears twice: first, on the social level, and later, on the individual level; first, between people (interpsychological), and then inside the child (intrapsychological)."[17]

In concrete experimental practice, the idea of *internalization* of psychological tools acquired two different, and ultimately even conflicting, forms. Internalization as the process of transformation of external actions into internal psychological functions was thoroughly studied by such followers of Vygotsky as Peter Zinchenko, Alexander Zaporozhets, and Peter Galperin. Their studies undoubtedly had much in common with Piaget's concept of the development of intelligence through the internalization of sensory-motor schemas. Vygotsky himself, however, was much more interested in the problem of internalization of symbolic psychological tools and social relations. He was greatly impressed by the works of the French sociological school of Emile Durkheim and by related ideas of Maurice Halbwachs, Charles Blondel, and Pierre Janet, who studied the internalization of so-called collective representations.

To understand in what direction Vygotsky's thought

was moving, consider the following problem: How does the indicatory gesture appear in a child's behavioral repertoire? At first it is simply an unsuccessful grasping movement directed at an object. Vygotsky used the term "gesture-in-itself" to designate this stage of the development of gesture. When mother comes to the aid of the child, the situation acquires a different character. Gesture "in-itself" becomes gesture "for-others." Others (mother in our case) interpret the child's grasping movement as an indicatory gesture, thus turning it into a socially meaningful communicative act. Only afterward does the child become aware of the communicative power of his movement. He then starts addressing his gesture to adults, rather than to an object, which was the focus of his interest in the first place. It is essential that the child be the last person who consciously apprehends the meaning of his own gesture. Only at this later stage does a gesture become a "gesture-for-oneself."

The focus of Vygotsky's research program in the period 1926–1930 happened to be the experimental study of the mechanism of transformation of natural psychological functions into the higher functions of logical memory, selective attention, decision making, and comprehension of language. Besides Alexander Luria and Alexei Leontiev, who joined Vygotsky as early as 1924, his group of collaborators included Lidia Bozhovich, Alexander Zaporozhets, Natalia Morozova, Roza Levina, Liya Slavina, Lev Sakharov, and Zhozephina Shif. Studies were developing along three avenues of research: instrumental, developmental, and cultural-historical.

The instrumental approach centered on the use of external means, that is, psychological tools in facilitating of the development of higher forms of memory, attention, and decision making. Here the 1932 study of Alexei Leontiev on natural and instrumentally mediated memory remains a classic.[18] In that study children were asked to memorize several colors "forbidden" according to the rules of the game required by the study (that is, these colors were not to be named while answering the experimenter's questions). Colored cards were offered to the children as possible aids. The results showed that children of preschool age failed to make use of the colored cards. They made as many mistakes, naming forbidden colors, with cards as without them. Adolescents, on the contrary, used cards extensively, separating out forbidden ones and consulting them before they answered. The percentage of mistakes was much higher when the experiment was conducted without cards. It is interesting that for adults the performance with cards was not significantly better than without them, although in both cases it was better than for adolescents. Vygotsky explained this as a result of internalization. Adults do not cease to use psychological tools to structure their memory, but their tools are emancipated from the material form of a color card. The external sign that schoolchildren require is transformed by adults into an internal sign.

In considering the developmental and cultural-historical approaches, it must be borne in mind that throughout his career, Vygotsky insisted on the developmental (*geneticheskii*—from genesis) method of study as essential for scientific psychology. Vygotsky's use of the term *geneticheskii* requires some terminological classification. He used it with reference to a philosophical tradition in the Hegelian and Marxist modes, according to which the essence of any phenomenon could be apprehended only through a study of its origin and history. For that reason one term, development, was applied to both the individual (ontogenetic) and the cultural-historical evolution of mental functions.

In calling his psychology developmental, Vygotsky meant much more than a mere analysis of the ontogenetic unfolding of behavior. As a matter of fact, the very idea of development as unfolding and maturation was alien to him. Vygotsky perceived psychological development as a dynamic process full of upheavals, sudden changes, and reversals. He singled out two major misunderstandings that limit the progress of developmental psychology. One is a reductionist position that tries to explain the higher forms of behavior and mental life by means of principles established for elementary functions. The second one, a mirror image of the first that historically appeared as a sort of corrective measure, simply transfers the explanatory principle, like that of structure or gestalt, found in the investigation of higher forms of behavior to the study of lower ones. These two misleading tendencies are equally blind to the important fact that the principles of natural development do not coincide with those of cultural development.

Vygotsky suggested that the new developmental approach must be built upon three concepts: higher mental functions, cultural development, and mastering one's own behavioral processes. Vygotsky further elaborated that "the structure of behavioral development to some degree resembles the geological structure of the earth's core. Research has established the presence of genetically differentiated layers in human behavior."[19] The older layers do not die out when the new emerges, but are superseded by it. The conditional reflex, for example, is "copied" in intellectual action, simultaneously existing and not existing in it. Thus psychology is faced with a double task: to be able to distinguish the lower stages imbedded in the higher, but also to reveal how the higher stages mature out of the lower ones. One and the same psychological formation (for example, a concept) may have a number of "geologically" different layers, and will play different roles depending on which layer is activated. The task of developmental study, therefore, cannot be confined to the investigation of the progressing complexity of such functions as perception, attention, and memory; it must also inquire into the inner evolution going on in psychological formations that at the first glance may seem to be well developed. (A summary of Vygotsky's earliest developmental studies were set forth in his monograph *History of the Development of Higher Mental Functions,* which was finished in 1931, but published, in unabridged form, only in 1983.[20])

Although Vygotsky's theory embraced all higher mental functions, Vygotsky himself was primarily interested in the development of language in its relation to thought. Language and speech occupy a special place in Vygotsky's psychological system because they play a double role. On the one hand, they are a psychological tool that helps to form other mental functions; on the other hand, they are one of these functions, which means that they also undergo a cultural development. Vygotsky's work in this field became his most popular book: *Myshlenie i rech—Thought and Language.*[21]

Like many of his other works, Vygotsky's *Myshlenie i rech* is in the form a critical dialogue in which the survey of conflicting approaches is interspersed with experimental data and theoretical constructions. The participants in this imaginative dialogue in *Myshlenie i rech* are William Stern, Karl Bühler, Wolfgang Köhler, Robert Yerkes, and, above all, Jean Piaget.

A few words are in order here concerning Vygotsky's presentation of experimental material. Quantitative methods and operationalistic descriptions were not a significant feature of Soviet psychology in the 1920s, and Vygotsky, in particular, emphasized ideas and arguments in his monographs intended for the general educated audience, reserving experimental details for technical reports. After all, the number of professional psychologists in Russia at that time was so insignificant that each of them knew all the others, making it easy for them to clarify the experimental details in the technical reports of their fellow psychologists. As a result, *Myshlenie i rech* may strike some nowadays as inadequately grounded in experimental data, even as careless. However, the studies by Vygotsky's followers have shown that the basic findings are sound, and that argument may arise only as to the interpretation of these findings.

Vygotsky's first objective in *Myshlenie i rech* was to show that thought and speech have different roots, merging only at a certain moment in ontogenesis, after which these two functions develop together under reciprocal influence. In its historical context, this thesis constituted a critique of those who either identified thought with speech (J. B. Watson) or, on the contrary, absolutized their differences. Vygotsky's thesis called instead for an *interfunctional* interpretation of higher mental functions. As was mentioned earlier, Vygotsky's initial concept of higher mental function focused on the transformation of natural functions into cultural functions under the influence of psychological tools. Further research convinced him that of even more importance was the interaction of different higher mental functions, forming thereby so-called functional systems: "Studying the development of thought and speech in childhood, we found that the process of their development depends not so much on the changes within these two functions, but rather on changes in the primary relations between them. . . . Their relations and connections do not remain constant. That is why the leading idea is that there is no constant formula of relation between thought and speech that would be applicable to all stages and forms of development or involution. Each of these stages has its own characteristic form of relation between these two functions."[22]

Vygotsky elaborated this thesis in his critical review of

the phylo- and ontogenetic studies of Köhler, Yerkes, and Bühler (*Myshlenie i rech,* chapter 4). He concluded that the primate shows certain elements of humanlike intelligence in its use of primitive tools and implements and that at the same time its language has such human aspects as phonetics, emotional expression, and primordial social meaningfulness. What is lacking in the primate, Vygotsky held, is a close reciprocal relation between thought and language—their interfunctional relations are in a prehistorical stage. In ontogenesis Vygotsky also made a distinction between the roots of speech and those of thought. A child's development knows preintellectual speech as well as nonverbal thought; only with the establishment of interfunctional systemic unity does thought become verbal, and speech become intellectual.

Vygotsky was able to establish the concept of interfunctional relations on an experimental basis only to the extent (and even then only partially) of the sign-concept connection (*Myshlenie i rech,* chapter 5); his follower Alexander Luria succeeded, however, in basing this concept on much richer material, and eventually made it a cornerstone of his neuropsychological theory. Vygotsky's experiments in concept formation were designed in accordance with the Ach-Sakharov sorting test, in which a triplet of letters, that is, a "sign," was affixed to each object to be sorted. Vygotsky described his experimental procedures as a method of double stimulation, presuming that the physical properties of objects to be grouped constitute one form of stimulation, while triplets of words provide the other, semiotic, stimulation. Experimental data obtained indicated to him a long and complex developmental process leading from classification based on unorganized congeries of physical characteristics of objects, through the stages of "complex" and "pseudoconceptual" thinking, to mature forms of classification based on conceptual thinking.

Vygotsky's hypothesis concerning the "geological" character of concepts was fully confirmed. For example, "flat, triangular, and green" turned out to be a dynamic formation, having different characteristics at different stages of psychological development. One of the most important discoveries in Vygotsky's study is "pseudoconceptual" thinking: a form of child's reasoning that phenotypically coincides with reasoning in the adult and yet has a different, preconceptual nature. In this respect Vygotsky's study resembled very much those of Heinz Werner. It is not surprising that Werner's followers enthusiastically used Vygotsky's sorting test in their studies of the preconceptual thinking of schizophrenic patients.[23] Vygotsky observed in addition that preconceptual, and even mythological, thinking not only is characteristic of children and the mentally ill, but also forms the basis of the everyday, normal reasoning of adults. This latter insight, like many others, was neglected by Vygotsky's followers, and the problem of preconceptual forms of everyday intelligence has remained practically untouched in Soviet studies.

In the work of Vygotsky's student Zhozephina Shif the study of concept formation was extended to its educational setting (*Myshlenie i rech*, chapter 6). Different forms of childhood experience were put into correspondence with stages in the development of concept formation. In this connection, Vygotsky had distinguished two basic forms of experience, which give rise to two different, albeit interrelated, groups of concepts: the "scientific" and the "spontaneous." Scientific concepts originate in the highly structured and specialized activity of classroom instruction and impose on a child logically defined concepts; spontaneous concepts emerge from the child's own reflections on everyday experience. Vygotsky made it a point to argue that scientific concepts, far from being assimilated in a ready-made form, actually undergo substantial development, which essentially depends on the existing level of a child's general ability to comprehend concepts. This level of comprehension, in its turn, is connected with the development of spontaneous concepts. Spontaneous concepts, in working their way "upward," toward greater abstractness, clear a path for scientific concepts in their "downward" development toward greater concreteness.

Two forms of learning responsible for concept formation were thus distinguished. One of them, systematically organized learning in an educational setting, later attracted the attention of Soviet psychologists and was thoroughly investigated in the works of Peter Galperin and Vasili Davydov.[24] The much less articulated spontaneous learning turned out to be perceived rather as an obstacle on the road to concept formation, and its characteristic features were mostly neglected. There is a certain irony in this turn of events, for Vygotsky argued at length against Piaget's preoccupation with spontaneous concepts at the expense of scientific concepts. Vygotsky's followers made the opposite mistake by neglecting spontaneous concepts and centering all their attention instead on scientific concepts. As a result, concept formation in children became a one-sided process.

A study of concept formation in educational setting led Vygotsky to another insight, namely, the dialogical character of learning. In his analysis Vygotsky departed from what he perceived as the inability of Piaget's theory to reconcile the spontaneous character of a child's reasoning with the scientific—and thus the adult—nature of concepts learned at school. Where Piaget saw confrontation, Vygotsky sought dialogue. Vygotsky was also critical of those methods of mental testing that routinely took into account only the problem-solving progress made by the child who is left on his own. Vygotsky argued that the progress in concept formation by a child achieved in cooperation with an adult would be a much more sensitive gauge of the child's intellectual abilities. In this connection, Vygotsky used the term *zo-ped*, "the zone of proximal development": the place at which a child's empirically rich but disorganized spontaneous concepts "meet" the systematicity and logic of adult reasoning. As a result of such a "meeting," the weaknesses of spontaneous reasoning are compensated by the strengths of scientific logic. The depth of *zo-ped* varies, reflecting children's relative abilities to appropriate adult structures. The final product of this child-adult cooperation is a solution, which, being internalized, becomes an integral part of the child's own reasoning.

The last of the major problems discussed in *Myshlenie i rech* is the phenomenon of inner speech (chapters 2 and 7). The problem of inner speech enters Vygotsky's discourse twice: the first time in the context of polemics with Piaget concerning child egocentrism, and the second time in connection with a problem of the personal senses of words. Vygotsky challenged Piaget's thesis that the inherent autism of a child's thought manifests itself in egocentric speech. According to Piaget, autism is the original, earliest form of thought; logic and socialized speech, from his point of view, appear rather late, and egocentric thought is the genetic link between autism and logic. Vygotsky, who repeated some of Piaget's experiments, insisted, however, that the earliest speech of the child is already social. At a certain age this original social speech becomes rather sharply divided into egocentric speech, that is, speech-for-oneself, and communicative speech-for-others. Egocentric speech, splintered off from general social speech, gives rise to inner speech. Inner speech is therefore a rather late product of the transformation of a speech that earlier had served the goals of communication into individualized verbal thought.

In Piaget's view, however, the uniqueness of speech-for-oneself, which is incomprehensible to others, is rooted in the child's original autism and egocentrism, and ultimately in the pleasure principle. In the course of the child's development this individual specch dies out, giving place to socialized speech, which is easily understood by any interlocutor, and which is ultimately connected with the reality principle.

Without denying the phenomenon of autism as such, Vygotsky suggested that egocentric speech is rather a transitory form situated between social, communicative speech and inner speech. For Vygotsky the major problem was not that of socialization, but rather of individualization of the originally communicative speech-for-others. As was mentioned earlier, Vygotsky believed that the outward, interpsychological relations become the inner, intrapsychological mental functions. In the context of this idea, the transition from egocentric to inner speech manifests the internalization of an originally communicative function, which becomes individualized inner mental function. Peculiarities of grammar and syntax characteristic of inner speech indicate this submergence of communication-for-others into individualized reasoning-for-oneself: in inner speech, culturally prescribed forms of language and reasoning find their individualized realization. Culturally sanctioned symbolic systems are remodeled into individual verbal thought. The principal steps in this remodeling include the transition from overt dialogue to internal dialogue.

The problem of interpersonal communication and intrapersonal communication (*obschenie*) thus appeared at the forefront of Vygotsky's theory. An objective development of his ideas now required that the typology of semiotic means of mediation should be complemented by the typology of the overt and inner dialogues in which culture acquires its psychologically individualized form. Unfortunately Vygotsky had no time to develop this aspect of his study; he just outlined it, mentioning that the difference in the conditions of social interaction between children in different settings plays a decisive role in understanding the coefficients of egocentric speech. The children observed by Piaget, the children observed by William Stern in German kindergartens, and the children observed by Vygotsky—all had different social milieus and consequently different types of communication shaping the processes by which they developed verbal thought.

Vygotsky returned to the problem of inner speech in connection with a study of generalization versus contextualization of word meaning. He made a distinction between word meaning (*znachenie*), which reflects a generalized concept, and word sense (*smysl*), which depends on the context of speech. The sense of a word is the sum of all the psychological events aroused in a person's consciousness by the word. It is a dynamic, complex, fluid whole, which has several zones of unequal stability. Meaning is only one of the zones of sense, the most stable and precise zone. A word acquires its sense from the context in which it appears; in different contexts, it changes its sense.

According to Vygotsky, the predominance of sense over meaning, of sentence over word, and of context over sentence are rules of inner speech. While meaning stands for socialized discourse, sense represents an interface between one's individual (and thus incommunicable) thinking and verbal thought comprehensible to others. Inner speech is not an internal aspect of talking; it is a function in itself. It remains, however, a form of speech, that is, thought connected with words. But while in external speech thought is embodied in words, in inner speech words must sublimate in order to bring forth a thought. In inner speech two important processes are interwoven: the transition from external communication to inner dialogue and the expression of intimate thoughts in linguistic form, thus making them communicative. Inner speech becomes a psychological interface between, on the one hand, culturally sanctioned symbolic systems and, on the other hand, private "language" and imagery. The concretization of psychological activity in this context appears as a psychological mechanism for creating new symbols and word senses capable of eventually being incorporated into the cultural stock.

This was a return on Vygotsky's part to the enigmatic problem of artistic and intellectual creativity, which, apparently, had not left his mind since *The Psychology of Art* (1925). In Vygotsky's view, the process of artistic or intellectual creation is antipodal to the process of internalization. In creative activity, inner context-dependent senses gradually unfold their meanings as symbols-for-others. Vygotsky remarked (*Myshlenie i rech,* chapter 7) that in titles like *Don Quixote,* the entire sense of a book is contained in one name. Initially such a name is meaningful only in the context of a plot conceived in the author's head. But in being "exteriorized," that is, becoming a literary fact, Don Quixote ceases to be merely the name of a character and acquires meaning immediately recognized by any educated person. Name, thus, becomes a generalized concept.

Vygotsky intrepidly overstepped here the border of strictly psychological discussion, plunging into the much broader subjects of human creativity and cultural formation. This was not strange for Vygotsky, however; after all, he had started as a literary critic, and for a number of years, considered psychology a temporary diversion from his main studies, which were literature and art. But, as it turned out, psychological "diversions" were to occupy him for the rest of his life. He remained, however, an outsider with respect to psychology, no matter how paradoxical it sounds nowadays, when he is widely regarded as the father of Soviet psychology. His approach was essentially "methodological," focused on the elaboration of what is or ought to be the *subject* of psychological inquiry, and which *method* of study psychology should take on to fit its objectives; but such a task belongs not so much to professional psychology as to philosophy. Moreover, from *The Psychology of Art* on, Vygotsky refused to consider experimentally elicited behavior or mental operations as the sole legitimate material for psychological research. He emphasized that psychological inquiry is akin to criminal investigation, relying on circumstantial, indirect evidence; in such roundabout investigation, works-of art, manifestations of unconscious and cultural-anthropological data, play no less important role than direct responses. It is not surprising, therefore, that Vygotsky the philosopher and humanist was mostly rejected by professional psychology, dominated as it was by behaviorists in the West and reflexologists in the East. His "methodological" approach and his concern with semiotic means of psychological mediation were innovative, but they challenged the accepted views of the discipline of psychology.

Although *Myshlenie i rech* undoubtedly marks a high point in Vygotsky's career, it was by no means its conclusion. There were other avenues of research opened by Vygotsky, many of which he only partly explored. One was the study of the mediating role of signs taken in their cultural-historical context. The concept of historical transformation of higher mental functions under the influence of changing forms of mediation was theoretically elaborated by Vygotsky and Luria in their book *Essays in the History of Behavior* (1930). To reinforce their theoretical conjectures with empirical observations, Vygotsky and Luria organized an expedition to remote parts of Soviet Central Asia, the objective of which was to study the psychological changes that followed the rapid and radical socioeconomic and cultural restructuring taking place in the 1930s in Soviet Uzbekistan, where historically distinctive layers of society then coexisted: living on high mountain pastures "as if nothing had happened," collective farm workers receiving minimal schooling, and students studying at a teachers' college.

The study included experiments in classification, concept formation, and problem solving. It concluded that illiterate peasants failed to perform abstract acts of classification, either grouping objects according to principes of usefulness or lumping them all together according to the dictates of practical situations; farm workers who had received minimal schooling accepted the task of abstract classification without difficulty, but used the situational mode as well, especially when they tried to reason independently; and young people who had had a year or two of school training easily picked up the abstract notions of class, group, and similarity—the process of abstract categorization seemed to them a natural and self-evident procedure.

The conclusion of this field study, which was executed by Luria and coworkers, fully confirmed the basic tenets of Vygotsky and Luria's cultural-historical theory. For illiterate peasants, speech and reasoning simply echoed the patterns of practical, situational activity, while for people with some education the relation was reversed: abstract categories and word meanings dominated situational experience and restructured it. Although this study opened interesting perspectives on cross-cultural research and suggested parallels with ontogenetic material, it came under fire from critics for its alleged resem-

blance to the "bourgeois speculations" of Emile Durkheim.
The results were refused publication, and the very theme
of cultural development was forbidden in the Soviet
Union for the next forty years. Only in 1974 did Luria
publish his material.[25]

Vygotsky was aware of the possible one-sidedness of
his research program, which was devoted almost exclusively to the development of intellectual functions. On
the last pages of *Myshlenie i rech* he wrote that "thought
does not beget another thought," that the last "whys" of
psychological inquiry inevitably lead to the problem of
motivation. It is not surprising; therefore, that one of the
last works of Vygotsky, which remained unfinished, addressed the problem of emotions. The first part of this
work bears the title *A Study of Emotions: A Historical-
Psychological Investigation* and was finished in 1933 (published in 1984).[26] In *A Study of Emotions* Vygotsky
returned to the problem he had raised in *The Historical
Meaning of the Crisis in Psychology* (1926), namely, the phenomenon of the "gravitation" of modern psychological
systems to the opposite poles of naturalism and mentalism, except that the subject of the later work is the James-
Lange theory of emotions, as viewed in its relation to the
Cartesian dualistic tradition. *A Study of Emotions* demonstrates that the frequently mentioned resemblance between James-Lange theory and Spinoza's concept of
passions in reality does not exist. It further argues that
unlike Descartes—who is the real precursor of James-
Lange theory—Spinoza sought a synthetic concept of
emotions that would eliminate Cartesian dualism. Vygotsky showed here how the dualistic approach inevitably
divided psychology, be it of the seventeenth or the twen-
tieth century, into mechanistic naturalism and metaphysical mentalism. One may only speculate that in the second
part of his work Vygotsky would have attempted to draw

parallels between Spinoza's synthetic approach and his own struggle in behalf of a nonnaturalistic scientific psychology.

The picture of Vygotsky's work and achievements would be incomplete if I were to fail to mention his involvement in applied research. There are three major areas where Vygotsky matched his experimental studies with practical applications: educational psychology, studies of mentally and physically handicapped children, and psychopathology. The application of the concept of higher mental function to educational psychology was summarized in *The Pedology of the Adolescent* (1929).[27] The title is a reflection of the thinking of those times, when pedology was a widely used term, meant to designate an interdisciplinary approach to child development, a sort of a scientific basis for pedagogics. Vygotsky, naturally, also used this term, having no idea that in the mid-1930s pedology would be banned as a "bourgeois deviation" and former pedologists blacklisted.

Vygotsky's interest in both the development and involution of higher mental functions led him to tackle the problem of the development of higher mental functions in physically and mentally handicapped children. Vygotsky was instrumental in the establishment of the Institute for the Study of Handicapped Children, which still remains the leading Soviet research center dealing with the problems of handicapped. Some of Vygotsky's students, notably Zhozephina Shif, became prominent specialists in this field. Numerous papers of Vygotsky addressing the problem of cognitive rehabilitation of handicapped children were reprinted in volume 5 of his *Collected Papers* (1983).

Finally, a study of preconceptual forms of thinking in children led Vygotsky to a broader study of preconceptual intelligence, including psychopathologies. Vygotsky identified some characteristic features of "schizophrenic logic" and speech. Results of his studies were published in English as "Thought in Schizophrenia" (1934)[28] and inspired further studies in this direction by the American psychologists Eugenia Hanfmann and Jacob Kasanin.

III

The early 1930s were destined to become a critical period in the development of Soviet psychology. Stalin, who had pronounced 1929 "the year of great breakthrough," was clearly tightening party control over the fringes of culture and science. Soviet psychologists could hardly show any group resistance, for they were engaged in a bitter struggle with each other. Each of the rival groups claimed to be the closest to the Marxist ideal of objective science. At the height of their polemics, ideological labels and political insinuations were used liberally. In this atmosphere of intolerance, psychology became an easy prey to the party apparatchiks, and soon all independent trends in psychology were suppressed. From then on Soviet psychologists were expected to derive psychological categories directly from the works of Marx, Engels, and Lenin.[29]

Such a turn of events seriously undermined Vygotsky's research program, which relied upon such "bourgeois" theories and methods as psychoanalysis, Gestalt psychology, and the cross-cultural analysis of consciousness. All these trends were labeled anti-Marxist, and Vygotsky's work pronounced "eclectic" and "erroneous." Luria's field study in the cross-cultural development of thinking was severely criticized for its alleged bias against national minorities. Luria was also forced to renounce his interest in psychoanalysis. One might guess that these events had something to do with Luria's decision to change his field of study and to concentrate on the clinical aspects of neuropsychology.[30] Alexei Leontiev also obviously ran into some troubles. The exact circumstances remain obscure because the official Soviet biography of Leontiev simply states that "in 1930 the constellation of circumstances forced Alexei Nikolaevich [Leontiev] to resign from the Academy of Communist Education and to leave his [teaching] position at the State Institute of Cinematography."[31]

Vygotsky, who was already gravely ill, continued working in Moscow until 1934, when an attack of tuberculosis led to his death. Even before the death of their leader, a group of Vygotsky's students, which included Leontiev, Zaporozhets, and Bozhovich, had decided on leaving Moscow for the Ukrainian city of Kharkov, where they eventually established a program in developmental psychology. Studies conducted by the Kharkov group between 1934 and 1940 centered on the problem of internalization and the relation in a child between external activities and corresponding mental operations. The Kharkovites developed an extensive experimental program for comparing the external sensory-motor activity of a child with his mental actions and outlining their respective morphologies. It was their general conclusion that the structure of cognitive processes more or less repeats the structure of external operations. From this circle of studies came some of the notions that much later, in the 1960s, were to be accepted as the basic premises of Soviet developmental psychology, among them Zaporozhets's concept of "perception as action" and Peter Galperin's concept of the "step-by-step formation of intellectual actions."

The Kharkovites solved the problem of the relation between consciousness and activity in the following way: "The development of the consciousness of a child occurs as a result of the development of the system of psychological operations, which, in their turn, are determined by the actual relations between a child and reality."[32] This insistence on the "actual relations with reality" became a major point of disagreement between the Kharkovites and Vygotsky. As Michael Cole has accurately observed, "As even a superficial reading of this work indicates, Leontiev and the young researchers who worked with him established a good deal of a distance between themselves and their teacher Vygotsky."[33]

It is very tempting to attribute this distancing to extrascientific factors. In 1936 a special Decree of the Communist Party was issued condemning pedology (roughly, interdisciplinary educational psychology). Vygotsky's theory, which had been severely criticized before, now became a real heresy because its author had collaborated with pedologists. Moreover, the thesis of "actual relations with reality" fitted the Soviet dialectical-materialistic credo of the 1930s much better than Vygotsky's more complex cultural-historical model.

Nevertheless, there are solid grounds for believing that Leontiev's revisionism, apart from its ideological benefits, did have serious scientific underpinnings—that even if Vygotsky had not become a "persona non grata," Leontiev and his group most probably would still have challenged some of his basic notions. Ideological cautiousness, honest scientific disagreement, and also a misunderstanding of certain of Vygotsky's ideas—all were intricately interwoven in the phenomenon that later became known as Leontiev's theory of activity.

As I have mentioned, the dispute centered on the problem of the relations between consciousness, activity, and reality. The Kharkovites insisted that it is practical acquaintance with and the use of objects that leads the child toward the cognitive mastery of situations which hardly departs from Vygotsky's thesis "from action to thought." And yet the studies that stand behind this view resemble those on generalization and transfer far more than those on the effect of the involvement of psychological tools—the Kharkovites have played down the role of signs as the chief mediators. This is an attack not on a peripheral, but on a central notion of the cultural-historical theory.

As the Kharkovite Peter Zinchenko has argued, "One of the most basic of all problems, the conceptualization of the nature of mind, was incorrectly resolved. The central characteristic of the human mind was thought to be *mastery* of the natural or biological mind through the use of auxiliary psychological means. Vygotsky's fundamental error is contained in this thesis, in which he misconstrued the Marxist conception of the historical and social determination of the human mind. Vygotsky understood the Marxist perspective idealistically. The conditioning of the human mind by social and historical factors was reduced to the influence of human culture on the individual. The source of mental development was thought to be the interaction of the subject's mind with a cultural, ideal reality rather than his actual relationship to reality."[34] In a word, Zinchenko claimed that practical activity provides a mediation between the individual and reality, while Vygotsky insisted that such an activity, in order to fulfill its role as a psychological tool, must necessarily be of a semiotic character.

Vygotsky's theory was attacked by Zinchenko both in general and in particular. Zinchenko's general, theoretical, critique centered on Vygotsky's inclination to oppose the natural, biological functions to the higher, culturally mediated, psychological functions. Zinchenko argued that such an approach will ruin any attempt to understand the early stages of mental development as psychological rather than as physiological: "This loss of the 'mental' in the biological stage of development produced a situation in which the human mind was contrasted with purely physiological phenomena."[35] Vygotsky in this view, had overinflated the role of semiotic means of mediation: "[Vygotsky] began with the thesis that the mastery of the sign-means was the basic and unique feature of human memory processes. He considered the central feature of any activity of remembering to be the relation of the means to the object of that activity. But in Vygotsky's thinking, the relation of the means to the object was divorced from the subject's relation to reality considered in its actual and complete content. In the strict sense, the relation between the means and the object was logical rather than psychological. But the history of social development cannot be reduced to the history of the development of culture. Similarly, we cannot reduce the development of the human mind—the development of memory in particular—to the development of the relation of 'external' and 'internal' means to the object of activity. The history of cultural development must be included in the history of society's social and economic development; it must be considered in the context of the particular social and economic relations that determine the origin and development of culture. In precisely this sense, the development of 'theoretical' or 'ideal' mediation must be considered in the context of the subject's real, practical relations with reality, in the context of that which actually determines the origin, the development, and the content of mental activity."[36]

Concerning memory studies (the focus of his own experimental work), Zinchenko suggested approaching involuntary memory as a psychological, rather than as a physiological, phenomenon and seeking its roots in children's practical activities. Zinchenko's experiments revealed that a child remembers either pictures or numbers depending upon which one of these two groups of stimuli plays an active role in the child's activity, which in both cases was not an activity of memorization but of classification. Zinchenko emphasized that it is the involvement of the stimuli in the activity of classification that ensures their involuntary memorization. Involuntary memory in the child thus appeared, on the one hand, as a psychological rather than as a natural, biological function and, on the other hand, as a process intimately connected with practical activity, rather than with the means of semiotic mediation. In order to challenge Vygotsky's position, Zinchenko would have his readers believe—incorrectly, in my opinion—that Vygotsky saw no difference between natural, eidetic memory and involuntary memorization. Zinchenko also choose to ignore Luria's cross-cultural study, which had showed, in the framework of the concept of psychological tools, a number of stages in the development of higher mental functions, one of them closely resembling the phenomenon of practical thinking revealed in the experiments of the Kharkovites.

The major theoretical disagreement between the Kharkovites' position and Vygotsky's was epitomized by Zinchenko's statement that "social development cannot be reduced to the history of the development of culture." While in Vygotsky's theory, activity as a general explanatory principle finds its concretization in the specific, culturally bound types of semiotic mediation, in the doctrine of the Kharkovites, activity assumes a double role: as a general principle and as a concrete mechanism of mediation. However, in order to be socially meaningful, the concrete actions have to be connected in some way with human social and economic relations with reality. The task of elaborating this overall structure of activity was taken up by Leontiev.

The first sketch of Leontiev's theory of psychological activity appeared in his *Essays on the Development of the Mind* (1947), which was followed by the very popular *Problems of the Development of the Mind* (1959/1982) and *Activity, Consciousness, and Personality* (1978). Leontiev suggested the following breakdown of activity—activity corresponding to a motive, action corresponding to a goal, and operation dependent upon conditions: "The main thing which distinguishes one activity from another, however, is the difference of their objects. It is exactly the object of an activity that gives it a determined direction. According to the terminology I have proposed, the object of an activity is its true motive."[37]

Entering human activity, its object loses its apparent naturalness and appears as an object of collective, social experience: "Consequently, it is the activity of others that provides an objective basis for the specific structure of individual activity. Historically, that is, in terms of its origin, the connection between motive and object of activity reflects objective social, rather than natural relations."[38] For example, food as a motive for human activity already presupposes a complex structure of the division of labor. Such a division provides a basis for differentiation of activities and actions: "The actions that realize activity are aroused by its motive but appear to be directed toward a goal. . . . For satisfying the need for food [one] must carry out actions that are not aimed directly at getting food. For example, the purpose of a given individual may be preparing equipment for fishing. . . ."[39] Motives thus belong to the socially structured reality of production and appropriation, while actions belong to the immediate reality of practical goals. "When a concrete process is taking place before us, external or internal, then from the point of its relation to motive, it appears as human activity, but when it is subordinated to purpose, then it appears as an action or accumulation of a chain of actions."[40] Psychologically, activity has no constituent elements other than actions. "If the actions that constitute activity are mentally subtracted from it, then absolutely nothing will be left of activity."[41] And yet activity is not an additive phenomenon; it is realized in actions, but its overall social meaning cannot be devised from the individual actions.

At this point Leontiev's concept of activity ran into serious theoretical trouble, which did not fail to catch the attention of his opponents, Sergei Rubinstein and his students. While discussing human activity (*Tätigkeit*) in general, Leontiev used such categories of Marxist social philosophy as production, appropriation, objectivation, and disobjectivation. These categories apply to the social-historical subject, rather than to the psychological individual. At the same time, "actual relations with reality" were sought by Leontiev in the concrete practical actions and operations of the individual. The intermediate link between these two facets of activity—which Vygotsky identified as culture in general and the semiotic systems in particular—has been lost because of the rejection of Vygotsky's position. Rubinstein, who noticed this gap in Leontiev's theoretical schema, accused him of "illegitimate identification of the psychological problem of mastering operations with the social process of the disobjectivation of the social essence of Man."[42]

Rejecting semiotic mediation, and insisting on the dominant role of practical actions, the Kharkovites had obliged themselves to elaborate the connection between the philosophical categories of production and objectivation and the psychological category of action. Leontiev, however, was reluctant to provide such an elaboration, substituting for it a standard "sermon" on the alienation of activity under capitalism versus the free development of personality in socialist society.[43] Moreover, when Leontiev made an attempt to outline the forms of human consciousness corresponding to activity, he chose to use the categories of meaning and sense, rather than those of internalized operations. In this way he unwittingly acknowledged the advantage of Vygotsky's approach. This theoretical inconsistency also did not pass unnoticed by his critics, who claimed that "although the concept of object orientedness of the psyche aims at derivation of the specificity of psyche from the practical, and even the material, activity of society, actually it turns out that this *practical activity* . . . becomes identified as a system of *social meanings.* . . . One important point remained, however, unnoticed here, namely, that although social modes of action do find their fixation in meanings, the latter represent the forms of *social consciousness,* and by no means the forms of *social practice.*"[44]

Unfortunately, Rubinstein's students made no distinction between Leontiev and Vygotsky, and their critiques remained mostly unheeded by those who chose to work in the framework of Vygotsky's tradition. Moreover, this critique was often perceived as an assault on the cultural-historical theory as such.

Beginning in the late 1950s the relations between Leontiev's concept of activity and Vygotsky's theoretical legacy took a new form. As was the case with many others, Vygotsky, and his ideas, was "rehabilitated" in the course of de-Stalinization. Some of his works were reprinted, and some published for the first time.[45] Once again it became fashionable to be considered his follower. By this time, former Kharkovites were solidly established in Moscow: Leontiev had become chairman of the Division of Psychology at Moscow University; Zaporozhets had founded and become director of the new Institute for Pre-School Education; and Galperin, Bozhovich, and Elkonin had attained senior professorships at Moscow University and the Moscow Institute of Psychology.

In 1963, Leontiev's *Problems of the Development of the Mind* won the Lenin Prize for scientific research and thus achieved the status of official Soviet psychological doctrine. It was not difficult for Leontiev under these circumstances to gain the status of Vygotsky's official interpreter; indeed, his interpretation enjoyed a wider circulation than the original texts. Gradually Vygotsky came to be regarded as a mere predecessor of Leontiev, a predecessor who made some theoretical mistakes later rectified in Leontiev's theory. In his preface to the 1956 edition of Vygotsky's *Selected Psychological Investigations,* Leontiev reasserted his own interpretation of activity, suggesting that Vygotsky's emphasis on signs as the principal psychological tools was not essential for cultural-historical theory, and that his own theory was in fact the authentic realization of Vygotsky's research program.[46]

In the later 1970s, however, Leontiev's theory came under critical scrutiny. This criticism originated partly in the works of the younger psychologists, like Vasili Davydov and Vladimir Zinchenko, who, although brought up in the shadow of Leontiev's theory, managed to recognize its limits and disadvantages. Another factor prompting reevaluation was the rediscovery of some of Vygotsky's works, published as the *Collected Papers* (1982–1984). The critical trend was further strengthened by certain Soviet philosophers interested in the problem of activity.

Leontiev's theory of activity, having been elevated to the level of an all-embracing psychological doctrine, had run into the problem against which Vygotsky had warned in his early paper "Consciousness as a Problem of Psychology of Behavior" (1925): using the notion of activity at one and the same time as an explanatory principle and as a subject of concrete psychological study. By "explaining" the phenomena of activity by means of the principle of activity, a vicious circle was created (mentioned by Vygotsky in his critique of mentalism—"consciousness through consciousness"—and behaviorism—"behavior through behavior").

In philosophically elaborated form, the distinction between activity as an explanatory principle and activity as a subject of scientific inquiry was made by Eric Yudin.[47] Yudin's point of departure was the restoration of the connection between the notion of activity and its original meaning as elaborated in the philosophy of Hegel and Marx, an effort justified by the fact that the psychologists often neglected the theoretical roots of the very concepts over which they argued. Yudin emphasized that it was Hegel who had made activity a universal explanatory principle, thus reversing the individualistic model of human conduct advanced by the empiricists. In Hegel's philosophical theory, the individual appears as an "organ" of activity; activity, in its role as the ultimate explanatory principle, cannot be reduced to the manifestations of individual consciousness—on the contrary, these manifestations are referred to activity as their real source.

Yudin further pointed out that activity could also become a subject of concrete scientific study; but in this case (and this is a crucial point)—the structural elements elaborated in behalf of activity as an explanatory principle will be irrelevant. Activity as a subject of psychological study should have its own system of structural elements, and even its own explanatory principles. One and the same notion of activity cannot successfully carry out both functions simultaneously. But this is precisely what had happened in Leontiev's theory—structural elements of activity (activity-action-operation and motive-goal-condition) once suggested as the elaboration of the explanatory principle, were later used in the context of the subject of study.

It was another philosopher of psychology, Georgy Schedrovitsky, who, addressing a colloquium on Vygotsky in 1979, challenged the myth of succession and suggested that Leontiev's theory substantially deviated from Vygotsky's program. Schedrovitsky emphasized that the principle of semiotic mediation and the role of culture in Vygotsky's theory were by no means accidental or transient; only with their help could the tautological explanation of activity through activity be avoided.

The polemics surrounding Vygotsky's theoretical legacy continue. All leading Soviet psychologists feel obliged to express their views on this subject: Some have addressed the problem of semiotic mediation;[48] some have attempted to reintegrate Vygotsky's ideas concerning signs as mediators into Leontiev's theory.[48] But what is probably more important, Vygotsky's theory "has gone public"; it has broken the linguistic, cultural, and ideological barriers and is about to become a topic of international interest and study.

IV

The first attempts to acquaint the Western, and particularly the American, audience with Vygotsky's ideas were undertaken as early as the 1930s, when Jacob Kasanin commissioned and subsequently translated Vygotsky's paper "Thought in Schizophrenia" (1934). Some excerpts from *Myshlenie i rech* were published in 1939.[50] But in those years only a very narrow circle of American psychologists, primarily those associated with Heinz Werner and Kurt Goldstein, appreciated Vygotsky's contributions. At a time when neobehaviorism and learning theory remained the grass-roots ideology of American psychology, one could hardly expect enthusiastic acceptance of Vygotsky's cognitive and cultural-historical ideas.

Things changed in the 1960s, when American psychology gradually freed itself from the spell of behavioristic mentality and the Soviets rediscovered Vygotsky and reprinted his works. The growing popularity of Jean Piaget also contributed to the change in intellectual climate that made Vygotsky's ideas welcome. Finally, in 1962

Myshlenie i rech was published in English as *Thought and Language* (Cambridge, MA: MIT Press, 1962).

With that publication Vygotsky became well known to those interested in developmental psychology and psycholinguistics. And yet that important development was marred by omissions made by translators and editors set on removing those portions of Vygotsky's work, including certain essential psychological discussions and broader philosophical ideas, that they perceived as redundant or obsolete. As a result, Vygotsky the theoretician and polemicist somehow disappeared from this English version of *Thought and Language,* and American psychologists, being on the whole unaware that they were dealing with an edited rather than a complete version of Vygotsky's work, were led into various misunderstandings. For example, Jerry Fodor's review of *Thought and Language* went so far as to criticize Vygotsky for the lack of an articulated philosophical position: "Psychologists have not been able to stop doing philosophy. . . . But they *have* often managed to stop noticing when they are doing philosophy, and from not doing it consciously, it is a short step to not doing it well. Vygotsky's book is a classic example of this state of affairs. What Vygotsky wanted to do was pursue a straightforward 'scientific' investigation. . . ."[51] The irony is that these remarks repeat almost verbatim Vygotsky's critique of Piaget—a critique that was omitted in the English translation.

For a while Vygotsky remained known as the author of just one book. The situation changed in the late 1970s, however, when, mostly as a result of the efforts of Michael Cole and James Wertsch, a broader range of Vygotsky's writings, including some chapters from *The History of the Development of Higher Mental Functions,* started to appear in English.[52] But what is probably more important, Vygotsky's ideas ceased to be viewed as an exotic fruit of Soviet psychology and started to take root in the American soil. Such Vygotskian concepts as inner speech, psychological tools, semiotic mediation, and the "zone of proximal development" proved their heuristic value in a number of experimental studies subsequently collected in *Culture, Communication, and Cognition: Vygotskian Perspectives,* edited by J. Wertsch.[52] These later developments marked the close of the introductory period in the process by which the West familiarized itself with Vygotsky and justified a revised, accurate English-language edition of *Myshlenie i rech.*

This new translation is based on the 1934 edition of *Myshlenie i rech,* the only one actually prepared—although imperfectly—by Vygotsky himself. In it I have sought to follow Vygotsky's line of thought as closely and fully as possible, departing from it only when it repeats itself or when the logic of Russian discourse cannot be directly rendered in English. Substantial portions of the 1962 translation made by the late Eugenia Hanfmann and Gertrude Vakar have been retained.

One last word. Being well aware that he was losing in his struggle with tuberculosis, Vygotsky had no time for the luxury of including well-prepared references in *Myshlenie i rech.* Often he simply named a researcher without mentioning any exact work. At the same time, many of his references are now obscure figures. Therefore to place Vygotsky's work in its proper context requires explanatory notes. Such notes, to be found immediately after the text, were specially prepared for this edition. Those taken from Vygotsky's text are indicated by his initials, L.V.; all others were written by myself. The notes also contain portions from Piaget's "Comments," published as a supplement to the first edition of *Thought and Language.*[54]

Alex Kozulin
Boston University, 1985

Note on the Title

Although *Myshlenie i rech* should be rendered in English as *Thought and Speech,* it has been decided to retain the rendering *Thought and Language,* which has become the standard English translation since the first MIT Press edition.

Author's Preface

This book is a study of one of the most complex problems in psychology, the interrelation of thought and speech. As far as we know, this problem has not yet been investigated experimentally in a systematic fashion. We have attempted at least a first approach to this task by conducting experimental studies of a number of separate aspects of the total problem: experimentally formed concepts, written language in its relation to thought, inner speech, etc. The results of these studies provide a part of the material on which our analyses are based.

Theoretical and critical discussions are a necessary precondition of and a complement to the experimental part of the study and constitute a large portion of our book. The working hypotheses that serve as starting points for our fact-finding experiments had to be based on a general theory of the genetic roots of thought and speech. In order to develop such a theoretical framework, we reviewed and carefully analyzed the pertinent data in the psychological literature. We subjected to critical analysis those contemporary theories that seemed richer in their scientific potential, and that thus could become a starting point for our own inquiry. Such an inquiry from the very beginning has been in opposition to theories that, although dominant in contemporary science, nevertheless call for review and replacement.

Inevitably our analysis encroached on neighboring disciplines, such as linguistics and the psychology of education. In discussing the development of scientific concepts in childhood we made use of a working hypothesis concerning the relation between the educational process and mental development that we had evolved elsewhere using a different body of data.

The structure of this book is perforce complex and multifaceted; yet all its parts are oriented toward a central task, the genetic analysis of the relation between thought and the spoken word. Chapter 1 poses the problem and discusses the method. Chapters 2 and 3 are critical analyses of the two most influential theories of the development of language and thinking, Piaget's and Stern's. Chapter 4 attempts to trace the genetic roots of thought and language; it serves as a theoretical introduction to the main part of the book, the two experimental investigations described in the next two chapters. The first of these investigations (chapter 5) deals with the general developmental course of word meanings in childhood; the second (chapter 6) is a comparative study of the development of the "scientific" and the spontaneous concepts of the child. The last chapter [chapter 7] attempts to draw together the threads of our investigations and to present the total process of verbal thought as it appears in the light of our data.[1]

It may be useful to enumerate briefly the aspects of our work that we believe to be novel and consequently in need of further careful checking. Apart from our modified formulation of the problem and the partially new method, our contribution may be summarized as follows: (1) providing experimental evidence that meanings of words undergo evolution during childhood, and defining the basic steps in that evolution; (2) uncovering the singular way in which the child's "scientific" concepts develop, compared with his spontaneous concepts, and formulating the laws governing their development; (3) demonstrating the specific psychological nature and linguistic function of written speech in its relation to thinking; and (4) clarifying, by way of experiments, the nature of inner speech and its relation to thought. The evaluation of our findings and of the interpretations we have given them is hardly the author's province and must be left to our readers and critics.

The author and his associates have been exploring the field of language and thought for almost ten years, in the course of which some of the initial hypotheses were revised, or abandoned as false.[2] The main line of our investigation, however, has followed the direction taken from the start. In this work we have tried to explicate the ideas that our previous studies contained only implicitly. We fully realize the the inevitable imperfections of this study, which is no more than a first step in a new direction. Yet we feel that in uncovering the problem of thought and speech as the focal issue of human psychology, we have made an essential contribution to progress. Our findings point the way to a new theory of consciousness, which is barely touched upon at the end of this book.

Thought and Language

1

The Problem and the Approach

The study of thought and language is one of the areas of psychology in which a clear understanding of interfunctional relations is particularly important. As long as we do not understand the interrelation of thought and word, we cannot answer, or even correctly pose, any of the more specific questions in this area. Strange as it may seem, psychology has never investigated the relation systematically and in detail. Interfunctional relations in general have not as yet received the attention they merit. The atomistic and functional modes of analysis prevalent during the past decade treated psychic processes in isolation. Methods of research were developed and perfected with a view to studying separate functions, while their interdependence and their organization in the structure of consciousness as a whole remained outside the field of investigation.

The unity of consciousness and the interrelation of all psychological functions were, it is true, accepted by all; the single functions were assumed to operate inseparably, in an uninterrupted connection with one another. But this unity of consciousness was usually taken as a postulate, rather than as a subject of study. Moreover, in the old psychology the unchallengeable premise of unity was combined with a set of tacit assumptions that nullified it for all practical purposes. It was taken for granted that the relation between two given functions never varied; that perception, for example, was always connected in an identical way with attention, memory with perception, thought with memory. As constants, these relations could be, and were, factored out and ignored in the study of the separate functions. Because the relations remained in fact inconsequential, the development of consciousness was seen as determined by the autonomous development of the single functions. Yet all that is known about psychic development indicates that its very essence lies in the change of the interfunctional structure of consciousness. Psychology must make these relations and their developmental changes the main problem, the focus of study, instead of merely postulating the general interrelation of all functions. This shift in approach is imperative for the productive study of language and thought.

A look at the results of former investigations of thought and language will show that all theories offered from antiquity to our time range between *identification,* or *fusion,* of thought and speech on the one hand, and their equally absolute, almost metaphysical *disjunction* and *segregation* on the other. Whether expressing one of these extremes in pure form or combining them, that is, taking an intermediate position but always somewhere along the axis between the two poles, all the various theories on thought and language stay within the confining circle.

We can trace the idea of identity of thought and speech from the speculation of psychological linguistics that thought is "speech minus sound" to the theories of modern American psychologists and reflexologists who consider thought a reflex inhibited in its motor part. In all these theories the question of the relation between thought and speech loses meaning. If they are one and the same thing, no relation between them can arise.

Those who identify thought with speech simply close the door on the problem.

At first glance it seems that the adherents of the opposite view—those who propound the idea of the independence of thought from speech—are in better position. In regarding speech as the outward manifestation, the mere vestment, of thought, and in trying (as does the Würzburg school)[1] to free thought from all sensory components including words, they not only pose but in their own way attempt to solve the problem of the relation between the two functions. Actually, however, they are unable to pose it in a manner that would permit a real solution. And if they do not avoid it, then they try to cut through the knot of the problem instead of untying it. Having made thought and speech independent and "pure," and having studied each apart from the other, they are forced to see the relation between them merely as a mechanical, external connection between two distinct processes. The analysis of verbal thinking into two separate, basically different elements precludes any study of the intrinsic relations between language and thought.

As an example we may recall a recent attempt of this kind. It was shown that speech movements facilitate reasoning. In a case of a difficult cognitive task involving verbal material, inner speech helped to "imprint" and organize the conscious content. The same cognitive process, taken now as a sort of activity, benefits from the presence of inner speech, which facilitates the selection of essential material from the nonessential. And finally, inner speech is considered to be an important factor in the transition from thought to external speech. This example is revealing for it shows that once analyzed into constituent elements, the verbal thinking becomes a system whose structural connections appear as mechanical and external to the system itself.

The fault thus lies in the *methods of analysis* adopted by previous investigators. To cope successfully with the problem of the relation between thought and language, we must ask ourselves first of all what method of analysis is most likely to ensure its solution.

Two essentially different modes of analysis are possible in the study of psychological structures. It seems to us that one of them is responsible for all the failures that have beset former investigators of the old problem, which we are about to tackle in our turn, and that the other is the only correct way to approach it.

The first method analyzes complex psychological wholes into *elements*. It may be compared to the chemical analysis of water into hydrogen and oxygen, neither of which possesses the properties of the whole and each of which possesses properties not present in the whole. The student applying this method in looking for the explanation of some property of water—why it extinguishes fire, for example—will find to his surprise that hydrogen burns and oxygen sustains fire. These discoveries will not help him much in solving the problem. Psychology winds up in the same kind of dead end when it analyzes verbal thought into its components, thought and word, and studies them in isolation from each other. In the course of analysis, the original properties of verbal thought have disappeared. Nothing is left to the investigator but to search out the mechanical interaction of the two elements in the hope of reconstructing, in a purely speculative way, the vanished properties of the whole.

In essence, this type of analysis, which leads us to products in which the properties of the whole are lost, may not be called analysis in the proper sense of this word. It is generalization, rather than analysis. The chemical formula for water is equally applicable to the water in a great ocean and to the water in a raindrop. That is why by analyzing water into its elements we shall get its most general characteristics rather than the individually specific.

This type of analysis provides no adequate basis for the study of the multiform concrete relations between thought and language that arise in the course of the development and functioning of verbal thought in its various aspects. Instead of enabling us to examine and explain specific instances and phases, and to determine concrete regularities in the course of events, this method produces generalities pertaining to all speech and all thought. It leads us, moreover, into serious errors by ignoring the unitary nature of the process under study. The living union of sound and meaning that we call the word is broken up into two parts, which are assumed to be held together merely by mechanical associative connections.

Psychology, which aims at a study of complex holistic systems, must replace the method of analysis into elements with the method of analysis into units. What is the unit of verbal thought that is further unanalyzable and yet retains the properties of the whole? We believe that such a unit can be found in the internal aspect of the word, in *word meaning*.

Few investigations of this internal aspect of speech have been undertaken so far. Word meaning has been lost in the ocean of all other aspects of consciousness, in the same way as phonetic properties detached from meaning have been lost among the other characteristics of vocalization. Contemporary psychology has nothing to say about the specificity of human vocalization, and concomitantly it has no specific ideas regarding word meaning, ideas that would distinguish it from the rest of cognitive functions. Such a state of affairs was characteristic of the old associationistic psychology, and it remains a sign of contemporary Gestalt psychology. In the word we recognized only its external side. Yet it is in the internal aspect, in word meaning, that thought and speech unite into verbal thought.

Our experimental, as well as theoretical analysis, suggests that both Gestalt psychology and association psychology have been looking for the intrinsic nature of word meaning in the wrong directions. A word does not refer to a single object, but to a group or to a class of objects. Each word is therefore already a generalization. Generalization is a verbal act of thought and reflects reality in quite another way than sensation and perception reflect it. Such a qualitative difference is implied in the proposition that there is a dialectical leap not only between total absence of consciousness (in inanimate matter) and sensation but also between sensation and thought. There is every reason to suppose that the qualitative distinction between sensation and thought is the presence in the latter of a *generalized* reflection of reality, which is also the essence of word meaning; and consequently that meaning is an act of thought in the full sense of the term. But at the same time, meaning is an inalienable part of word as such, and thus it belongs in the realm of language as much as in the realm of thought. A word without meaning is an empty sound, no longer a part of human speech. Since word meaning is both thought and speech, we find in it the unit of verbal thought we are looking for. Clearly, then, the method to follow in our exploration of the nature of verbal thought is semantic analysis—the study of the development, the functioning, and the structure of this unit, which contains thought and speech interrelated.

This method combines the advantages of analysis and synthesis, and it permits adequate study of complex wholes. As an illustration, let us take yet another aspect of our subject, also largely neglected in the past. The primary function of speech is communication, social intercourse. When language was studied through analysis into elements, this function, too, was dissociated from the intellectual function of speech. The two were treated as though they were separate, if parallel, functions, without attention to their structural and developmental interrelation. Yet word meaning is a unit of both these functions of speech. That understanding between minds is impossible without some mediating expression is an axiom for scientific psychology. In the absence of a system of signs, linguistic or other, only the most primitive and limited type of communication is possible. Communication by means of expressive movements, observed mainly among animals, is not so much communication as a spread of affect. A frightened goose suddenly aware of danger and rousing the whole flock with its cries does not tell the others what it has seen but rather contaminates them with its fear.

The rational, intentional conveyance of experience and thought to others requires a mediating system, the prototype of which is human speech born of the need of communication during work. In accordance with the dominant trend, psychology has until recently depicted the matter in an oversimplified way. It was assumed that the means of communication was the sign (the word or sound); that through simultaneous occurrence a sound could become associated with the content of any experience and then serve to convey the same content to other human beings.

Closer study of the development of understanding and communication in childhood, however, has led to the conclusion that real communication requires meaning—that is, generalization—as much as signs. In order to convey one's experience or thought, it is imperative to refer them to some known class or group of phenomena. Such reference, however, already requires generalization. Therefore, communication presupposes generalization and development of word meaning; generalization, thus, becomes possible in the course of communication. The higher, specifically human forms of psychological communication are possible because man's reflection of reality is carried out in generalized concepts. In the sphere of emotions, where sensation and affect reign, neither understanding nor real communication is possible, but only affective contagion.

Edward Sapir brilliantly showed this in his works: "The world of our experience must be enormously simplified and generalized before it is possible to make a symbolic inventory of all our experiences of things and relations, and this inventory is imperative before we can convey ideas. The elements of language, the symbols that ticket off experience, must therefore be associated with whole groups, delimited classes, of experience rather than with the single experiences themselves. Only so is communication possible, for the single experience lodges in an individual consciousness and is, strictly speaking, incommunicable" (Sapir, 1971, p. 12).

Sapir, therefore, considers a word meaning not as a symbol of a singular sensation, but as a symbol of a concept. And actually, if I like to convey the feeling of cold, I may do this with the help of expressive gestures, but real understanding and communication will be achieved only through generalization and conceptual designation of my experience. Such generalization would refer my experience to the class of phenomena known to my interlocutor. That is why certain thoughts cannot be communicated to children even if they are familiar with the necessary words. The adequately generalized concept that alone ensures full understanding may still be lacking. Lev Tolstoy, in his educational writings, says that children often have difficulty in learning a new word not because of its sound, but because of the concept to which the word refers: "There is a word available nearly always when the concept has matured" (Tolstoy, 1903, p. 143).

Therefore, we all have reasons to consider a word meaning not only as a union of thought and speech, but also as a union of generalization and communication, thought and communication.

The conception of word meaning as a unit of both generalizing thought and social interchange is of incalculable value for the study of thought and language. It permits true causal-genetic analysis, systematic study of the relations between the growth of the child's thinking ability and his social development. The interrelation of generalization and communication may be considered a secondary focus of our study.

It may be well to mention here some of the problems in the area of language that were not specifically explored in our studies. Foremost among them is the relation of the phonetic aspect of speech to meaning. We believe that the recent important advances in linguistics are largely due to the changes in the method of analysis employed in the study of speech.

Traditional linguistics, which divorced phonetic and semantic aspects of speech, tried to achieve their secondary unity through the combination of meaning and sound taken as independent elements. It used the single sound as the unit of linguistic analysis. But sound detached from meaning immediately loses all the characteristics that make it a sound of human speech. As a result, traditional linguistics concentrated on the physiology and acoustics rather than the psychology of speech.

As has been correctly pointed out in modern phonology, it is a meaning of certain sounds in their capacity of signs that makes these sounds a unit of human speech. Sound-in-itself, sound that lacks meaning, cannot serve as a unit of speech. Therefore, an actual unit of speech is not a sound but a phoneme, the smallest indivisible phonetic unit that retains all basic properties of the vocal side of speech taken in its significative function.[2]

The introduction of the phoneme as a unit of analysis has benefited psychology as well as linguistics. The concrete gains achieved by the application of this method conclusively prove its value. If in the old psychology the entire field of interfunctional relations has been impenetratable to investigation, then now it becomes open for those who are willing to employ the method of analysis into units.

When we approach the problem of the interrelation between thought and language and other aspects of mind, the first question that arises is that of intellect and affect.[3] Their separation as subjects of study is a major weakness of traditional psychology, since it makes the thought process appear as an autonomous flow of "thoughts thinking themselves," segregated from the fullness of life, from the personal needs and interests, the inclinations and impulses, of the thinker. Such segregated thought must be viewed either as a meaningless epiphenomenon incapable of changing anything in the life or conduct of a person or else as some kind of primeval force exerting an influence on personal life in an inexplicable, mysterious way. The door is closed on the issue of the causation and origin of our thoughts, since deterministic analysis would require clarification of the motive forces that direct thought into this or that channel. By the same token, the old approach precludes any fruitful study of the reverse process, the influence of thought on affect and volition.

Unit analysis points the way to the solution of these vitally important problems. It demonstrates the existence of a dynamic system of meaning in which the affective and the intellectual unite. It shows that every idea contains a transmuted affective attitude toward the bit of reality to which it refers. It further permits us to trace the path from a person's needs and impulses to the specific direction taken by his thoughts, and the reverse path from his thoughts to his behavior and activity. This example should suffice to show that the method used in this study of thought and language is also a promising tool for investigating the relation of verbal thought to consciousness as a whole and to its other essential functions.

What remains to be done in this chapter is to outline our research program. We shall start with a critical analysis of [Piaget's] theory of thought and language. Although we consider this theory as the best of its kind, we developed our own theoretical position in exactly an opposite direction. Further, we shall discuss the theoretical aspects of the ontogenesis and philogenesis of speech and thought. The major issue here will be the genetic roots of thought and language, for exactly at this point misunderstanding often leads to a wrong attitude toward the problem in general. The focus of this part of our work is an experimental study of concept formation in children. We shall start with a study of experimentally produced, artificial concepts and shall later proceed toward the real concepts spontaneously formed by children. Finally, we shall conclude our work with an analysis of structure and function of verbal thought in general.

Our leading idea throughout the work will be that of development.

2

Piaget's Theory of the Child's Speech and Thought

I

Psychology owes a great deal to Jean Piaget. It is not an exaggeration to say that he revolutionized the study of the child's speech and thought. He developed the clinical method for exploring children's ideas that has since been widely used. He was the first to investigate the child's perception and logic systematically; moreover, he brought to his subject a fresh approach of unusual amplitude and boldness.[1]

To get some idea of the new paths and perspectives that Piaget brought to the study of the child's thought and language, one need only read Edouard Claparède's excellent introduction to Piaget's *The Language and Thought of the Child:* "Whereas, if I am not mistaken, the problem of child mentality has been thought of as one of quantity, Mr. Piaget has restated it as a problem of quality. Formerly, any progress made in the [study of the] child's intelligence was regarded as the result of a certain number of additions and subtractions, such as an increase in new experience and elimination of certain errors—all of them phenomena which it was the business of science to explain. Now, this progress is seen to depend first and foremost upon the fact that this intelli-

gence undergoes a gradual change of character"
(Claparède, 1959, p. xiii).[2]

Like many another great discovery, Piaget's idea is simple to the point of seeming self-evident. It had already
been expressed in the words of J. J. Rousseau, which
Piaget himself quoted, that a child is not a miniature
adult and his mind not the mind of an adult on a small
scale. Behind this truth, for which Piaget provided experimental proof, stands another simple idea—the idea
of evolution, which suffuses all of Piaget's studies with a
brilliant light.

For all its greatness, Piaget's work bears the stigmata of
crisis characteristic of all modern psychology. In this respect, Piaget's theory shares the fate of such theories as
those of Sigmund Freud, Charles Blondel, and Lucien
Levy-Bruhl.[3] All of them are the offsprings of the crisis
in psychology. This crisis stems from the sharp contradiction between the factual material of science and its
methodological and theoretical premises—a contradiction deeply rooted in history of knowledge, revealing a
dispute between the materialistic and idealistic world
concepts.

The historical development of psychology has led to a
situation in which, to repeat the words of Franz Brentano, there are many psychologies, but there is no one,
unified psychology.[4] We may add that there are so many
psychologies precisely because there is no one psychology. As long as we lack a generally accepted system incor-
porating all available psychological knowledge, any
important factual discovery inevitably leads to the creation of a new theory to fit the newly observed facts.

Freud, Levy-Bruhl, and Blondel, each created his
own system of psychology. The prevailing duality
[materialism versus idealism] is reflected in the incongruity between these theoretical systems, with their
metaphysical, idealistic overtones, and the empiric bases

on which they are erected. This duality is a sign of the crisis, when a step forward in the acquisition of data is accompanied by two steps backward in theoretical interpretation. In modern psychology, great discoveries are made daily, only to be shrouded in ad hoc theories, prescientific and nearly metaphysical.

Piaget tries to escape this fatal duality by sticking to facts. He deliberately avoids generalizing even in his own field and is especially careful not to step over into the related realms of logic, the theory of cognition, or the history of philosophy. Pure empiricism seems to him the only safe ground: "This means that the essays before us are first and foremost a collection of facts and documents, and that the bond between the various chapters is not that of systematic exposition, but of unity of method applied to a diversity of material" (Piaget, 1959, p. xviii).

Indeed, his forte is the unearthing of new facts, their painstaking analysis, their classification—the ability, as Claparède puts it, to *listen* to their message. An avalanche of facts, great and small, opening up new vistas or adding to previous knowledge, tumbles down on child psychology from the pages of Piaget. His clinical method proves a truly invaluable tool for studying the complex structural wholes of the child's thought in its evolutional transformations. It unifies his diverse investigations and gives us coherent, detailed, real-life pictures of the child's thinking.

The new facts and the new method have led to many problems, some entirely new to scientific psychology, others appearing in a new light; among them are the problem of logic and grammar in the child's speech, the problem of introspection in children and its functional role in the development of logical operations, and the problem of comprehension of verbal thought in communication between children and adults.

Piaget, however, did not escape the duality characteristic of psychology in the age of crisis. He tried to hide behind the wall of facts, but facts "betrayed" him, for they led to problems. Problems gave birth to theories, in spite of Piaget's determination to avoid them by closely following the experimental facts and disregarding for the time being that the very choice of experiments is determined by hypotheses. But facts are always examined in the light of some theory and therefore cannot be disentangled from philosophy. Who would find a key to the richness of the new facts must uncover the *philosophy of fact:* how it was found and how interpreted. Without such an analysis, fact will remain dead and mute.

Because of all this, our prime goal will be to study the theoretical and methodological aspects of Piaget's work. Here we cannot follow the path of his own thought, for it moves from one group of facts to another in such a way as purposively to avoid generalization. We, in our turn, are primarily interested in a principle that would help to unite all these data. The first question that should be raised in this connection is the objective interrelatedness of all the characteristic traits of the child's thinking observed by Piaget. Are these trends fortuitous and independent, or do they form an orderly whole, with a logic of its own, around some central, unifying fact? Piaget believes that they do. In answering the question, he passes from facts to theory, and incidentally shows how much his analysis of facts was influenced by theory, even though in his presentation the theory follows the findings.

According to Piaget, the bond uniting all the specific characteristics of the child's logic is the egocentrism of the child's thinking. To this core trait he relates all the other traits he found, such as intellectual realism, syncretism, and difficulty in understanding relations. He describes egocentrism as occupying an intermediate position, genetically, structurally, and functionally, between autistic and directed thought.

The idea of the polarity of directed and undirected (or as Eugen Bleuler proposed to call it, autistic) thought is borrowed from psychoanalysis.[5] Piaget says (Piaget, 1959, p. 43),

Directed thought is conscious, i.e., it pursues an aim which is present to the mind of the thinker; it is intelligent, which means that it is adapted to reality and tries to influence it; it admits of being true or false (empirically or logically true), and it can be communicated by language. Autistic thought is subconscious, which means that the aims it pursues and the problems it tries to solve are not present in consciousness; it is not adapted to reality, but creates for itself a dream world of imagination; it tends, not to establish truths, but to satisfy desires, and it remains strictly individual and incommunicable as such by means of language. On the contrary, it works chiefly by images, and in order to express itself, has recourse to indirect methods, evoking by means of symbols and myths the feeling by which it is led.

Directed thought is social. As it develops, it is increasingly influenced by the laws of experience and of logic proper. Autistic thought, on the contrary, is individualistic and obeys a set of special laws of its own: "Now between autism and intelligence there are many degrees, varying with their capacity for being communicated. These intermediate varieties must therefore be subject to a special logic, intermediate too between the logic of autism and that of intelligence. The chief of those intermediate forms, i.e., the type of thought which like that exhibited by our children seeks to adapt itself to reality, but does not communicate itself as such, we propose to call *egocentric* thought" (Piaget, 1959, p. 45).

While its main function is still the satisfaction of personal needs, it already includes some mental adaptation, some of the reality orientation typical of the thought of adults. The egocentric thought of the child "stands midway between autism in the strict sense of the word and socialized thought" (Piaget, 1969, p. 208). This is Piaget's basic hypothesis.

It is important to note that throughout his work Piaget stresses the traits that egocentric thought has in common with autism rather than the traits that divide them. In the summary at the end of his book [*Judgment and Reasoning in the Child*], he states emphatically, "Play, when all is said and done, is the supreme law of egocentric thought" (Piaget, 1969, p. 244).

The same tendency to emphasize the close similarity between egocentric thought and autistic thought is particularly pronounced in Piaget's treatment of the phenomenon of syncretism. Syncretism, which is one of the most characteristic features of the child's thought, has—according to Piaget—more in common with autistic thinking and the logic of dreams than with logical thinking proper.

Here again Piaget considers the mechanism of syncretic thought as intermediate between logical thinking and that process psychoanalyses have rather boldly described as the "symbolism" of dreams. Sigmund Freud has shown that two main factors contribute to the formation of the images of dreaming: condensation, by which several disparate images melt into one, and displacement, by which the qualities belonging to one object are transferred to another.

Following Hans Larsson, Piaget assumes that somewhere between condensation and displacement, on the one hand, and generalization (which is a form of condensation), on the other, there must be some intermediate links.[6] Syncretism is one of the most important of these links.

It remains to clarify the ontogenetic relations of

egocentrism to the logic of dreams, autism, and rational reasoning.

Piaget holds that egocentrism stands between extreme autism and the logic of reason chronologically as well as structurally and functionally. His conception of the development of thought is based on the premise taken from psychoanalysis that the child's thought is originally and naturally autistic and becomes realistic thought only under long and sustained social pressure. This does not, Piaget points out, devaluate the intelligence of the child: "Logical activity isn't all there is to intelligence" (Piaget, 1969, p. 201). Imagination is important for finding solutions to problems, but it does not take care of verification and proof, which the search for truth presupposes. The need to verify thought—that is, the need for logical activity—arises late. This lag is to be expected, says Piaget, since thought begins to serve immediate satisfaction much earlier than to seek truth; the most spontaneous form of thinking is play, or wishful imaginings that make the desired seem obtainable. Up to the age of seven or eight, play dominates in the child's thought to such an extent that it is very hard for the child to distinguish deliberate invention from fantasy that the child believes to be the truth.

We find the same idea in Freud, who claims that the pleasure principle precedes the reality principle.

To sum up, autism is seen as the original, earliest form of thought; logic appears relatively late; and egocentric thought is the genetic link between them.[7]

This conception, though never presented by Piaget in a coherent, systematic fashion, is the cornerstone of his whole theoretical edifice. True, he states more than once that the assumption of the intermediate nature of the child's thought is hypothetical, but he also says that this hypothesis is so close to common sense that it seems little more debatable to him than the fact itself of the child's egocentrism. He traces egocentrism to the nature of the practical activity of the child and to the late development of social attitudes: "But surely from the genetic point of view, we must start from the child's activity, if we want to explain his thought. Now, this activity is unquestionably egocentric and egotistical. The social instinct is late in developing. The first critical stage occurs at the age of seven or eight, and it is precisely at this age that we can place the first period of reflection and logical unification. . . ." (Piaget, 1969, p. 209).

Before this age, Piaget tends to see egocentrism as all-pervading. All the phenomena of the child's logic in its rich variety he considers directly or indirectly egocentric. Of syncretism, an important expression of egocentrism, he says unequivocally that it permeates the child's entire thinking, both in the verbal and in the perceptual spheres. After seven or eight, when socialized thinking begins to take shape, the egocentric features do not suddenly vanish. They disappear from the child's perceptual operations but remain crystallized in the more abstract area of purely verbal thought.

His conception of the prevalence of egocentrism in childhood leads Piaget to conclude that egocentrism of thought is so intimately related to the child's psychic nature that it is impervious to experience. The influences to which adults subject the child "do not imprint themselves upon the child as on a photographic plate; they are 'assimilated,' i.e., deformed by the living being who comes under their sway, and they are incorporated into his own substance. It is this psychological substance (psychologically speaking) of the child's, or rather this structure and functioning peculiar to his thought, that we have tried to describe, and in certain measure, to explain" (Piaget, 1969, p. 256).

This passage epitomizes the nature of Piaget's basic assumptions and brings us to the general problem of social and biological uniformities in psychic development, to which we shall return in section III. First, let us examine the soundness of Piaget's conception of the child's egocentrism in the light of the facts on which it is based.

II

If one takes into account phylo- and ontogenetic development, one immediately recognizes that the autistic thought can be neither the most primitive nor the original form of mental development.

Even if one assumes the evolutionary point of view and considers child development in purely biological terms, even then autistic thinking fails to suit the role assigned to it by Freud and Piaget. Autistic thinking is neither the first step, nor is it the basis upon which all further developmental stages might be built. It is also incorrect to portray autistic thinking as a form of hallucinatory imagination prompted by the pleasure principle, which allegedly precedes the reality principle.

It is quite remarkable that it was a biologically oriented psychologist, Eugen Bleuler, who developed a critique of the aforementioned concept of child autism. Bleuler mentions that the very term "autistic thinking" has already become a source of confusion. There are certain attempts to link it to schizophrenic autism, egotistic reasoning, etc. That is why Bleuler chose to use the term "irrealistic" thinking as opposed to realistic, rational thinking. Already in this change of name one may find a telling sign of that revision that the notion of autism is currently undergoing.

In his study of autistic thinking Bleuler (1912) directly addresses the problem of the genetic relation between autistic and rational reasoning: "Since realistic thinking and the complex forms of satisfaction of realistic needs suffer earlier in the course of illness, and autistic think-ing, later, from this French psychologists led by Pierre Janet concluded that the 'reality function' occupies higher position and is more complex.[8] Freud's position in this question is absolutely clear. He claims that the mech-anisms of pleasure satisfaction are the primary ones. He assumes that a baby whose needs are all satisfied by its mother lives a purely autistic life resembling that of a chicken still in the egg. A baby 'hallucinates' about the satisfaction of his visceral needs, manifests his irritation by crying and motor reaction, and then experiences hal-lucinatory satisfaction" (Bleuler, 1912, pp. 25–26).

As we see, Bleuler refers to the very same concept of autism on which the psychoanalytical approach to child behavior has been built, and which serves as a starting point for Piaget's theory, which places egocentric thought between this original autism and rational thinking. Bleuler rejects this position using developmental argu-ments that, from our point of view, are invincible (Bleuler, 1912, pp. 26–27):

I cannot agree with that. I do not see a hallucinatory satisfac-tion in a baby, but I do see a satisfaction after the actual intake of food. And I must say that the chicken finds its way out of the egg not with the help of imagination, but because it physically and chemically assimilates available nutritious substances.

Observing more grown-up children, I also fail to find any predisposition toward an imaginary apple at the cost of a real one. A mentally retarded person, as well as a savage, is a real-istic "politician"; and when the savage makes his autistic er-rors—in the same way as we do—he makes them where his reason and experience turn out to be insufficient: in his ideas about the cosmos, or certain natural phenomena, or sources of disease, etc. In the mentally retarded person not only realistic but also autistic thinking is simplified. I cannot imagine a living creature who would not be concerned first of all with the reac-tion to reality. I also cannot imagine how the autistic function, which requires a complex memory, can exist below a certain stage of development. Animal psychology, if we disregard some observations on higher animals, knows only the reality function.

This contradiction can be easily resolved: autistic function is not as primitive as the simplest forms of reality function, but it is more primitive than the higher, well-developed forms of reality function, which we find in man. Lower animals have only the reality function. No living being would have the autistic function alone; at a certain moment the autistic function joins the reality function and from then on they evolve together.

And actually, as soon as one turns from the general thesis of the superiority of the pleasure principle over realistic thinking to the actual process of phylogenetic development, one sees that the primacy of autism is biological nonsense. To let the pleasure principle become a starting point of development is to make the origin of thinking and intelligence absolutely obscure. The same is true for ontogenetic development, for we cannot ignore the obvious fact, mentioned by Bleuler, that satisfaction comes from the intake of food and not through hallucination about pleasure.

Later we shall try to show that Bleuler's formula of the genetic relations between autistic thinking and realistic thinking is not absolutely satisfactory. It is sufficient, however, to emphasize that we do agree with Bleuler that (a) autistic function is a late product of development and (b) the idea of the primacy of autism is biologically invalid.

Bleuler places the appearance of autistic function at the fourth stage of the mental development of a child. At this stage of mental development a child is able to combine concepts without direct stimulation from the external world. Accumulated past experience may be extended to new unknown situations. At this stage coherent thinking may be carried out based exclusively on memory images, rather than on fortuitous stimuli and needs (Bleuler, 1912, pp. 28–29):

Only at this stage can the autistic function appear. Only here may appear such images connected with intensive pleasure that will satisfy the needs generated by these images themselves in a fantastic way. [Only here] is the human being able to dissociate the unpleasant aspects of the external world and to substitute for them some pleasant features that are products of his own imagination. The irreal function, therefore, cannot precede the real one, but must undergo a parallel development.[9]

As thinking becomes more and more complex and differentiated, it becomes better adjusted to external reality and less dependent on affects. At the same time, emotionally significant events of the past and projections to the future become more influential. The multitude of the possible combinations of thoughts make possible an endless fantasy, which is also prompted by the emotional memories and affective anticipations of future events.

In the course of development these two modes of intelligence turn into two divergent tendencies until they become mutual antagonists. When a balance between these two modes of intelligence is lost, then we have either a pure dreamer, who lives in fantastic combinations and disregards reality, or a sober realist, who lives only in the present and does not try to foresee the future. In spite of phylogenetic parallelism in the development of realistic thinking and irrealistic thinking, the former one turns out to be better developed and when a disease strikes it suffers more.

Bleuler poses an interesting question, namely: How does it happen that the autistic function, which appears rather late in phylogenesis, manages to be substantially present already in two-year-olds, directing the greater part of their psychological activity? The answer to this question is suggested by the fact that the development of speech creates a favorable condition for autistic thinking, while autistic function, in its turn, is beneficial for the development of intellectual skills. The combinatory abilities of the child's mind are enhanced by dreaming, just as his motor skills are enhanced by outdoor games.

But if we accept this revision of the genetic place of autism, similar revision must be undertaken in respect to its functional and structural aspects. The central issue here turns out to be a question whether autistic thought is conscious or not. Freud and Piaget made the unconscious character of autistic thought a starting point of their theories. Egocentric thought is also viewed as not fully conscious. It occupies an intermediate position between the conscious reasoning of adults and unconscious dream activity: "For insofar as he is thinking only for himself, the child has no need to be aware of the mechanism of his reasoning," says Piaget (1969, p. 213). Piaget, however, tries to avoid the expression "unconscious reasoning," which he considered ambiguous, and talks instead about the logic of action in opposition to the logic of thought: "Most of the phenomena of child logic can be traced back to general causes. The roots of this logic and of its shortcomings are to be found in the egocentrism of child thought up to the age of seven or eight, and in the unconsciousness which this egocentrism entails" (Piaget, 1969, p. 215).

Piaget scrutinizes the problem of insufficient introspective abilities in children, and comes to conclusion that the widely accepted belief according to which the egocentric people are more aware of themselves is not correct: "The concept of autism in psychoanalysis throws full light upon the fact that the incommunicable character of thought involves a certain degree of unconsciousness" (Piaget, 1969, pp. 209–210).

Child egocentrism, therefore, involves a certain unconsciousness, which in its turn explains some features of the child's logic. Piaget's experimental study of child introspection confirmed this idea.

Strictly speaking, a thesis about the unconscious

character of autistic and egocentric thinking serves as one of the central themes in Piaget's theory. But this thesis has also been challenged by Bleuler, who observed that Freud's use of the concepts of the unconscious and autism made them almost indistinguishable. Bleuler emphasized that these two concepts must be considered as separate: "Autistic thinking, in principle, can be conscious as well as unconscious" (Bleuler, 1912, p. 19).

Finally, the very idea that autistic thinking and its egocentric variant are divorced from reality has been challenged: "Depending on what basis the autistic thinking is developing, we are able to distinguish two variants of autism. . . . The autism of a healthy alert man does have a connection with reality and firmly established concepts" (Bleuler, 1912, pp. 14–15).

As we shall show later in this book, Bleuler's hypothesis of two different forms of autism is particularly true in what concerns the child's thought. One of these forms is intimately connected with the child's actual environment and subsequently is reality oriented. The other form, which reveals itself in dreams, is divorced from reality and distorts it.

We have thus found that autistic thinking, in neither its genetic, structural, nor functional aspects, shows itself as a primeval force and basis for the development of thought. Egocentric thought, therefore, may not be considered as an intermediary between such a hypothetical beginning and the higher stages in the development of mind. The place and the role of egocentrism must therefore be reconsidered.

III

As we have seen, the concept of the child's egocentrism is a major focus of the entire psychological theory of Piaget. Apparently the chaotic multitude of disparate traits of the child's logic finds its structural order and generative cause in the principle of egocentrism. That is why a challenge to the primacy of egocentrism is a challenge to Piaget's entire theoretical construction.

In the preceding chapter we made an attempt to provide a critical review of Piaget's concept of egocentrism taken in a theoretical context. However, the final verdict can be passed only after scrutiny of the data on which Piaget based his doctrine. A theoretical critique, therefore, must now yield the floor to experimental findings. We shall then test Piaget's facts by comparing them with the results of our own experiments.

The factual basis of Piaget's theory is provided by his investigation of the child's use of language. His systematic observations led him to conclude that all conversations of children fall into two groups, the egocentric and the socialized. The difference between them lies mainly in their functions: "This talk is egocentric," explains Piaget, "partly because the child speaks only about himself, but chiefly because he does not attempt to place himself at the point of view of his hearer" (Piaget, 1959, p. 9). The child does not try to communicate, expects no answers, and often does not even care whether anyone listens to him. It is similar to a monologue in a play: "The child talks to himself as though he were thinking aloud. He does not address anyone" (Piaget, 1959, p. 9). What Piaget is calling egocentric speech is a running accompaniment to whatever the child may be doing. The function of socialized speech is quite different; here a child does attempt to an exchange with others—he begs, commands, threatens, conveys information, asks questions.

Piaget's experiments showed that by far the greater part of the preschool child's talk is egocentric. He found that from 44 to 47% of the total recorded talk of children in their seventh year was egocentric in nature. This figure, he says, must be considerably increased in the case of younger children. Further investigations with six- and seven-year-olds proved that even socialized speech at that age is not entirely free of egocentric thinking. Furthermore, besides his expressed thoughts, the child has a great many unexpressed thoughts. Some of these, according to Piaget, remain unexpressed precisely because they are egocentric, i.e., incommunicable. To convey them to others, the child would have to be able to adopt their point of view: "To put it quite simply, we may say that the adult thinks socially, even when he is alone, and that the child under seven thinks egocentrically, even in the society of others" (Piaget, 1959, p. 40).

According to Piaget, the function of egocentric speech is to "chant" one's thoughts or actions. Such a speech has many vestiges of the chanting cries mentioned in Janet's essay on language. Not only words, which help to bring rhyme to the child's activity, but thoughts themselves are also egocentric.

Thus the coefficient of egocentric thought must be much higher than the coefficient of egocentric speech. But it is data on speech, which can be measured, that furnish the documentary proof on which Piaget bases his conception of child egocentrism.

What is the reason for the prevalence of egocentrism in children before seven? Why do they not communicate their ideas to each other? "What is the reason for this? It is, in our opinion, twofold. It is due, in the first place, to the absence of any sustained social intercourse between the children of less than seven or eight, and in the second place, to the fact that the language used in the fundamental activity of the child—play—is one of gestures, movements, and mimicry as much as of words. There is, as we have said, no real social life between children of less than seven or eight" (Piaget, 1959, p. 40).

On the one hand, exactly between seven and eight the desire to work with others manifests itself for the first time. It is Piaget's opinion that just at this age the egocentric talk loses some of its importance. At the same time, "If language of the child of about six-and-a-half is still so far from being socialized, and if the part played in it by the egocentric forms is so considerable in comparison to information and dialogue, etc., the reason for this lies in the fact that childish language includes two distinct varieties, one made up of gestures, movements, mimicking, etc., which accompany or even completely supplant the use of words, and the other consisting solely of the spoken word" (Piaget, 1959, p. 42).

The fact of the prevalence of egocentric speech over communicative speech in younger children became the real foundation of Piaget's theory. The ties that connect the hypothesis of the child's egocentrism with the data on egocentric speech, far from being just a matter of convenient organization of research material, reveal the inner logic of Piaget's theoretical position. That is why we decided to make the problem of egocentric speech a focus of our critical inquiry. Our goal, therefore, is to reveal the philosophy behind Piaget's system, its theoretical unity, which is neither clear nor obvious at first glance. As we have mentioned above, such an inquiry cannot but be based on experimental and clinical evidence.

IV

Piaget emphasizes that egocentric speech does not provide communication. It is rather chanting, rhyming, and accompanying the major melody of the child's activity. Egocentric speech changes nothing in the leading melody of activity. Between them there is a sort of concordance, but no essential connections. Egocentric speech, in Piaget's description, appears as a by-product of the child's activity, as a stigma of the child's cognitive egocentrism.

Egocentric speech is, therefore, useless. It plays no essential role in child behavior. It is speech for the child's sake, which is incomprehensible for others and which is closer to a verbal dream than to a conscious activity.

But if such speech plays no positive role in child behavior, if it is a mere accompaniment, it is but a symptom of weakness and immaturity in the child's thinking, a symptom that must disappear in the course of child development. Useless and unconnected with the structure of activity, this accompaniment should become weaker and weaker until it completely disappears from the routine of the child's speech.

Data collected by Piaget seemingly supports this point of view. The coefficient of egocentric speech decreases with age and reaches zero at the age of seven or eight—which means that egocentric speech is not typical for schoolchildren. Piaget, however, assumes that the loss of egocentric speech does not preclude children from remaining cognitively egocentric. Egocentric thought simply changes the form of its manifestation, appearing now in abstract reasoning and in the new symptoms that have no semblance to egocentric talk. In conformity with his idea of the uselessness of egocentric speech, Piaget claims that this speech "folds" and dies out at the threshold of school age.

We in our turn conducted our own experiments aimed at understanding the function and fate of egocentric speech.[10] The data obtained led us to a new comprehension of this phenomenon that differs greatly from that of Piaget. Our investigation suggests that egocentric speech does play a specific role in the child's activity.

In order to determine what causes egocentric talk, what circumstances provoke it, we organized the children's activities in much the same way Piaget did, but we added a series of frustrations and difficulties. For instance, when a child was getting ready to draw, he would suddenly find that there was no paper, or no pencil of the color he needed. In other words, by obstructing his free activity we made him face problems.

We found that in these difficult situations the co-efficient of egocentric speech almost doubled, in comparison with Piaget's normal figure for the same age and also in comparison with our figure for children not facing these problems. The child would try to grasp and to remedy the situation in talking to himself: "Where's the pencil? I need a blue pencil. Never mind, I'll draw with the red one and wet it with water; it will become dark and look like blue."

In the same activities without impediments, our co-efficient of egocentric talk was even slightly lower than Piaget's. It is legitimate to assume, then, that a disruption in the smooth flow of activity is an important stimulus for egocentric speech. This discovery fits in with two premises to which Piaget himself refers several times in his book. One of them is the so-called law of awareness, which was formulated by Claparède and which states that an impediment or disturbance in an automatic activity makes the author aware of this activity. The other premise is that speech is an expression of that process of becoming aware.

Indeed the above-mentioned phenomena were observed in our experiments: egocentric speech appeared when a child tries to comprehend the situation, to find a solution, or to plan a nascent activity. The older children behaved differently: they scrutinized the problem, thought (which was indicated by long pauses), and then found a solution. When asked what he was thinking about, such a child answered more in line with the "thinking aloud" of a preschooler. We thus assumed that the same mental operations that the preschooler carries out through voiced egocentric speech are already relegated to soundless inner speech in schoolchildren.

Our findings indicate that egocentric speech does not long remain a mere accompaniment to the child's activity. Besides being a means of expression and of release of tension, it soon becomes an instrument of thought in the proper sense—in seeking and planning the solution of a problem. An accident that occurred during one of our experiments provides a good illustration of one way in which egocentric speech may alter the course of an activity: A child of five-and-a-half was drawing a streetcar when the point of his pencil broke. He tried, nevertheless, to finish the circle of wheel, pressing down on the pencil very hard, but nothing showed on the paper except a deep colorless line. The child muttered to himself, "It's broken," put aside the pencil, took watercolors instead, and began drawing a *broken* streetcar after an accident, continuing to talk to himself from time to time about the change in his picture. The child's accidentally provoked egocentric utterance so manifestly affected his activity that it is impossible to mistake it for a mere byproduct, an accompaniment not interfering with the melody. Our experiments showed highly complex changes in the interrelation of activity and egocentric talk. We observed how egocentric speech at first marked the end result or a turning point in an activity, then was gradually shifted toward the middle and finally to the beginning of the activity, taking on a directing, planning function and raising the child's acts to the level of purposeful behavior. What happens here is similar to the well-known developmental sequence in the naming of drawings. A small child draws first, then decides what it is that he has drawn; at a slightly older age, he names his drawing when it is half-done; and finally he decides beforehand what he will draw.

The revised conception of the function of egocentric speech must also influence our conception of its later fate and must be brought to bear on the issue of its disappearance at school age. Experiments can yield indirect evidence but no conclusive answer about the causes of this disappearance.

There is, of course, nothing to this effect in Piaget, who believes that egocentric speech simply dies off. The development of inner speech in the child receives little specific elucidation in his studies. But since inner speech and voiced egocentric speech fulfill the same function, the implication would be that if, as Piaget maintains, egocentric speech precedes socialized speech, then inner speech also must precede socialized speech—an assumption untenable from the genetic point of view.

However, Piaget's theoretical position apart, his own findings and some of our data suggest that egocentric speech is actually an intermediate stage leading to inner speech. Of course, this is only a hypothesis, but taking into account the present state of our knowledge about the child's speech, it is the most plausible one. If we compare the amount of what might be called egocentric speech in children and adults, we would have to admit that the "egocentric" speech of adults is much richer. From the point of view of functional psychology, all silent thinking is nothing but "egocentric" speech. John B. Watson would have said that such speech serves individual rather than social adaptation. The first feature uniting the inner speech of adults with the egocentric speech of children is its function as speech-for-oneself. If one turns to Watson's experiment and asks a subject to solve some problem thinking aloud, one would find that such thinking aloud of an adult has a striking similarity to the egocentric speech of children. Second, these two forms also have the same structural characteristics: out of context they would be incomprehensible to others because they omit to mention what is obvious to the speaker. These similarities lead us to assume that when egocentric speech disappears, it does not simply atrophy but "goes underground," i.e., turns into inner speech.

Our observation that at the age when this change is taking place children facing difficult situations resort now to egocentric speech, now to silent reflection, indicates that the two can be functionally equivalent. It is our hypothesis that the processes of inner speech develop and become stabilized approximately at the beginning of school age and that this causes the quick drop in the egocentric speech observed at this stage.

Observations made by Auguste Lemaître and some other authors support this hypothesis.[11] It was shown that the inner speech of schoolchildren is labile and unsettled. This is an indication that what we observe is a developmentally immature process that is still unstable and indefinite.

The above-mentioned experiments and considerations hardly support Piaget's hypothesis concerning the egocentrism of six-year-olds. At least the phenomenon of egocentric speech, viewed from our perspective, fails to confirm his assumptions.

The cognitive function of egocentric speech, which is most probably connected with the development of inner speech, by no means is a reflection of the child's egocentric thinking, but rather shows that under certain circumstances egocentric speech is becoming an agent of realistic thinking. Piaget assumed that if 40–47% of the speech of a child of six-and-a-half is egocentric, then his thinking must be egocentric within the same range. Our investigation showed, however, that there can be no connection between egocentric talk and egocentric thinking whatsoever—which means that the major implication drawn from Piaget's data might be wrong.

We thus have an experimental fact that has nothing to do with the correctness or falsity of our own hypothesis concerning the fate of egocentric speech. This is the factual evidence that the child's egocentric speech does not reflect egocentric thinking, but rather carries out an opposite function, that of realistic thinking.

Actually Piaget carried out three different studies in support of his point of view on egocentrism. We centered on the first one, which is dedicated to egocentric speech, because it was this first study that allowed Piaget to formulate his hypothesis. The other two just substantiated and expanded the first one and brought about no major alterations.

V

We now turn to those positive conclusions that can be drawn from our critique of Piaget's theory.

Limited in scope as our findings are, we believe that they help one to see in a new and broader perspective the general direction of the development of speech and thought. In Piaget's view, the two functions follow a common path, from autistic to socialized speech, from subjective fantasy to the logic of relations. In the course of this change, the influence of adults is deformed by the psychic processes of the child, but it wins out in the end. The development of thought is, to Piaget, a story of the gradual socialization of deeply intimate, personal, autistic mental states. Even social speech is represented as following, not preceding, egocentric speech.

The hypothesis we propose reverses this course. Let us look at the direction of thought development during one short interval, from the appearance of egocentric speech to its disappearance, in the framework of language development as a whole.

We consider that the total development runs as follows: The primary function of speech, in both children and adults, is communication, social contact. The earliest speech of the child is therefore essentially social. At first it is global and multifunctional; later its functions become differentiated. At a certain age the social speech of the child is quite sharply divided into egocentric speech and communicative speech. (We prefer to use the term *communicative* for the form of speech that Piaget calls *socialized,* as though it had been something else before becoming social. From our point of view, the two forms, communicative and egocentric, are both social, though their functions differ.) Egocentric speech emerges when the child transfers social, collaborative forms of behavior to the sphere of inner-personal psychic functions. The child's tendency to transfer to his inner processes the behavior patterns that formerly were social is well known to Piaget. He describes in another context how arguments between children give rise to the beginnings of logical reflection. Something similar happens, we believe, when the child starts conversing with himself as he has been doing with others. When circumstances force him to stop and think, he is likely to think aloud. Egocentric speech, splintered off from general social speech, in time leads to inner speech, which serves both autistic and logical thinking.

Egocentric speech as a separate linguistic form is the highly important genetic link in the transition from vocal to inner speech, an intermediate stage between the differentiation of the functions of vocal speech and the final transformation of one part of vocal speech into inner speech. It is this transitional role of egocentric speech that lends it such great theoretical interest. The whole conception of speech development differs profoundly in accordance with the interpretation given to the role of egocentric speech. Thus our schema of development— first social, then egocentric, then inner speech—contrasts both with the traditional behaviorist schema—vocal speech, whisper, inner speech—and with Piaget's sequence—from nonverbal autistic thought through ego-centric thought and speech to socialized speech and logical thinking.

We mentioned the behavioristic schema only because it happened to look so similar, methodologically, to Piaget's. Its author, John Watson, suggested that the transition from voiced speech to inner speech must involve an intermediate whispering stage. Developing the same idea of an intermediate stage, which he assumed to be egocentric, Piaget linked with its help autistic thought and logical reasoning.

We see how different is the picture of the development of the child's speech and thought depending on what is considered to be a starting point of such development. In our conception, the true direction of the development of thinking is not from the individual to the social, but from the social to the individual.[12]

VI

Our somewhat protracted analysis of Piaget's concept of egocentrism is now coming to an end. We have shown that from the phylo- and ontogenetic points of view the concept of the child's egocentrism illegitimately polarizes autistic thinking and realistic thinking. We have also shown that the factual basis of Piaget's doctrine, i.e., a study of egocentric speech, failed to support the thesis of a direct manifestation of egocentric thought in egocentric speech. Finally, we have attempted to show that egocentric speech by no means is a mere by-product of the child's activity. On the contrary, as our data have revealed, egocentric speech is actively involved in the child's activity, facilitating the transition from overt to inner speech.

The first and most serious conclusion that can be drawn from our critical analysis concerns the alleged opposition of two forms of thinking: autistic and realistic. This opposition served as a basis for Piaget's theory as well as for the psychoanalytical approach to child development. We think that it is incorrect to oppose the principle of satisfaction of needs to the principle of adaptation to reality. The very concept of need, if taken from the perspective of development, necessarily contains the notion of satisfaction of need through a certain adjustment to reality.

As Bleuler mentioned, in the passage quoted earlier, the infant satisfies his need, not through "hallucination about pleasure," but through an actual intake of food. And when the older child prefers a real apple to an imaginary one, it happens not because he abandoned his need for the sake of adjustment to reality, but exactly because his thinking and actions are guided by his need.

Adjustment to objective reality does not exist for the sake of adjustment in itself. All adaptations are regulated by needs. The latter statement is obviously a truism, and one may only wonder how the theories we have just reviewed managed to overlook it.

Need and adaptation must be considered in their unity. What we have in well-developed autistic thinking, i.e., an attempt to attain an imaginary satisfaction of desires that failed to be satisfied in real life, is a product of a long development. Autistic thinking, therefore, is a late product of the development of realistic, conceptual thinking. Piaget, however, chose to borrow from Freud the idea that the pleasure principle precedes the reality principle. Moreover, in doing this, he took up in addition the entire metaphysics of the pleasure principle, which instead of remaining a technical and biologically subordinated moment, appeared as a primeval vital force, a *primum movens*, i.e., a generator of the entire psychological development.

Piaget considered one of the major achievements of

psychoanalysis to be its demonstration that autism does not know the adaptation to reality, because for the ego it is pleasure that dominates life: "Thus the sole function of autistic thought is to give immediate and unlimited satisfaction to desires and interests by deforming reality so as to adapt it to the ego" (Piaget, 1969, p. 244).

Once he separated pleasure and need from adaptation to reality, Piaget was forced by the power of logic to divorce realistic thinking from all needs, interests, and desires, and to confine it to a sphere of *pure thought*. But such pure thought does not exist in nature, as there is no need without adaptation and no child's thinking for the sake of pure inquiry that would go unconnected with needs, wishes, and interests: "It strives not for truth, but for satisfaction of drives," says Piaget about autistic thought. But does desire always exclude reality? And is there a child's thought that would seek to establish truth for truth's sake irrespective of practical needs? Only hollow abstract formulas and logical fictions, only metaphysical hypostases can be defined in such a way, but never the real routes of the child's thinking.

In his comments on Aristotle's critique of the Pythagorean concept of numbers and Plato's concept of Ideas, separated from real things, V. I. Lenin wrote the following (Lenin, 1961, p. 372):

Primitive idealism: the universal (concept, idea) is a particular being. This appears wild, monstrously (more accurately, childishly) stupid. But is not modern idealism, Kant, Hegel, the idea of God, of the same nature (absolutely of the same nature)? Tables, chairs, and the ideas of table and chair; the world and the idea of the world (God); thing and "noumen," the unknowable "Thing-in-itself"; the connection of the earth and the sun, nature in general—and law, logos, God. The dichotomy of human knowledge and the possibility of idealism (=religion) are given already in the first, elementary abstraction.

The approach of the (human) mind to a particular thing, the taking of a copy (= a concept) of it, is not a simple immediate act, a dead mirroring, but one which is complex, split into two, zig-zag-like, which includes in it the possibility of the flight of fantasy from life; more than that: the possibility of the transformation (moreover, an unnoticeable transformation, of which man is unaware) of the abstract concept, idea, into a fantasy (*in letzer Instanz* = God). For even in the simplest generalization, in the most elementary general idea ("table" in general), there is a certain bit of fantasy.

It is hardly possible to express the idea of unity and contradiction of imagination and thought in more clear-cut way. Imagination and thought appear in their development as the two sides of opposition, whose unity is already present in the very first generalization, in the first concept formed by man.

This coexistence of unity and opposition, this zigzag character of the development of fantasy and thought, which reveals itself in the "flight" of imagination on the one hand, and its deeper reflection upon real life on the other (for there is a piece of fantasy in any general concept)—all these moments help us to find a correct way to study realistic thinking and autistic thinking.

We have shown that the egocentric speech of a child, far from being detached from the child's activity, is actually its integral component. We saw that this speech becomes gradually intellectualized and starts serving as a mediator in purposive activity and in planning complex actions. Activity and practice are, thus, those moments that help us to uncover previously unknown aspects of egocentric speech.

Piaget argues that "things do not shape a child's mind." But we have seen that in real situations when the egocentric speech of a child is connected with his practical activity, things do shape his mind. Here, by "things" we mean reality, neither as passively reflected in the child's perception nor as abstractly contemplated, but reality that a child encounters in his practical activity.

VII

Modern psychology in general and child psychology in particular reveal a tendency to combine psychological and philosophical issues. The German psychologist Narziss Ach aptly summarized this trend when he remarked at the end of a session, "But this is experimental philosophy!"[13] And indeed many issues in the complex field of thinking in childhood border on epistemology, logic, and other branches of philosophy. Piaget's study under review constantly touches upon one or another of these philosophical issues.

Piaget himself perceives such philosophizing as a danger. He warns against the "premature" generalization, in which he sees a risk of introducing a biased logical system. His explicit intention is to remain within the framework of the analysis of facts, and not to plunge into the philosophy of these facts. At the same time, he cannot but admit that logic, epistemology, and history of philosophy are more closely connected with the study of the child's intelligence than one may imagine. Because of that, time and again, Piaget inadvertently touches upon one or another of these issues, but with remarkable consistency checks himself and breaks off.

In his introduction to *The Language and Thought of the Child,* Claparède emphasized that Piaget happily combines the attitude of the natural scientist who "has a special talent for letting the material speak for itself" with deep erudition in philosophical questions: "He knows every nook and cranny and is familiar with every pitfall of the old logic—the logic of the textbooks; he shares the hopes of the new logic, and is acquainted with the delicate problems of epistemology. But this thorough mastery of other spheres of knowledge, far from luring him into doubtful speculation, has on the contrary enabled him to draw the line very clearly between psychology and philosophy, and to remain rigorously on the side of the first. His work is purely scientific" (Claparède, 1959, pp. xv–xvi).

We cannot agree with the latter statement of Claparède, for in spite of his express intention to avoid theorizing, Piaget does not succeed in keeping his work within the bounds of pure factual science. Deliberate avoidance of philosophy is itself a philosophy. And what sort of philosophy it represents we shall now discuss, taking as an example Piaget's views on the place of causal explanation in science.

Piaget attempts to refrain from considering causes in presenting his findings. In doing so, he comes dangerously close to what he calls in the child "precausality," though he himself may view his abstention as a sophisticated "supracausal" stage, in which the concept of causality has been outgrown. He proposes to replace the explanation of phenomena in terms of cause and effect by a genetic analysis in terms of temporal sequences and by the application of a mathematically conceived formula of the functional interdependence of phenomena.

Thus developmental relations and functional interdependence replaced the functional explanation (Piaget, 1969, p. 200):

But what do we mean by explaining psychological phenomena? As Baldwin has shown in his subtle analysis, without the genetic method in psychology, we can never be sure of not taking effects for causes, nor even of having formulated problems of explanation aright. The relation of cause and effect must, therefore, be superseded by that of genetic progression, which adds the notion of functional dependence, in the mathematical sense of the word, to that of antecedent and consequent. This will give us the right to say of two phenomena A and B, that A is a function of B, as B is a function of A, and yet leave us the possibility of taking the earliest phenomenon, i.e., genetically speaking, the most explicative, as the starting-point of our description.

Thus, Piaget suggests that the relation of cause and effect must be superseded by that of genetic and functional explanation. He missed here a point, brilliantly formulated by Goethe, that the ascension from the effect to the cause is pure historical understanding. Piaget also neglected the well-known thesis of Francis Bacon, that real knowledge is knowledge that goes to causes. In his attempt to substitute functional explanation for the genetic explanation of causes, Piaget, without noticing this, made vacuous the very concept of development. In his schema everything is contingent: A may be viewed as a function of B, but at the same time, B also may be viewed as a function of A.

Such a position relieves Piaget of the necessity to answer the question concerning causes and factors of development. All that he can do is to pick those phenomena that look more promising in terms of genetic explanation (Piaget, 1969, p. 201):

What, then, are these explicative phenomena? The psychology of thought is always faced at this point with two fundamental factors, whose connexion it is her task to explain: the biological factor, and the social factor. The mind becomes conscious of itself, and consequently exists psychologically speaking only when it is in contact with objects or with other minds. We have here two different planes, theoretically independent of one another, and which logically one would wish to keep separate; but in practice, these two planes will always be associated, so long as the child has parents who represent Society to him, and so long as he experiences sensations which constitute a biological environment. Describe the evolution of thought from the purely biological point of view, or as threatens to be the fashion, from the purely sociological point of view, and you risk leaving half the real process in the shade. These two poles must both be kept in view, and nothing must be sacrificed; but in order to make a beginning, we must choose one language at the expense of others. We have chosen the language of sociology, but wish to emphasize the point that there need be nothing exclusive in the choice. We reserve the right to revert to the biological explanation of child thought and to bring our present description into accordance with it. All we have attempted to do as a beginning, was to order our description from the point of view of social psychology, taking the most characteristic phenomenon as our starting-point, namely, egocentrism of child thought.

We, thus, arrive at the paradoxical conclusion that the presentation of material can be transformed from the sociological into the biological. The choice of sociological point of view appears as an arbitrary decision of the author, who is free to pick up any one of the available languages of description at the expense of the others. Such a position is not casual for Piaget, and it sheds some light on how he views the role of the social factor in child development in general.

Piaget's book is permeated with the idea of the gradual socialization of the structures and functions of thought. In the preface to the Russian edition of his work, Piaget directly expresses this thought (Piaget, 1932, pp. 55–56):

The dominant idea for this work is the idea of social determinants in the formation of the child's thought. The child's thought cannot be derived from the inborn psychobiological factors and the factors of the physical environment alone. This does not mean we assert that a child merely reflects ideas and opinions of his milieu, which would be trivial. What I wish to say is that the very structure of thought depends upon the social milieu. When an individual thinks for himself, thinks egocentrically, then his thoughts are subordinated to his fantasy, his desires, and his personality trends. This is a special case of the child's psyche, a case that reveals a number of peculiar forms of thought, but that has nothing to do with rational thinking. When, however, an individual experiences a systematic influence of certain social factors, as is the case with the authority of adults with respect to children, then individual thought forms according to "external" rules. . . . In the course of mutual cooperation between individuals, the rules of such cooperation provide thought with some sort of discipline, the latter being a foundation of reasoning in both its aspects, practical and theoretical.

Egocentrism, coercion, and cooperation are, thus, the three axes between which the developing thought of a child is in continuous oscillation. The thought of the adult also gravitates to one of these axes, depending on whether it is autistic or belongs to a certain type of social organization.

Seemingly, the above statement unequivocally pronounces the social factor to be the decisive one in child development. And yet, as we have seen, it only reflects Piaget's one-time decision to choose the sociological approach. As he himself mentioned, the biological approach is almost equally feasible. This brings us to the problem of the relation between the biological and social factors of development in Piaget's theory.

This relation, as presented by Piaget, looks more like a breakdown. Biological factors appear as primeval, original forces composing the psychological substance of the child's mind. Social factors act as an external, "alien" force, which using coercion replaces the original biological modes of mental life. It is not strange, therefore, that Piaget places coercion as a middle term between autism and cooperation. Coercion is the notion that reflects Piaget's understanding of the mechanism through which social factors enter the child's mind.

In this respect Piaget's point of view has much in common with that of psychoanalysis. In psychoanalysis as well, the milieu is considered to be "alien" and coercive, a force that limits the expression of individual desires, changes them, and directs them along roundabout paths.

We have already seen how Piaget uses the concept of assimilation to account for the role of social factors in child development. These factors penetrate the child's psychological substance, but this substance in itself is determined by autistic, biological factors. Piaget does not see a child as a part of the social whole. Social factors are shown as an external force that enters the child's mind and dislodges the forms of thinking inherent in the child's intelligence. This aspect of Piaget's theory was very accurately described by Claparède (1959, pp. xii–xiii):

Our author shows us in fact that the child's mind is woven on two different looms, which are as it were placed one above the other. By far the most important during the first years is the work accomplished on the lower plane. This is the work done by the child himself, which attracts to him pell-mell and crystallizes round his wants all that is likely to satisfy these wants. It is the plane of subjectivity, of desires, games, and whims, of the *Lustprinzip* as Freud would say. The upper plane, on the contrary, is built up little by little by the social environment, which presses more and more upon the child as time goes on. It is the plane of objectivity, speech, and logical ideas, in a word the plane of reality. As soon as one overloads it, it bends, creaks, and collapses, and the elements of which it is composed fall on the lower plane, and become mixed up with those that properly belong there. Other pieces remain half-way, suspended between Heaven and Earth. One can imagine that an observer whose point of view was such that he did not observe this duality of planes, and supposed the whole transition to be taking place on one plane, would have an impression of extreme confusion, because each of these planes has a logic of its own which protests loudly at being coupled with that of the other.

As we see, the characteristic feature of the child's thinking appears to be a result of the work of two different looms, the first of which works on the plane of subjectivity, desires, and whims. Even if Piaget and Claparède were not mentioning Freud, it would be clear nevertheless that what we have here is the biological concept attempting to derive the specificity of the child's psyche from his biological nature.

The principal conclusion made here by Piaget, and further developed in his later works, portrays the child's life as existing in a dual reality. The first of these realities corresponds to the child's original, inherent, and natural intelligence; the second one appears as a product of the logical forms of thinking forced upon the child from outside. These two realities are incompatible; each has a logic of its own that "protests loudly" at being coupled with that of the other. Autistic thought, according to Piaget, produces its own reality, the reality of a dream.

Then the following question should be answered: Which one of these two planes of thought, which one of these two realities, is more important for a child? Claparède clearly stated that the subjective plane is the most important during the first years of life. Piaget, as we shall see later, adds that our reality is much less real for a child than his own reality of a dream. Following this line of argument, one can do nothing but accept that the child's soul is a dweller of two worlds, and his thought, to quote the Russian poet Tiutchev, "struggles at the gates, as if of a double existence."

"Does there exist for the child only one reality?" asks Piaget, "that is to say one supreme reality which is a touchstone of all others (as is the world of the senses for one adult, the world constructed by science, or even the invisible world of the mystic for another)? Or does the child find himself, according as he is in an ego-centric or in a socialized state of being, in the presence of two worlds which are equally real, and neither of which succeeds in supplanting the other? It is obvious that the second hypothesis is the more probable" (Piaget, 1969, p. 245).

Piaget believes that there may be several realities for

the child, and these realities may be equally real in turn, instead of being arranged in a hierarchy, as with us. During the first stage of a child's development, which lasts two to three years, reality may be said to be simply and solely what is desired. Freud's "pleasure principle" deforms and refashions the world to its liking. The second stage marks the appearance of two heterogeneous but equal realities—the world of play and the world of observation: "Childish play may therefore be said to constitute an autonomous reality, by which we mean that 'true' reality to which it stands in contrast is far less true for the child than for us" (Piaget, 1969, p. 248).

The latter idea does not belong exclusively to Piaget. Recently the same thought has been clearly expressed by Eliasberg in his study of so-called autonomous child speech.[14] Eliasberg comes to the conclusion that the image of the world that appears in language forms does not correspond to a child's nature, which reveals itself in his play and drawings. Only through the speech of adults does a child acquire the categorical forms of subjective and objective, I and you, here and over there, now and then—*das alles vollig unkindgemass.* And, following the lines of Goethe, Eliasberg claims that two souls live in a child, the childish one, full of different relations, and the second one, which emerges under the influence of adults and experiences the world in categories. Such a conclusion is simply the natural outcome of the original view of social and biological factors as alien to each other.

VIII

Piaget, thus, suggests a very peculiar theory of socialization indeed. For one thing, socialization is a force that is alien to the child's nature. Socialization occurs when the child's egocentrism is overridden. The child himself would never arrive at logical thought: "He enlarges sen-

sible reality . . . by means of the verbal and magic reality
which he puts on the same plane. These things are not
sufficient in themselves to make the mind feel any need
for verification, since things themselves have been made
by the mind" (Piaget, 1969, p. 203).

To say such a thing means to claim that the external
reality plays no substantial role in the development of a
child's thought. It is the "collision" of our thought with
the thought of others that engenders doubt and calls for
verification: "If there were not other people, the disap-
pointments of the experience would lead to overcompen-
sation and dementia. We are constantly hatching an
enormous number of false ideas, conceits, Utopias, mys-
tical explanations, suspicions, and megalomaniac fan-
tasies, which disappear when brought into contact with
other people. The social need to share the thought of
others and to communicate our own with success is at the
root of our need for verification. Proof is the outcome of
argument. All this, moreover, is common knowledge for
contemporary psychology" (Piaget, 1969, p. 204).

It is hardly possible to express better the idea that the
need for logical thinking and the search for truth in general come from the communication between the consciousness of a child and the consciousness of others. By
its philosophical nature this idea is very close to the doctrine of Emile Durkheim and those sociologists who derive
time, space, and reality from the social organization of
human life. It also closely resembles the thesis of Alexander Bogdanov that the objective character of physical reality, as it is present in our experience, is ultimately
verified through the social organization of the experiences of others.[15]

There is little doubt that here Piaget's thought comes
close to that of Ernst Mach, especially if one remembers
Piaget's position concerning the problem of causality.[16]
In this respect Piaget follows Claparède and his "law of

consciousness," which states that the conscious realization of a problem occurs when the automatic adaptation of one's actions fails to achieve its goal: "How did the individual ever come to ask questions about cause, aim, or place, etc? This problem of origins is the same as that of knowing how the individual gradually came to interest himself in the cause, the aim, and the place of things, etc. And there is good reason for believing that his interest was only directed to these 'categories' when his action was unadapted to one of them. Need creates consciousness, and the consciousness of cause (or of aim, or of place, etc.) only arose in the mind when the need was felt for adaptation in relation to the cause" (Piaget, 1959, p. 228).

When it works within the framework of automatic adaptation the mind does not know categories. The execution of the automatic act does not contain any problem, and therefore there is no need for conscious realization.

Following this line of Claparède's argument, Piaget adds that (Piaget, 1959, pp. 229–230)

in a sense, we have gone further along the path of functional psychology in asserting that the fact of becoming conscious of a category will alter its actual nature. If, therefore, we accept the formula: "The child is cause long before having any idea of cause" it must be remembered that we do so only for the sake of convenience. It is only as a concession to language (and one which if we are not careful will involve us in a thoroughly realistic theory of knowledge entirely outside the scope of psychology) that we can talk of "causality" as a relation entirely independent of the consciousness which may be had of it. As a matter of fact, there are as many types of causality as there are types and degrees of becoming conscious of it. When the child "is cause," or acts as though he knew one thing was cause of another, this, even though he has not consciously realized causality, is an early type of causality, and, if one wishes, the functional equivalent of causality. Then, when the same child becomes conscious of the relation in question, this realization, just because it depends upon the needs and interests of the moment, is capable of assuming a number of different types—

animistic causality, artificialistic, finalistic, mechanistic (by contact), or dynamic (force), etc. The list of types can never be considered complete, and the types of relation used nowadays by adults and scientists are probably only as provisional as those which have been used by the child and the savage.

Denying the objective character of causality, and other categories, Piaget assumes the idealistic and psychologistic position, and advises that the "genetician will therefore have to note the appearance and use of these categories at every stage of intelligence traversed by the child, and to bring these facts under the functional laws of thought" (Piaget, 1959, pp. 230–231). Piaget rejects both scholastic realism and Kantian apriorism, and praises the position of pragmatic empirists who "have given to the theory of the categories a turn which it is no exaggeration to characterize as psychological, since the task they have set themselves is to define the categories according to their genesis in the history of thought and to their progressive use in the history of the sciences" (Piaget, 1959, p. 230). As we see, Piaget not only takes a position of subjective idealism, but contradicts his own data, which, as he admits, may carry him to a realistic theory of thinking.

It comes as no surprise that in his later studies Piaget names realism, artificialism, and animism as three major features of the child's mentality (Piaget, 1927). In this study Piaget made an attempt to find experimental support for Mach's thesis of the lack of an inherent distinction between physical reality and the psychological reality. Piaget observed that Mach's thesis in itself is purely theoretical, and that Baldwin's "genetic logic" is also a subjective rather than an experimental concept. Therefore a new study of the child's logic may become an experimental proof of Mach's formula. Trying to produce this necessary proof, Piaget ran into a contradiction, for he portrayed the original state of the child's mind as a realistic one. Developing his argument, Piaget came to the following formula of the relation between logic and reality: "Experience forms thought, and thought forms experience. There is a certain relationship between reason and reality. The problem of this relationship primarily belongs to epistemology, but the same problem also emerges in genetic psychology as the following: either the evolution of logic determines the actual categories of causality, or otherwise actual causality determines logic" (Piaget, 1927, p. 337).

Piaget pointed out that there is a similarity, even a certain parallelism, between the actual categories of experience and those of formal logic. From his point of view, there exists, for example, not only logical egocentrism but also ontological egocentrism. The logical and ontological categories of a child undergo a parallel development.

The final statement of Piaget regarding this question is very cautious. He considers agnosticism, which would allow him to remain on the borderline of idealism and materialism. Actually, however, he rejects the objectivity of logical categories, thus siding with Mach: "Once we have established the fact of parallelism of logic and experience, we have to inquire whether the content of concrete thinking determines logical forms, or, probably otherwise, logical forms determine the content of thinking. But in this form the question has no sense; only if we change 'logical' into 'psychological' may we acquire a sensible answer. However, we would refrain from suggesting what kind of answer this can be" (Piaget, 1927, p. 342).

IX

If we were to summarize the central flaws in Piaget's theory, we would have to point out that it is reality and the relations between a child and reality that are missed in his theory. The process of socialization appears as a direct communication of souls, which is divorced from the practical activity of a child.

The acquisition of knowledge and logical forms involved are considered as products of the adjustment of one set of thoughts to another. The practical confrontation with reality plays no role in this process. If left to himself, a child would develop only delirious thinking. Reality would never teach him any logic.

This attempt to derive the logical thinking of a child and his entire development from the pure dialogue of consciousnesses, which is divorced from practical activity and which disregards the social practice, is the central point of Piaget's theory.

In his comments on Hegel's *Logic*, V. I. Lenin mentions philosophical and psychological idealistic views that have much in common with those discussed above (Lenin, 1961, p. 190 and p. 217):

When Hegel endeavors—sometimes even huffs and puffs—to bring man's purposive activity under the categories of logic, saying that this activity is the 'syllogism' (*Schluss*), that the subject (man) plays the role of a 'member' in the logical 'figure' of the 'syllogism,' and so on, then that is not merely stretching a point, a mere game. This has a very profound, purely materialistic content. It has to be inverted: the practical activity of man had to lead his consciousness to the repetition of the various logical figures thousands of millions of times in order that these figures could obtain the significance of axioms. . . . Man's practice, repeating itself a thousand million times, becomes consolidated in man's consciousness by figures of logic. Precisely (and only) on account of this thousand-million-fold repetition, these figures have the stability of a prejudice, an axiomatic character.

It is no surprise that abstract verbal thought, as Piaget has shown, is incomprehensible to a child. Communication without action remains unintelligible: "Naturally, when children are playing together, or are all handling the same material, they understand each other, because, however elliptical their language may be, it is accompanied by gesture and mimicry which is a beginning of action and serves as an example to the interlocutor. But it can be questioned whether verbal thought and language itself are really understood among children, whether in other words, children understand each other when they speak without acting. This problem is of fundamental importance, since it is on the verbal plane that the child makes the chief effort of adaptation to adult thought and to the acquisition of logical habits" (Piaget, 1969, pp. 207–208).

This idea, namely, that the acquisition of logical thinking comes from the comprehension of verbal thought that is independent of action, lies at the foundation of Piaget's discovery of the lack of understanding among children. It was Piaget himself who clearly demonstrated that the logic of action precedes the logic of thought, and yet he insists that thinking is separated from reality. And naturally, if the function of thinking is to reflect upon reality, this actionless thinking appears as a parade of phantoms and a chorus of shadows rather than the real thinking of a child. That is why Piaget's study, which attempts to supersede the laws of causality by the principles of development, loses this very notion of development. Piaget does not put the specificity of a child's thinking in such a relation to logical thinking as to show how the latter is evolving in the child's psyche. On the contrary, Piaget tries to show how logic penetrates the child's thinking, deforms, and finally dislodges it.

It is not surprising, therefore, that to the question whether a child's logic produces a coherent system, Piaget answers that the truth must lie between two extremes: A child reveals the originality of his mental organization, but its development depends on circumstances. Piaget, thus, clearly indicates that the originality of a child's thinking is inherent, and does not appear as a product of development. Development, therefore, is not self-development, but obeys the "logic" of circumstance. But where there is no self-development, there can be no development in a strict sense of this term, only a dislodging of one form by another.

It is sufficient to discuss one example to make our point of view clear. Piaget attempted to show that a child's thought is illogical and irrational. But if a child's thought is exclusively syncretic, then how is it possible for him to adapt? The same question, some time ago, had been posed to Lucien Levy-Bruhl in connection with his theory of primitive alogism.

In the light of these facts, Piaget's conclusions call for clarification concerning two important points. First, the peculiarities of the child's thought discussed by Piaget, such as syncretism, do not extend over quite so large an area as Piaget believes. We are inclined to think (and our experiments bear us out) that the child thinks syncretically in matters of which he has no knowledge or experience but does not resort to syncretism in relation to familiar things or things within easy reach of practical checking—and the number of these things depends on the method of education. Also, within syncretism itself we must expect to find some precursors of the future causal conceptions that Piaget himself mentions in passing. The syncretic schemata themselves, despite their fluctuations, lead the child gradually toward adaptation; their usefulness must not be underrated. Sooner or later, through strict selection, reduction, and mutual adaptation, they will be sharpened into excellent tools of investigation in areas where hypotheses are of use.

The second point calling for reappraisal and limitation is the applicability of Piaget's findings to children in general. His experiments led him to believe that the child was impervious to experience. Piaget draws an analogy that we find illuminating: Primitive man, he says, learns from experience only in a few special, limited cases of practical activity—and he cites as examples of these rare cases agriculture, hunting, and manufacturing: "But even this momentary and partial contact with facts does not react in any way upon the orientation of [primitive man's] thought. This applies even more strongly to the child. . . ." (Piaget, 1969, p. 203).

We would not call agriculture and hunting negligible contacts with reality in the case of primitive man; they are practically his whole existence. Piaget's view may hold true for the particular group of children he studied, but it is not of universal significance. He himself tells us the cause of the special quality of thinking he observed in his children: "On the contrary, the child never really comes into contact with things because he does not work. He plays with them, or simply believes them without trying to find the truth" (Piaget, 1969, p. 203).

The developmental uniformities established by Piaget apply to the given milieu, under the conditions of Piaget's study. They are not laws of nature, but are historically and socially determined. Piaget has already been criticized by Stern for his failure sufficiently to take into account the importance of the social situation and milieu. Whether the child's talk is more egocentric or more social depends not only on his age but also on the surrounding conditions. Piaget observed children at play together in a particular kindergarten, and his coefficients are valid only for this special milieu.

When a child's activity consists entirely of play, it is accompanied by extensive soliloquizing. Marta Muchow of Hamburg pointed out that the structural organization of activity in kindergarten is of decisive importance.[17] In Genevan as well as in Montessori kindergartens, where children simply play with each other, the coefficient of egocentric speech is higher than that in German kindergartens, where there is more group activity.[18]

Even more pronounced is the social aspect in a child's speech at home, where the very process of learning how to speak is thoroughly socialized. At home a child has so much to ask and to understand, has so many practical and ideal needs to be satisfied that the desire to understand and to be understood appears very early (see C. and W. Stern, 1928, pp. 148–149).

What we are concerned about at this moment is not so much egocentric speech data as the nature of the relations that stand behind these data. The relations discovered by Piaget turned out to be valid only for the social milieu in which his subjects live. One may imagine how substantial must be the differences in data collected in Genevan and Soviet kindergartens. Piaget directly addresses this problem when he writes in the preface to the Russian edition of his book that "when one works, as I do, with one and the same social milieu in Geneva, one is unable to give relative weights to the social and individual contributions in the development of a child's thought. In order to achieve this goal one should be able to study children in the most varied and contrasting social milieus" (Piaget, 1932, p. 56). Piaget emphasized that this goal makes a collaboration between Western and Soviet psychologists particularly valuable.

We too are convinced that the study of thought development in children from different social environments, and especially of children who unlike Piaget's children, work, must lead to results that will permit the formulation of laws having a much wider sphere of application.

On the last pages of Goethe's *Faust,* a chorus praises the eternal elevating feminine qualities. In recent times, child psychology, through its spokesman Volkelt, praised the "primitive unity that is distinctive to the normal psyche of a child and that characterizes the essence and the high value of the eternally childish" (Volkelt, 1930, p. 138).[19] Thus, Volkelt revealed a major trend in child psychology, whose aim is the discovery of the timelessly childish in the child's character. But the real aim of psychology should be rather to discover the "historically childish." This stone that the builders rejected should be the cornerstone.[20]

3

Stern's Theory of Language Development

The part of William Stern's system that is best known and has actually gained ground over the years is his intellectualistic conception of speech development in the child. (C. and W. Stern 1928) Yet it is precisely this conception that plainly reveals the limitations and inconsistencies of Stern's philosophical and psychological personalism, its idealistic foundations and scientific invalidity.[1]

Stern himself describes his point of view as "personalistic-genetic." We shall discuss the personalistic principle later on. Let us see first how Stern deals with the genetic aspect, and let us state from the outset that his theory, like all intellectualistic theories, is by its very nature antidevelopmental.

Stern distinguishes three roots of speech: the expressive, the social, and the "intentional" tendencies. While the first two underlie also the rudiments of speech observed in animals, the third is specifically human. Stern defines *intentionality* in this sense as a directedness toward a certain content, or meaning: "At a certain stage of his psychic development," he says, "man acquires the ability to mean something when uttering sounds, to refer to something objective" (C. and W. Stern 1928, p. 126). In substance, such intentional acts are already acts of thought; their appearance denotes intellectualization and objectification of speech.

Some of the modern cognitive psychologists, notably Karl Bühler and Reimut, also emphasize the logical factor in the child's speech.[2] Although Stern considers their emphasis on that factor excessive, he, nevertheless, fully endorses their orientation. He indicates a precise moment in speech development when "intentionality penetrates and supplies speech with its specifically human characteristics" (C. and W. Stern, 1928, p. 127).

We have no quarrel with the statement that advanced human speech possesses objective meaning and therefore presupposes a certain level in the development of thinking, and we agree that it is necessary to take account of the close relation that exists between language and logical thinking. The trouble is that Stern regards intentionality, a trait of advanced speech that properly calls for a genetic explanation (i.e., how it came into being in the evolutionary process), as one of the *roots* of speech development, a driving force, an innate tendency, almost an urge, at any rate something primordial, on a par genetically with the expressive and the communicative tendencies—which indeed are found at the very beginnings of speech. In viewing intentionality in this way ("*die 'intentionale' Triebfeder des Sprachdranges*"), he substitutes an intellectualistic explanation for the genetic one.

This method of "explaining" a thing by the very thing that needs explaining is the basic flaw of all intellectualistic theories and of Stern's in particular—hence its general hollowness and its antigenetic quality (traits belonging to advanced speech are relegated to its beginnings). Stern answers the question of why and how speech acquires meaning by saying: from the intentional tendency, i.e., the tendency toward meaning. We are reminded of Molière's physician who explained the sleep-inducing effect of opium by its soporific properties. Stern insists that at a certain stage of his intellectual development, the human being acquires an ability [*Fähigkeit*] to infer some objective content when he voices words. But what is this if not an explanation of Molière's physician?

From Stern's famous description of the great discovery made by the child of one-and-a-half or two, we can see to what exaggerations overemphasis on the logical aspects can lead. At that age the child first realizes that each object has its permanent symbol, a sound pattern that identifies it—i.e., that each thing has a *name*. Stern believes that a child in the second year of his life can become aware of symbols and of the need for them, and he considers this discovery already a thought process in the proper sense: "The understanding of the relation between sign and meaning that dawns on the child at this point is something different in principle from the simple use of sound images, object images, and their associations. And the requirement that *each* object of whatever kind have its name may be considered a true generalization made by the child—possibly his first" (Stern, 1914, pp. 109–110).

Are there any factual or theoretical grounds for assuming that a child of one-and-a-half or two has an awareness of the symbolic function of language and a consciousness of a general rule, a general concept? All the studies made of this problem in the last twenty years suggest a negative answer to this question.

Everything we know of the mentality of the child of one-and-a-half or two clashes with the idea that he might be capable of such complex intellectual operations. Both observation and experimental studies indicate that he grasps only much later the relation between sign and meaning, or the functional use of signs; this is quite beyond a child of two. Furthermore, systematic experimental investigations have shown that grasping the relation between sign and meaning and the transition to operating with signs never result from an instantaneous discovery or invention by the child. Stern believes that the child discovers the meaning of language once and for all. Actually, this is an extremely complex process, which has its "natural history" (i.e., its early beginnings and transitional forms on the more primitive developmental levels) and also its "cultural history" (again with its own series of phases, its own quantitative, qualitative, and functional growth, its own dynamics and laws).

Stern virtually ignores the intricate ways leading to the ripening of the sign function; his conception of linguistic development is immensely simplified. The child suddenly discovers that speech has meaning. Such an explanation of how speech becomes meaningful truly deserves to be grouped with the theory of the deliberate invention of language, the rationalistic theory of the social contract, and other famous intellectualistic theories. All of them disregard the genetic realities and do not really explain anything.

Factually, too, Stern's theory fails to stand up. Wallon, Koffka, Piaget, Delacroix, and many others in their studies of normal children, and K. Bühler in his study of deaf-mute children, have found (1) that the discovery by the child of the tie between word and object does *not* immediately lead to a clear awareness of the symbolic relation of sign and referent, characteristic of well-developed thought; that the word for a long time appears to the child as an attribute or a property of the object rather than as a mere sign; that the child grasps the external structure object-word before he can grasp the internal relation sign-referent; and (2) that the discovery made by the child is not in reality a sudden one, the exact instant of which can be defined. A series of long and complicated "molecular" changes leads up to that critical moment in speech development.[3]

That Stern's basic observation was correct, that there is indeed a moment of discovery that to gross observation appears unprepared, has been established beyond doubt during the twenty years since his study was first published. The decisive turning point in the child's linguistic, cultural, and intellectual development discovered by Stern does exist—though he was wrong to interpret it intellectualistically. Stern points out two objective symptoms of the occurrence of the critical change: the appearance of inquiries about names of objects and the resulting sharp, saccadic increases in the child's vocabulary, both of major importance for the development of speech.

The active search for words on the part of the child, which has no analogy in the development of "speech" in animals, indicates a new phase in his development. The child's speech ceases to be a signaling, and becomes a signifying function. From the use of sounds a child turns to their active production. Some psychologists (for example, Wallon and Delacroix) used to question the universality of this symptom, and gave it different explanations. Nevertheless, there is no doubt that it is at that time that the "grandiose signality of speech," to quote Pavlov, emerges for a child from the mass of all other signals and assumes a specific function in behavior, the function of signification. To have established this fact on a firm objective basis is one of Stern's great achievements. Against such a background, the gap in his explanation of these facts is all the more striking.

In contrast with the two other roots of language, the expressive and the communicative, whose development has been traced from the lower social animals to anthropoids and to man, the "intentional tendency" appears out of nowhere; it has no history and no derivation. According to Stern, it is basic, primordial; it springs up spontaneously "once and for all"; it is the propensity enabling the child to discover the function of speech by way of purely logical operation.

To be sure, Stern does not state this explicitly. He even reproaches Reimut and Ament for reading too much logic into the child's speech. However, objectively, while arguing with the antiintellectualistic theories of speech of Wundt, Meumann, and Idelberger, Stern assumes the same intellectualist position as Reimut and Ament.[4] Stern views himself as a "moderate," but he actually goes much further then Ament. Ament's intellectualism has an empirical character, while in Stern it becomes metaphysical. Ament naively overestimates the child's ability to reason logically. Stern makes a graver mistake in assigning to intellect the metaphysical position of primacy as the origin, the unanalyzable first cause, of meaningful speech.

Paradoxically, intellectualism of this kind proves especially inadequate in the study of intellectual processes, which at first glance would seem to be its legitimate sphere of application. It was Wolfgang Köhler who exposed this inadequacy. But Stern's work itself testifies to the same effect. One might expect, for instance, that much light would be thrown on the relation between speech and thought when the meaningfulness of language is regarded as the result of an intellectual operation. Actually, however, such an approach, stipulating as it does an already formed intellect, blocks an investigation of the involved dialectical interactions of thought and speech. Stern's treatment of this cardinal aspect of the problem of language is full of inconsistencies and is the weakest part of his work (C. and W. Stern, 1928).

Such important topics as inner speech, its emergence, and its connection with thought are barely touched upon by Stern. He reviews the results of Piaget's investigation of egocentric speech merely in his discussion of children's conversations, ignoring the functions, the structure, and the developmental significance of that form of speech. Altogether, Stern fails to relate the complex functional and structural changes in thinking to the development of speech.

Even when Stern gives a correct characterization of a

developmental phenomenon, his theoretical framework prevents him from drawing the obvious conclusions from his own observations. Nowhere is this fact more apparent than in his failure to see the implications of his own "translation" of the child's very first words into the language of adults. The interpretation given to the first words of the child is the touchstone of every theory of child speech; it is the focal point at which all the major trends in modern speech theories meet and cross. One might say without exaggeration that the whole structure of a theory is determined by its translation of the first words of the child.

Stern believes that they should be interpreted neither from the purely intellectualistic nor from the purely affective-conative point of view. He acknowledges Meumann's great merit in opposing the intellectualistic theory that the child's first words actually designate objects as such (Meumann, 1902). He does not, however, share Meumann's assumption that the first words are merely expressions of the emotions and wishes of the child.

Stern points out that the "direction toward object" [*"Hindenten auf das Object"*] predominates in the children's first words over the moderately emotional tone (C. and W. Stern, 1928, p. 183). This is an extremely important moment. There is factual evidence that the "direction toward object" appears already in the very early pre-stages [*"ein primitivieren Entwincklungs-Stadien"*] of the development of child speech, prior to any intentionality. Stern himself recognized these facts. Seemingly, this evidence alone is a sufficient argument against the hypothesis of the primacy of intentionality.

There are some other facts reported by Stern that also speak against the principle of intentionality: for example, the mediating role of gestures in defining the meaning of the first words; the fact that objective reference overshadows the affective aspect; the indicative function of the first words, etc. (C. and W. Stern, 1928, pp. 160, 166).

Stern, however, turned down the only possible genetic explanation of these phenomena. He refused to accept the idea of intentionality developing from the indicatory gesture and the first word. He opted for the intellectualist shortcut according to which meaningfulness appears as a result of a tendency toward the meaningful, and neglected the longer, dialectical, way of genetic explanation.

This is how Stern translates first words: "The childish *mama*, translated into advanced speech, does not mean the word 'mother' but rather a sentence such as 'Mama, come here,' or 'Mama, give me,' or 'Mama, put me in the chair,' or 'Mama, help me' " (C. and W. Stern, 1928, p. 180).

When we observe the child in action, however, it becomes obvious that it is not only the word *mama* that means, say, "Mama, put me in the chair," but *the child's whole behavior at that moment* (his reaching out toward the chair, trying to hold on to it, etc.). Here the "affective-conative" directedness toward an object (to use Meumann's terms) is as yet inseparable from the "intentional tendency" of speech. The two are still a homogeneous whole, and the only correct translation of *mama*, or of any other early words, is the pointing gesture. The word, at first, is a conventional substitute for the gesture; it appears long before the child's crucial "discovery of language" and before he is capable of logical operations. Stern himself admits the mediatory role of gestures, especially pointing, in establishing the meaning of first words. The inescapable conclusion would be that pointing is, in fact, a precursor of the "intentional tendency." Yet Stern declines to trace the genetic history of that tendency. To him, it does not evolve from the affective object-directedness of the pointing act (gesture or first words)—it appears out of nowhere, and it accounts for the emergence of meaning.

The same antigenetic approach also characterizes Stern's treatment of all the other major issues discussed in his pithy book, such as the development of concepts and the main stages in the development of speech and thought. Nor can it be otherwise; this approach is a direct consequence of the philosophical premises of personalism, the system developed by Stern.

Stern tries to rise above the extremes of both empiricism and nativism. He opposes his own view of the development of speech, on the one hand, to Wundt's, who sees the child's speech as a product of environment, while the child's own participation is essentially passive, and, on the other hand, to the view of Ament, to whom primary speech (onomatopoeia and so-called nursery talk) is the invention of countless generations of children. Stern takes care not to disregard the part that imitation plays in speech development, or the role of the child's spontaneous activity, by applying to these issues his concept of "convergence": The child's conquest of speech occurs through a constant interaction of inner dispositions prompting the child to speech and external conditions— i.e., the speech of people around him—which provide both stimulation and material for the realization of these dispositions.

Convergence, to Stern, is a general principle to be applied to the explanation of all human behavior. Truly this is one more instance when we may say, with Goethe, "The words of science hide its substance." The sonorous word *convergence*, denoting here a perfectly unassailable methodological principle (i.e., that development should be studied as a process determined by the interaction of organism and environment), in fact releases the author from the task of analyzing the social, environmental factors in speech development. Stern does say quite emphatically, it is true, that social environment is the main factor in speech development, but in reality he limits its role to merely accelerating or slowing down the development, which obeys its own immanent laws. As we have tried to show by using the example of his explanation of how meaning emerges in speech, Stern greatly overrated the role of the internal organismic factors.

This bias is a direct outcome of the personalistic frame of reference. The "person" to Stern is a psychophysically neutral entity that "in spite of the multiplicity of its part-functions manifests a unitary, goal-directed activity" (Stern, 1905, p. 16). This idealistic, "monadic" conception of the individual person naturally leads to a theory that sees language as rooted in personal teleology— hence the intellectualism and the antigenetic bias of Stern's approach to problems of linguistic development. Applied to the eminently social mechanism of speech behavior, Stern's personalism, ignoring as it does the social side of personality, leads to patent absurdities. His metaphysical conception of personality, deriving all developmental processes from personal teleology, turns the real genetic relations between personality and language upside down; instead of a developmental history of the personality itself, in which language plays a far from minor role, we have the metaphysical theory that personality generates language out of the goal-directedness of its own essential nature.

4

The Genetic Roots of Thought and Speech

I

The most important fact uncovered through the genetic study of thought and speech is that their relation undergoes many changes. Progress in thought and progress in speech are not parallel. Their two growth curves cross and recross. They may straighten out and run side by side, even merge for a time, but they always diverge again. This applies to both phylogeny and ontogeny. The cases of pathological dissolution and involution of functions, as we shall try to prove later, also indicate that the *relation* between thought and speech is not an unchangeable one. In each case of disturbance or retardation there is a specific balance between impaired thought and impaired speech.

In animals, language and thought spring from different roots and develop along different lines. This fact is confirmed by Köhler's, Yerkes's, and other recent studies of apes (Köhler, 1921/1973; Yerkes and Learned, 1925). Köhler's experiments proved that the appearance in animals of an embryonic intellect—i.e., of thinking in the proper sense—is in no way related to language. The "inventions" of apes in making and using tools, or in finding detours for the solutions of problems, though undoubtedly rudimentary intellect, belong in a prelinguistic phase of thought development.

In Köhler's opinion, his investigations proved that the chimpanzee shows the beginning of an intellectual behavior of the same kind and type as man's. At the same time, he wrote that "a great many years spent with chimpanzees lead me to venture the opinion that, besides in the lack of speech, it is in the extremely narrow limits in *this* direction that the chief difference is to be found between anthropoids and even the most primitive human beings. The lack of an invaluable technical aid (speech) and a great limitation of those very important components of thought, so called 'images,' would thus constitute the causes that prevent the chimpanzee from attaining even the smallest beginnings of cultural development" (Köhler, 1973, p. 267).

The existence of humanlike intelligence, and the absence of any traces of humanlike speech in anthropoids, as well as the independence of the chimpanzee's actions from its "speech"—these are the major conclusions to be drawn from the Köhler's study.

There is a considerable disagreement among psychologists of different schools about the theoretical interpretation of Köhler's findings. The mass of critical literature that his studies have called forth represents a variety of viewpoints. Köhler himself somehow limited his task. He developed no general theory of intellectual actions. He chiefly discusses the factual findings and turns to theory only when he wants to show that intellectual actions cannot be reduced to those of trial and error, and that, therefore, a "chance theory" is inapplicable here.

Rejecting the "theory of chance," Köhler seems to be satisfied with this only *negatively* defined theoretical position. His position vis-à-vis the idealistic concept of unconscious of Eduard von Hartmann, Henri Bergson's "*élan vital*," and the "forces with purpose" of neo- and psychovitalists is also purely negative. For Köhler, all these theories, which explicitly or implicitly presuppose a force that lies beyond experience, are unscientific: "I therefore wish to emphasize that the alternative is not at all between chance and factors outside experience [*Agenten jenseits der Erfahrung*]" (Köhler, 1973, p. 211).

At the same time, both groups of Köhler's opponents, i.e., the biologically oriented psychologists (Edward Thorndike, Vladimir Vagner, and Vladimir Borovsky) and the psychologists-subjectivists (Karl Bühler, Johannes Lindworsky, and Erich Jaensch) challenged his major conclusion that the chimpanzee's intelligence cannot be explained in terms of trial-and-error learning.[1] They also disagreed with Köhler's opinion that the chimpanzee's intellectual operations are akin to human ones.

In this context it is particularly important that even those psychologists, like Borovsky, who do not see anything in the chimpanzee's actions beyond the mechanics of instinct and trial-and-error learning ("nothing at all except the already known process of habit formation"), do recognize (a) the factual findings of Köhler and (b) the independence of the chimpanzee's actions from its "speech" (Borovsky, 1927, p. 179). These latter are also recognized by the introspectionists, who shy away from lowering intelligence to the level of even the most advanced behavior of apes.

Bühler says quite rightly that "the achievements of the chimpanzee are quite *independent of language* and in the case of man even in later life, technical thinking, or thinking in terms of tools [*Werkzeugdenken*] is far less closely bound up with language and concepts than other forms of thinking" (Bühler, 1919/1930, pp. 50–51).

We shall return to this thought of Bühler later. Experimental psychological and clinical data we know about indicate that even for human adults, the relation between speech and thought varies depending on the form of verbal and intellectual activity.

Arguing with Hobhous's[2] concept of "practical reasoning" in animals and Yerkes's concept of "ideation" in apes, Borovsky posed the following question: "Is there in animals anything resembling the speech habits of men?" "It seems to me," answered Borovsky, "that at the present level of our knowledge there are no grounds to believe that apes or any other animals, except humans, have verbal habits" (Borovsky, 1927, p. 189).

The issue would be quite simple if apes had no rudiments of language, nothing at all resembling speech. We do, however, find in the chimpanzee a relatively well-developed "language"—in some respects (most of all phonetically) not unlike human speech. The remarkable thing about its language is that it functions apart from its intellect. Köhler, who studied chimpanzees for many years at the Canary Island Anthropoid Station, tells us that "it may be taken as positively proved that their gamut of phonetics is entirely 'subjective,' and can only express emotions, never designate or describe objects" (Köhler, 1973, p. 305). But chimpanzee and human phonetics have so many elements in common that we may confidently suppose that the absence of humanlike speech is not due to any peripheral causes. Henri Delacroix absolutely correctly observed that the gestures and mimicries of apes do not bear any objective reference; i.e., they do not carry out a function of signification (Delacroix, 1924, p. 77).

The chimpanzee is an extremely gregarious animal and responds strongly to the presence of others of its kind. Köhler describes highly diversified forms of "linguistic communication" among chimpanzees. First of these is their vast repertoire of affective expressions: facial play, gestures, vocalization; next come the movements expressing social emotions: gestures of greeting, etc. The apes are capable both of "understanding" one another's gestures and of "expressing," through gestures, desires involving other animals. Usually a chimpanzee will *begin* a movement or an action it wants another animal to perform or to share—e.g., will push the other and execute the initial movements of walking when "inviting" the other to follow it, or grab at the air when it wants the other to give it a banana. All these are gestures *directly* related to the action itself. Köhler mentions that the experimenter comes to use essentially similar elementary ways of communication to convey to the apes what is expected of them.

By and large, these observations confirm Wundt's opinion that pointing gestures, the first stage in the development of human speech, do not yet appear in animals, but that some gestures of apes are a transitional form between grasping and pointing (Wundt, 1900, p. 219). We consider this transitional gesture a most important step from unadulterated affective expression toward objective language.

There is no evidence, however, that animals reach the stage of objective representation in any of their activities. Köhler's chimpanzees played with colored clay, "painting" first with lips and tongue, later with real paintbrushes; but these animals—who normally transfer to play the use of tools and other behavior learned "in earnest" (i.e., in experiments) and, conversely, transfer play behavior to "real life"—never exhibited the slightest intent of representing anything in their drawings or the slightest sign of attributing any objective meaning to their products. Bühler says, "There are facts which warn us against overestimating the achievements of the chimpanzee. We know that no explorer has ever confused gorillas or chimpanzees with men. No traditional tools or methods of using them differing from tribe to tribe (which would point to the transmission from one generation to another of some invention) have ever been found among them. We do not know of any scratchings in sand or clay, which would constitute a *representational drawing* or even a mere ornament scribbled playfully, nor of any *representational language*, i.e., sounds signifying names. There must be some inner reason for all this" (Bühler, 1930, p. 15).

Yerkes seems to be the only one among modern observers of apes to explain their lack of speech otherwise than by "intrinsic causes." His research on the intellect of orangutans yielded data very similar to Köhler's; but he goes further in his conclusions: He admits "higher ideation" in orangs—on the level, it is true, of a three-year-old child at most (Yerkes, 1916, p. 132).

Yerkes deduces ideation merely from superficial similarities between anthropoid behavior and human behavior; he has no objective proof that orangs solve problems with the help of ideation, i.e., of "images," or trace stimuli. In the study of the higher animals, analogy may be used to good purpose within the boundaries of objectivity, but basing an assumption on analogy is hardly a scientific procedure.

Köhler, on the other hand, went beyond the mere use of analogy in exploring the nature of the chimpanzee's intellectual processes. He showed by precise experimental analysis that the success of the animals' actions depended on whether they could see all the elements of a situation simultaneously—this was a decisive factor in their behavior. If, especially during the earlier experiments, the stick they used to reach some fruit lying beyond the bars was moved slightly, so that the tool (stick) and the goal (fruit) were not visible to them at one glance, the solution of the problem became very difficult, often impossible. The apes had learned to make a longer tool by inserting one stick into an opening in another. If the two sticks accidentally crossed in their hands, forming an

X, they became unable to perform the familiar, much-practiced operation of lengthening the tool. Dozens of similar examples from Köhler's experiments could be cited.

Köhler considers the actual visual presence of a sufficiently simple situation an indispensable condition in any investigation of the intellect of chimpanzee's, a condition without which their intellect cannot be made to function at all; he concludes that the inherent limitations of imagery (or "ideation") are a basic feature of the chimpanzee's intellectual behavior. If we accept Köhler's thesis, then Yerkes's assumption appears more than doubtful.

In connection with his recent experimental and observational studies of the intellect and language of chimpanzees, Yerkes presents new material on their linguistic development and a new, ingenious theory to account for their lack of real speech. "Vocal reactions," he says, "are very frequent and varied in young chimpanzees, but speech in the human sense is absent" (Yerkes and Learned, 1925, p. 53). Their vocal apparatus is as well developed and functions as well as man's. What is missing is the tendency to imitate sounds. Their mimicry is almost entirely dependent on optical stimuli; they copy actions but not sounds. They are incapable of doing what the parrot does so successfully: "If the imitative tendency of the parrot were combined with the caliber of intellect of the chimpanzee, the latter undoubtedly would possess speech, since he has a voice mechanism comparable to man's as well as an intellect of the type and level to enable him to use sounds for purposes of real speech" (Yerkes and Learned, 1925, p. 53).

In his experiments, Yerkes applied four methods of teaching chimpanzees to speak. None of them succeeded. Such failures, of course, never solve a problem in principle. In this case, we still do not know whether or not it is possible to teach chimpanzees to speak. Not uncommonly the fault lies with the experimenter. Köhler says that if earlier studies of chimpanzee intellect failed to show that it had any, this was not because the chimpanzee really has none but because of inadequate methods, ignorance of the limits of difficulty within which the chimpanzee intellect can manifest itself, ignorance of its dependence on a comprehensive visual situation: "The experimenter should recognize," quipped Köhler, "that every intelligence test is a test, not only of the creature examined, but also of the experimenter himself" (Köhler, 1973, p. 265).

Without settling the issue in principle, Yerkes's experiments showed once more that anthropoids do not have anything like human speech, even in embryo. Correlating this with what we know from other sources, we may assume that apes are probably incapable of real speech.

What are the causes of their inability to speak, since they have the necessary voice apparatus and phonetic range? Yerkes sees the cause in the absence or weakness of vocal imitativeness. This may very well have been the immediate cause of the negative results of his experiments, but he is probably wrong in seeing it as the fundamental cause of the lack of speech in apes. The latter thesis, though Yerkes presents it as established, is belied by everything we know of the chimpanzee's intellect.

Yerkes had at his disposal an excellent means of checking his thesis, which for some reason he did not use and which we should be only too happy to apply if we had the wherewithal. We should exclude the auditory factor in training the animals in a linguistic skill. Language does not have to depend on sound. There are, for instance, the sign language of deaf-mutes and lip reading, which is also interpretation of movement. In the languages of primitive peoples, gestures are used along with sound, and play a substantial role (Levy-Bruhl, 1918). In principle, language does not depend on the nature of its material. If it is true that the chimpanzee has the intellect for acquiring something analogous to human language, and that the whole trouble lies in its lacking vocal imitativeness, then it should be able, in experiments, to master some conventional gestures whose psychological function would be exactly the same as that of conventional sounds. As Yerkes himself conjectures, the chimpanzees might be trained, for instance, to use manual gestures rather than sounds. The medium is beside the point; what matters is the *functional use of signs*, any signs that could play a role corresponding to that of speech in humans.

This method has not been tested, and we cannot be sure what its results might have been; but everything we know of chimpanzee behavior, including Yerkes's data, dispels the hope that they could learn functional speech. Not a hint of their using signs has ever been heard of. The only thing we know with objective certainty is not that they have "ideation" but that under certain conditions they are able to make very simple tools and resort to "detours," and that these conditions include a completely visible, utterly clear situation. In all problems not involving immediately perceived visual structures but centering on some other kind of structure—mechanical, for instance—the chimpanzees switched from an insightful type of behavior to the trial-and-error method pure and simple.

Are the conditions required for the apes' effective intellectual functioning also the conditions required for discovering speech or discovering the functional use of signs? Definitely not. Discovery of speech cannot, in any situation, depend on an optical setup. It demands an intellectual operation of a different kind. There are no indications whatever of such an operation's being within the chimpanzees' reach, and most investigators assume that they lack this ability. This lack may be the chief difference between chimpanzee and human intellect.

Köhler introduced the term *insight* (*Einsicht*) for the intellectual operations accessible to chimpanzees. The choice of term is not accidental. Gustav Kafka pointed out that Köhler seems to mean by it primarily *seeing* in the literal sense and only by extension "seeing" of relations generally, or comprehension as opposed to blind action (Kafka, 1922, p. 130).[3]

It must be said that Köhler never defines *insight* or spells out its theory. In the absence of theoretical interpretation, the term is somewhat ambiguous in its application: sometimes it denotes the specific characteristics of the operation itself, the structure of the chimpanzees' actions; and sometimes it indicates the psychological process preceding and preparing these actions, an internal "plan of operations," as it were. Bühler particularly insisted on the internal character of this process (Bühler, 1930, p. 12). Borovsky also assumes that if the ape shows no visible signs of "sizing up" the task, it must be doing this through inner muscular activity (Borovsky, 1927, p. 184).

Köhler advances no hypothesis about the mechanism of the intellectual reaction, but it is clear that however it functions and wherever we locate the intellect—in the actions themselves of the chimpanzee or in some preparatory internal process (cerebral or muscular-innervational)—the thesis remains valid that this reaction is determined, not by memory traces, but by the situation as visually presented. Even the best tool for a given problem is lost on the chimpanzee if it cannot see it simultaneously or quasi-simultaneously with the goal. By "quasi-simultaneous perception" Köhler means instances when tool and goal had been seen together a moment earlier, or when they had been used together so many times in an identical situation that they are to all intents and purposes simultaneously perceived psychologically (Köhler, 1973, pp. 99–100). Thus the consideration of "insight" does not change our conclusion that the chimpanzee, even if it possessed the parrot's gifts, would be exceedingly unlikely to conquer speech.

Yet, as we have said, the chimpanzee has a fairly rich language of its own. Yerkes's collaborator Learned compiled a dictionary of thirty-two speech elements, or "words," which not only resemble human speech phonetically but also have some meaning, in the sense that they are elicited by certain situations or objects connected with pleasure or displeasure, or inspiring desire, malice, or fear (Yerkes and Learned, 1925, p. 54). These "words" were written down while the apes were waiting to be fed and during meals, in the presence of humans and when two chimpanzees were alone. They are affective vocal reactions, more or less differentiated and to some degree connected, in a conditional-reflex fashion, with stimuli related to feeding or other vital situations: a strictly emotional language.

In connection with this description of ape speech, we should like to make three points. First, the coincidence of sound production with affective gestures, especially noticeable when the chimpanzees are very excited, is not limited to anthropoids—it is, on the contrary, very common among animals endowed with voice. Human speech certainly originated in the same kind of expressive vocal reactions.

Second, the affective states producing abundant vocal reactions in chimpanzees are unfavorable to the functioning of the intellect. Köhler mentions repeatedly that in chimpanzees, emotional reactions, particularly those of great intensity, rule out a simultaneous intellectual operation.

Third, it must be stressed again that emotional release as such is not the only function of speech in apes. As in other animals and in man, it is also a means of psychological contact with others of their kind.[4] Both in the chimpanzees of Yerkes and Learned and in the apes observed by Köhler, this function of speech is unmistakable. But it is not connected with intellectual reactions, i.e., with thinking. It originates in emotion and is clearly a part of the total emotional syndrome, but a part that fulfills a specific function, both biologically and psychologically. It is far removed from intentional, conscious attempts to inform or influence others. In essence, it is an instinctive reaction, or something extremely close to it.

There can hardly be any doubt that biologically this function of speech is one of the oldest and is genetically related to the visual and vocal signals given by leaders of animal groups. In a recently published study of the language of bees, Karl von Frisch (1923)[5] describes very interesting and theoretically important forms of behavior that serve interchange or contact and indubitably originate in instinct. In spite of the phenotypical differences, these behavioral manifestations are basically similar to the speech interchange of chimpanzees. This similarity points up once more the independence of chimpanzee "communications" from any intellectual activity.

We undertook this analysis of several studies of ape language and intellect to elucidate the relation between thinking and speech in the phylogenetic development of these functions. We can now summarize our conclusions, which will be of use in the further analysis of the problem.

1. Thought and speech have different genetic roots.

2. The two functions develop along different lines and independently of each other.

3. There is no clear-cut and constant correlation between them in phylogenesis.

4. Anthropoids display an intellect somewhat like man's

in certain respects (the embryonic use of tools) and a language somewhat like man's *in totally different respects* (the phonetic aspect of their speech, its release function, the beginnings of a social function).

5. The close correspondence between thought and speech characteristic of man is absent in anthropoids.

6. In the phylogeny of thought and speech, a prelinguistic phase in the development of thought and a preintellectual phase in the development of speech are clearly discernible.

II

Ontogenetically, the relation between thought and speech development is much more intricate and obscure; but here, too, we can distinguish two separate lines springing from two different genetic roots.

The existence of a prespeech phase of thought development in childhood has only recently been corroborated by objective proof. Köhler's experiments with chimpanzees, suitably modified, were carried out on children who had not yet learned to speak. Köhler himself occasionally experimented with children for purposes of comparison, and Bühler undertook a systematic study of a child on the same lines. The findings were similar for children and for apes.

"The child's actions," Bühler tells us, "were of exactly the same type as those we are familiar with in chimpanzees . . . indeed there is a phase in the life of the child, which one might well designate as the *CHIMPANZEE-AGE*. In the case of this particular child it was about the 10, 11 and 12 [sic] months. . . . It is in the chimpanzee-age, therefore, that the child makes its first small discoveries. They are, of course, exceedingly primitive discoveries, but they are of the greatest importance for its mental development" (Bühler, 1930, p. 48).

What is most important theoretically in these as well as in the chimpanzee experiments is the discovery of the independence of the rudimentary intellectual reactions from language. Noting this, Bühler comments, "It has been said that language is the prelude to the coming of man. That may be, but even before language comes *thinking in terms of tools*, i.e., the realization of mechanical connections and the invention of mechanical means for mechanical ends. To put it briefly, before the advent of speech, action comes to have a *subjective meaning*; i.e., it becomes consciously purposive" (Bühler, 1930, p. 51).

The preintellectual roots of speech in child development have long been known. The child's babbling, crying, even his first words, are quite clearly stages of speech development that have nothing to do with the development of thinking. These manifestations have been generally regarded as a predominantly emotional form of behavior. Not all of them, however, serve merely the function of release. Recent investigations of the earliest forms of behavior in the child and of the child's first reactions to the human voice, by Ch. Bühler, Hetzer, and Tudor-Hart,[6] have shown that the social function of speech is already clearly apparent during the first year, i.e., in the preintellectual stage of speech development. Quite definite reactions to the human voice were observed as early as during the third week of life, and the first specifically social reaction to a voice during the second month (Ch. Bühler, Hetzer, and Tudor-Hart, 1927, p. 124). These investigations also established that laughter, inarticulate sounds, movements, etc., are means of social contact from the first months of the child's life.

Thus the two functions of speech that we observed in

phylogenetic development are already present and obvious in the child less than one year old.

But the most important discovery is that at a certain moment at about the age of two the curves of development of thought and speech, till then separate, meet and join to initiate a new form of behavior. Stern's account of this momentous event was the first and the best. He showed how the will to conquer language follows the first dim realization of the purpose of speech, when the child "makes the greatest discovery of his life," that "each thing has its name" (Stern, 1914, p. 108).

This crucial instant, when speech begins to serve intellect, and thoughts begin to be spoken, is indicated by two unmistakable objective symptoms: (1) the child's sudden, active curiosity about words, his question about every new thing, "What is this?" and (2) the resulting rapid, saccadic increases in his vocabulary.

Before the turning point, the child does (like some animals) recognize a small number of words that substitute, as in conditioning, for objects, persons, actions, states, or desires. At that age the child knows only the words supplied to him by other people. Now the situation changes; the child feels the need for words and, through his questions, actively tries to learn the signs attached to objects. He seems to have discovered the symbolic function of words. Speech, which in the earlier stage was affective-conative, now, as was shown by Meumann, enters the intellectual phase. "This process," writes Stern, "may be called the intellectual one in a strict sense of this word. The understanding of the relation between sign and meaning, which appears at this stage, is something entirely different from the mere use of images and associations between them. The understanding that any object should have its own name becomes the first general concept acquired by the child" (Stern, 1914, p. 109).

At this point, the knot is tied for the problem of thought and language. Let us stop and consider exactly what it is that happens when the child makes his "great discovery," and whether Stern's interpretation is correct.

Bühler and Koffka both compare this discovery to the chimpanzee's inventions. Bühler observes, "Look at it from whatever side you will, at the decisive point a psychological parallel to the discoveries of the chimpanzee will appear" (Bühler, 1930, p. 58). The same idea has been developed by Koffka: "The function of naming things [*Namengebung*] is a discovery by the child that has a complete analogue in the inventions of chimpanzees. Both are structured actions. The name enters into the structure of the object, just as the stick becomes part of the situation of wanting to get the fruit" (Koffka, 1925, p. 243).[7]

We shall discuss the soundness of this analogy later, when we examine the functional and structural relations between thought and speech. For the present, we shall merely note that the "greatest discovery of the child" becomes possible only when a certain relatively high level of thought and speech development has been reached. In other words, speech cannot be "discovered" without thinking.

In brief, we must conclude that

1. In their ontogenetic development, thought and speech have different roots.

2. In the speech development of the child, we can with certainty establish a preintellectual stage, and in his thought development, a prelinguistic stage.

3. Up to a certain point in time, the two follow different lines, independently of each other.

4. At a certain point these lines meet, whereupon thought becomes verbal, and speech rational.

III

No matter how we approach the controversial problem of the relation between thought and speech, we shall have to deal extensively with *inner speech*. Its importance in all our thinking is so great that many psychologists, Watson among others, even identify it with thought—which they regard as inhibited, soundless speech. But psychology still does not know how the change from overt to inner speech is accomplished, or at what age, by what process, and why it takes place.

Watson says that we do not know at what point of their speech organization children pass from overt to whispered and then to inner speech because that problem has been studied only incidentally. Our own researches lead us to believe that Watson poses the problem incorrectly. There are no valid reasons to assume that inner speech develops in some mechanical way through a gradual decrease in the audibility of speech (whispering).

It is true that Watson mentions another possibility: "Perhaps," he says, "all three forms develop simultaneously" (Watson, 1919, p. 322). This hypothesis seems to us as unfounded from the genetic point of view as the following sequence: loud speech, whisper, inner speech. No objective data reinforce that *perhaps*. Testifying against it are the profound dissimilarities between external and inner speech, acknowledged by all psychologists including Watson.

"They really think aloud," observes Watson. "The reason why children are so talkative probably is due to the fact that at an early age their environment does not force a rapid shift from explicit to implicit language. . . . Even if we could roll out the implicit processes and record them on a sensitive plate or phonograph cylinder, it is possible that they would be so abbreviated, shortcircuited and economized that they would be unrecognizable unless their formation had been watched from the transition point where they are complete and social in character, to their final stage where they will serve for individual but not for social adjustments" (Watson, 1919, pp. 322–324).

There are no grounds for assuming that the two processes, so different *functionally* (social as opposed to personal adaptation) and *structurally* (the extreme, elliptical economy of inner speech, changing the speech pattern almost beyond recognition), may be *genetically* parallel and concurrent. Nor (to return to Watson's main thesis) does it seem plausible that they are linked together by whispered speech, which neither in function nor in structure can be considered a transitional stage between external speech and inner speech. It stands between the two only phenotypically, not genotypically.

Our studies of whispering in young children fully substantiate this. We have found that structurally there is almost no difference between whispering and speaking aloud; functionally, whispering differs profoundly from inner speech and does not even manifest a tendency toward the characteristics typical of the latter. Furthermore, it does not develop spontaneously until school age, though it may be induced very early; under social pressure, a three-year-old may, for short periods and with great effort, lower his voice or whisper. This is the one point that may seem to support Watson's view.

We discussed Watson's view not only because it is very typical of theories of language and thought, and not only because it helps to elucidate the opposition between the phenotypical and genetic approaches, but also because it contains a correct methodological moment. While disagreeing with Watson's thesis concerning the role of whispering, we believe that he has hit on the right methodological approach: To solve the problem, we must look for the intermediate link between overt and inner speech.

We are inclined to see that link in the child's egocentric speech, described by Piaget (see chapter 2). Observations made by Lemaître and some other authors who studied the inner speech of schoolchildren support our point of view. These observations showed that the inner speech of schoolchildren is labile and immature; i.e., it is a genetically "fresh" function. Besides its role of accompaniment to activity and its expressive and release functions, egocentric speech readily assumes a planning function, i.e., turns into thought proper quite naturally and easily.

If our hypothesis proves to be correct, we shall have to conclude that speech is interiorized psychologically before it is interiorized physically. Egocentric speech is inner speech in its functions; it is speech on its way inward, intimately tied up with the ordering of the child's behavior, already partly incomprehensible to others, yet still overt in form and showing no tendency to change into whispering or any other sort of half-soundless speech.

We should then also have the answer to the question of *why* speech turns inward. It turns inward because its function changes. Its development would still have three stages—not the ones Watson found, but these: external speech, egocentric speech, inner speech. We should also have at our disposal an excellent method for studying inner speech "live," as it were, while its structural and functional peculiarities are being shaped; it would be an objective method since these peculiarities appear while speech is still audible, i.e., accessible to observation and measurement.

Our investigations show that speech development follows the same course and obeys the same laws as the development of all the other mental operations involving the use of signs, such as counting and mnemonic memorizing.[8] We found that these operations generally develop in four stages. The first is the primitive or natural stage, corresponding to preintellectual speech and preverbal thought, when these operations appear in their original form, as they were evolved at the primitive level of behavior.

Next comes the stage that we might call "naive psychology," by analogy with what is called "naive physics"—the child's experience of the physical properties of his own body and of the objects around him, and the application of this experience to the use of tools: the first exercise of the child's budding practical intelligence.

This phase is very clearly defined in the speech development of the child. It is manifested by the correct use of grammatical forms and structures before the child has understood the logical operations for which they stand. The child may operate with subordinate clauses, with words like *because, if, when,* and *but,* long before he really grasps causal, conditional, or temporal relations. He masters syntax of speech before syntax of thought. Piaget's studies proved that grammar develops before logic and that the child learns relatively late the mental operations corresponding to the verbal forms he has been using for a long time.

With the gradual accumulation of naive psychological experience, the child enters a third stage, distinguished by external signs, external operations that are used as aids in the solution of internal problems. That is the stage when the child counts on his fingers, resorts to mnemonic aids, and so on. In speech development it is characterized by egocentric speech.

The fourth stage we call the "ingrowth" stage. The external operation turns inward and undergoes a profound change in the process. The child begins to count in his head, to use "logical memory," that is, to operate with inherent relations and inner signs. In speech development this is the final stage of inner, soundless speech. There remains a constant interaction between outer and inner operations, one form effortlessly and frequently changing into the other and back again. Inner speech may come very close in form to external speech—as was shown by Delacroix—or even become exactly like it when it serves as preparation for external speech—for instance, in thinking over a lecture to be given. There is no sharp division between inner and external behavior, and each influences the other.

In considering the function of inner speech in adults after the development is completed, we must ask whether in their case thought and linguistic processes are necessarily connected, whether the two can be equated. Again, as in the case of animals and of children, we must answer, "No."

Schematically, we may imagine thought and speech as two intersecting circles. In their overlapping parts, thought and speech coincide to produce what is called verbal thought. Verbal thought, however, does not by any means include all forms of thought or all forms of speech. There is a vast area of thought that has no direct relation to speech. The thinking manifested in the use of tools belongs in this area, as does practical intellect in general. Furthermore, investigations by psychologists of the Würzburg school have demonstrated that thought can function without any word images or speech movements detectable through self-observation. The latest experiments show also that there is no direct correspondence between inner speech and the subject's tongue or larynx movements.

Nor are there any psychological reasons to derive all forms of speech activity from thought. No thought process may be involved when a subject silently recites to himself a poem learned by heart or mentally repeats a sentence supplied to him for experimental purposes—Watson notwithstanding. Finally, there is "lyrical" speech, prompted by emotion. Though it has all the earmarks of speech, it can scarcely be classified with intellectual activity in the proper sense of the term.

We are therefore forced to conclude that the fusion of thought and speech, in adults as well as in children, is a phenomenon limited to a circumscribed area. Nonverbal thought and nonintellectual speech do not participate in this fusion and are affected only indirectly by the processes of verbal thought.

IV

We can now summarize the results of our analysis. We began by attempting to trace the genealogy of thought and speech, using the data of comparative psychology. These data are insufficient for tracing the developmental paths of prehuman thought and speech with any degree of certainty. The basic question, whether anthropoids possess the same type of intellect as man, is still controversial. Köhler answers it in the affirmative, others in the negative. But however this problem may be solved by future investigations, one thing is already clear: In the animal world, the path toward humanlike intellect is not the same as the path toward humanlike speech; thought and speech do not spring from one root.

Even those who would deny intellect to chimpanzees cannot deny that the apes possess something *approaching intellect*, that the highest type of habit formation they manifest is embryonic intellect.

Thorndike, who studied the behavior of marmosets, and who concluded that there are no signs of intelligence in it, nevertheless admitted that monkeys show the most advanced form of animal behavior. Thorndike's experiments showed that like humans, monkeys are able to drop ineffective movements and to acquire new effective movements almost instantly. In this respect they differ remarkably from the lower animals, like cats, dogs, and chickens, which are able only gradually to inhibit movements that turned out to be ineffective (Thorndike, 1901).

Some other authors, like Borovsky, question the very existence of an intellectual function superimposed upon habits, and not only in animals but also in humans. Obviously for them the problem of the humanlike character of the ape's intelligence must be reformulated.

In what concerns our own point of view, we believe that at least in their use of tools, apes prefigure human behavior. To Marxists, Köhler's discoveries do not come as a surprise. Marx said long ago that "the use and creation of implements of labor, although present in embryonic form in some species of animals, are a specific characteristic of the human process of labor" (Marx, 1920, p. 153). Georgy Plekhanov elaborated on this thought, saying that "zoology introduces into history a *homo* already capable of producing and implementing some primitive tools" (Plekhanov, 1922, p. 138). It is remarkable that Plekhanov mentions the production and use of tools, i.e., the intellectual operations, rather than instinctual activity, like building dams by beavers.[9]

Therefore, we may say that *theoretically* the most recent achievements of zoopsychology do not appear as something absolutely new for Marxism. Engels, while elaborating Hegel's distinction between reason and intelligence, pointed out, "Man and animals have all forms of intellectual activity in common; *induction, deduction, abstraction, analysis* (cracking a nut is a beginning of analysis), *synthesis* (animal cunning), and, as their unity, *experiment* (when an unexpected obstacle emerges). Typologically all these methods, i.e., all ordinary logical constructions employed by science, are common to animals and man. Only the developmental level differs" (Engels, 1925, p. 59).[10] Engels further speaks affirmatively about animal verbal behavior, mentioning an *objective* criterion of understanding that animals are able to achieve: "Teach the parrot to repeat obscenities (which is a favorite pastime of sailors returning from tropical countries) and to understand their meaning in a restricted sense, then tease it, and you would see that the parrot will let loose the choicest invective precisely as Berlin's *Frau* greengrocer would do. When begging, the parrot will use words for which it will be rewarded with a tidbit" (Engels, 1925, p. 93).[11]

We have no intention of alleging that Engels credited animals with the ability to think and speak on the human level, nor do we ourselves think so. Later we shall define the legitimate limits and actual meaning of Engels's statements. But for now we merely wish to elaborate that there are no good reasons to deny the presence in animals of embryonic thought and language of the same type as man's, which develop, again as in man, along separate paths.[12] An animal's ability to express itself vocally is no indication of its mental development. A great aptitude in the parrot for learning speech shows no connection with the level of its development of intelligence.

Let us now summarize the relevant data yielded by recent studies of children. We find that in the child, too, the roots and the developmental course of the intellect differ from those of speech—that initially thought is nonverbal and speech nonintellectual. Stern asserts that at a certain point the two lines of development meet, speech becoming rational and thought verbal. The child "discovers" that "each thing has its name," and begins to ask what each object is called.

Some psychologists, notably Delacroix, do not agree with Stern that this first "age of questions" occurs universally and is necessarily symptomatic of a momentous discovery (Delacroix, 1924, p. 286). Wallon suggested that there is a period when a child views a word as an attribute of, rather than as a substitute for, an object: "When a one-and-a-half-year-old asks the names of objects, nothing indicates that this is something more than a simple attribution. Only systematic generalization of such questions would prove that what we see is an embryonic function of signification, rather than passive and accidental association" (Delacroix, 1924, p. 287).

Koffka takes a stand between Stern's and that of his opponents. Like Bühler, he emphasizes the analogy between the chimpanzee's invention of tools and the child's discovery of the naming function of language, but the scope of this discovery, according to Koffka, is not as wide as Stern assumes. The word, in Koffka's view, becomes a characteristic of the structure of an object on equal terms with its other characteristics.

But a characteristic such as a name is detachable [*verschiedbar*] from the object. One may see things, without hearing their names: "We ourselves, in a naive way, will call a dress blue even in the dark when we actually cannot perceive its color. But since the name is a characteristic of all objects, a child completes all structures according to this rule" (Koffka, 1925, p. 244).

Bühler also observed that each new object appears for a child as a problem, a problem to which he has the general schema of a solution—enunciating a word—but not always the particular means—a definite word. When he lacks the word for a new object, he demands it from adults (Bühler, 1930, p. 57).

We believe that this view comes closest to the truth and resolves the dispute between Stern and Delacroix. The data on children's language (supported by anthropological data) strongly suggest that for a long time to a child the word is a property, rather than the symbol of an object; a child grasps the external structure of a word-as-object earlier than the inner symbolic structure.

We choose this "middle" hypothesis among the several

offered because we find it hard to believe on the basis of available data that a child of one-and-a-half to two years is able to "discover" the symbolic function of speech. Our point of view finds support in the experimental data, which show that the functional use of signs even more elementary than words is beyond the capacity of a child of this age. Studies in the child's speech also showed that for a long period of time a child is unaware of the symbolic role of language and uses words as simple attributes of things. Observations of handicapped children (notably the case of Helen Keller) revealed, according to Bühler, that deaf-and-mute children experience no instant discovery of speech, but rather acquire it gradually, through a series of "molecular" changes (Bühler, 1930, p. 59).

The hypothesis we prefer fits in with the general pattern of development in mastering signs that we outlined in the preceding section. Even in schoolchildren the functional use of a new sign is preceded by a stage of "naive psychology," i.e., by a period of mastering the external structure of the sign.

The preintellectual character of an infant's babbling is well known. Meumann suggested that the first words are also purely affective, expressing feelings and emotions; they are devoid of objective meaning, reflecting, like an animal's "language," purely subjective reactions (Meumann, 1902). Both Stern and Delacroix challenged some aspects of Meumann's position. But at the same time both of them agreed that the first words have no permanent and objective meaning, so that in this respect they are like the swearing of the "learned" parrot.

Thus, Stern's thesis of "discovery" calls for reappraisal and limitation. Its basic tenet, however, remains valid: It is clear that, ontogenetically, thought and speech develop along separate lines and that at a certain point these lines meet. This important fact is now definitely established, no matter how further studies may settle the details on which psychologists still disagree—whether this meeting occurs at one point or at several points, as a truly sudden discovery or after long preparation throught practical use and slow functional change, and whether it takes place at the age of two or at school age.

We shall now summarize our investigation of inner speech. Here, too, we considered several hypotheses, and we came to the conclusion that inner speech develops through a slow accumulation of functional and structural changes, that it branches off from the child's external speech simultaneously with the differentiation of the social and the egocentric functions of speech, and finally that the speech structures mastered by the child become the basic structures of his thinking.

This brings us to another indisputable fact of great importance: Thought development is determined by language, i.e., by the linguistic tools of thought and by the sociocultural experience of the child. Essentially, the development of inner speech depends on outside factors; the development of logic in the child, as Piaget's studies have shown, is a direct function of his socialized speech. The child's intellectual growth is contingent on his mastering the social means of thought, that is, language.

We can now formulate the main conclusions to be drawn from our analysis. If we compare the early development of speech and intellect—which, as we have seen, develop along separate lines both in animals and in very young children—with the development of inner speech and verbal thought, we must conclude that the later stage is not a simple continuation of the earlier. *The nature of the development itself changes*, from biological to sociohistorical. Verbal thought is not an innate, natural form of behavior, but is determined by a historical-cultural process and has specific properties and laws that cannot be found in the natural forms of thought and speech. Once we acknowledge the historical character of verbal thought, we must consider it subject to all the premises of historical materialism, which are valid for any historical phenomenon in human society. It is only to be expected that on this level the development of behavior will be governed essentially by the general laws of the historical development of human society.

The problem of thought and language thus extends beyond the limits of natural science and becomes the focal problem of historical human psychology, i.e., of social psychology. Consequently, it must be posed in a different way. This second problem presented by the study of thought and speech will be the subject of a separate investigation.[13]

5

An Experimental Study of the Development of Concepts

I

Until recently the student of concept formation was handicapped by the lack of an experimental method that would allow him to observe the inner dynamics of the process.

The traditional methods of studying concepts fall into two groups. Typical of the first group is the so-called method of definition, with its variations. It is used to investigate the already formed concepts of the child through the verbal definition of their contents. Two important drawbacks make this method inadequate for studying the process in depth. In the first place, it deals with the finished product of concept formation, overlooking the dynamics and the development of the process itself. Rather than tapping the child's thinking, it often elicits a mere reproduction of verbal knowledge, of ready-made definitions provided from without. It may be a test of the child's knowledge and experience, or of his linguistic development, rather than a study of an intellectual process in the true sense. In the second place, this method, concentrating on the word, fails to take into account the perception and the mental elaboration of the sensory material that give birth to the concept. The sensory material and the word are both indispensable parts of concept formation. Studying the word separately puts the process on the purely verbal plane, which is uncharacteristic of the child's thinking. The relation of the concept to reality remains unexplored; the meaning of a given word is approached through another word, and whatever we discover through this operation is not so much a picture of the child's concepts as a record of the relation in the child's mind between previously formed families of words.

The second group comprises methods used in the study of abstraction. They are concerned with the psychic processes leading to concept formations. The child is required to discover some common trait in a series of discrete impressions, abstracting it from all the other traits with which it is perceptually fused. Methods of this group disregard the role played by the symbol (the word) in concept formation; a simplified setting substitutes a partial process for the complex structure of the total process.

Thus each of the two traditional methods separates the word from the perceptual material and operates with one or the other. A great step forward was made with the creation of a new method that permits their combined treatment. The new method introduces into the experimental setting nonsense words that at first mean nothing to the subject. It also introduces artificial concepts by attaching each nonsense word to a particular combination of object attributes for which no ready concept and word exist. For instance, in Ach's experiments the word *gatsun* gradually comes to mean "large and heavy," the word *fal*, "small and light" (Ach, 1921).

In the course of the experiment, the whole process of comprehension of senseless "words" and the development of concepts unfolds in front of us. This method can be used with both children and adults, since the solution of the problem—due to the artificial character of the "words"—does not presuppose previous experience or knowledge on the part of the subject.

As we have mentioned above, one of the principal limitations of the method of definition lies in its abstraction from the real processes of problem solving confronting a child in his everyday life. The new method overcomes this limitation by focusing on the functional conditions of concept formation. It takes into account that a concept is not an isolated, ossified, and changeless formation, but an active part of the intellectual process, constantly engaged in serving communication, understanding, and problem solving.

Although Ach himself conducted no special experiments devoted to the study of concept formation in adolescents, he noticed that a fundamental change both in the form and the content of thinking does occur at this age under the influence of the transition from the use of preconceptual to the use of conceptual means of reasoning.

Franz Rimat conducted a carefully designed study of concept formation in adolescents, using a variant of this method. His main conclusion was that true concept formation exceeds the capacities of preadolescents and begins only with the onset of puberty. He writes, "We have definitely established that a sharp increase in the child's ability to form, without help, generalized objective concepts manifests itself only at the close of the twelfth year. . . . Thought in concepts, emancipated from perception, puts demands on the child that exceed his mental possibilities before the age of twelve" (Rimat, 1925, p. 112).

We are not going to discuss these experiments and their methodology here. What we are interested in is the general conclusion, that real concept formation and abstract reasoning appear only in adolescents. These findings challenge the position of some psychologists, who claimed that no radical changes in the intellectual function occur in adolescence and that all basic intellectual operations, which will be active later, are already formed by the age of three.

Ach's and Rimat's investigations disprove the view that concept formation is based on associative connections. Ach demonstrated that the existence of associations, however numerous and strong, between verbal symbols and objects is not in itself sufficient for concept formation. His experimental findings did not confirm the old idea that a concept develops through the maximal strengthening of associative connections involving the attributes common to a group of objects, and the weakening of associations involving the attributes in which these objects differ.

Ach's experiments showed that concept formation is a creative, not a mechanical passive, process; that a concept emerges and takes shape in the course of a complex operation aimed at the solution of some problem; and that the mere presence of external conditions favoring a mechanical linking of word and object does not suffice to produce a concept. In his view, the decisive factor in concept formation is the so-called determining tendency.

Before Ach, psychology postulated two basic tendencies governing the flow of our ideas: reproduction through association, and perseveration. The first brings back those images that had been connected in past experience with the one presently occupying the mind. The second is the tendency of every image to return and to penetrate anew into the flow of images. In his earlier investigations, Ach demonstrated that these two tendencies failed to explain purposeful, consciously directed acts of thought. He therefore assumed that such thoughts were regulated by a third tendency, the "determining tendency," set up by the image of the goal. Ach's study of concepts showed that no new concept was ever formed without the regulating effect of the determining tendency created by the experimental task.

According to Ach's schema, concept formation does not follow the model of an associative chain in which one link calls forth the next; it is an aim-directed process, a series of operations that serve as steps toward a final goal. Memorizing words and connecting them with objects does not in itself lead to concept formation; for the process to begin, a problem must arise that cannot be solved otherwise than through the formation of new concepts.

This characterization of the process of concept formation, however, is still insufficient. The experimental task can be understood and taken over by children long before they are twelve, yet they are unable until that age to form new concepts. Ach's own study demonstrated that children differ from adolescents and adults not in the way they comprehend the aim, but in the way their minds work to achieve it. Dmitri Usnadze's detailed experimental study of concept formation in preschoolers also showed that a child at that age approaches problems just as the adult does when he operates with concepts, but goes about their solution in an entirely different manner. We can only conclude that it is not the goal or the determining tendency but other factors, unexplored by these researchers, that are responsible for the essential difference between the adult's conceptual thinking and the forms of thought characteristic of the young child.

Uznadze singles out one particular functional moment, whose importance has been shown by Ach, namely, the communicative aspect of speech: "Word, obviously, is a tool of human mutual understanding. This moment plays a decisive role in concept formation. In the course of mutual comprehension between people a group of sounds acquires certain meaning, thus becoming a word or concept. Without this functional moment of mutual understanding, no one group of sounds would ever become a bearer of meaning, and no concept would ever appear" (Uznadze, 1966, p. 76).[1]

From the very beginning a child is brought up in a "verbal environment" and starts using the mechanisms of speech already after the second year of life: "Undoubtedly, he uses articulated words, rather than complexes of meaningless sounds, and in the course of development these words acquire more and more differentiated meanings" (Uznadze, 1966, p. 77).

At the same time it may be considered proved that only much later does a child reach a stage in the socialization of his thinking at which he can develop mature concepts: "Thus, we see that the real concept corresponding to the upper level in the socialization of thought appears relatively late. At the same time, children start using words and establish a mutual understanding with adults rather early. This implies that words take over the function of concepts and may serve as means of communication long before they reach the level of concepts characteristic of fully developed thought. A special study should reveal the development of such forms of thinking, which are not conceptual, but which provide a functional equivalent of concepts" (Uznadze, 1966, p. 77).

Uznadze's studies showed that these "functional equivalents" differ essentially in structure and quality from the mature concepts used by adolescents and adults. It must be taken into account, however, that this difference cannot be based on their functional roles—as it has been suggested by Ach—for it is exactly functional similarity that made these equivalents look like concepts.

We are faced, then, with the following state of affairs: A child is able to grasp a problem, and to visualize the goal it sets, at an early stage in his development; because the tasks of understanding and communication are essentially similar for the child and the adult, the child develops functional equivalents of concepts at an extremely early age, but the forms of thought that he uses in dealing with these tasks differ profoundly from the adult's in their composition, structure, and mode of operation. The main question about the process of concept formation—or about any goal-directed activity—is the question of the means by which the operation is accomplished. Work, for instance, is not sufficiently explained by saying that it is prompted by human needs. We must consider as well the use of tools, the mobilization of the appropriate means without which work could not be performed. To explain the higher forms of human behavior, we must uncover the means by which man learns to organize and direct his behavior.

The major weakness of Ach's method lies in its disregard of the genetic and dynamic aspects of concept formation. The means of concept formation, i.e., experimental words, are given from the very beginning of the experiment and do not change in its course. Moreover, the method of manipulation with these words is also predetermined in instruction. But words do not play the role of signs spontaneously. In the beginning they are indistinguishable from all other stimuli, from the objects that they must designate.

In spite of his critique of the associationistic theory of concept formation, Ach retained the traditional approach, which portrays concept formation as a process going from down up, i.e., from the separate objects to a few generalizing concepts. But, as Ach's own experiments have shown, such an approach does not reflect an actual process of concept formation. This process—to use Peter Vogel's words—cannot be confined to a one-way movement from the base of the pyramid of concepts to its top, from the concrete to the more abstract.

The experiments of Ach and Rimat, while they have the merit of discrediting once and for all the mechanistic view of concept formation, did not disclose the true nature of the process—genetically, functionally, or structurally. They took a wrong turn with their purely teleological interpretation, which amounts to asserting that the goal itself creates the appropriate activity via the determining tendency—i.e., that the problem carries its own solution.

Apart from its philosophical and methodological invalidity, such a view makes it impossible to understand why functionally equivalent goals in problem solving are achieved by children and adults with the help of drastically different forms of reasoning. From this point of view, the very process of the development of concepts remains obscure. Ach's and Rimat's studies did not provide a causal-dynamic explanation of concept formation, thus leaving this problem open.

II

To study the process of concept formation in its several developmental phases, we used the method worked out by one of our collaborators, Lev Sakharov (1930). It might be described as the "method of double stimulation": Two sets of stimuli are presented to the subject, one set as objects of his activity, the other as signs that can serve to organize that activity:[2]

The material used in the concept formation tests consists of 22 wooden blocks varying in color, shape, height, and size. There are 5 different colors, 6 different shapes, 2 heights (the tall blocks and the flat blocks), and 2 sizes of the horizontal surface (large and small). On the underside of each figure, which is not seen by the subject, is written one of the four nonsense words: *lag, bik, mur, cev*. Regardless of color or shape, *lag* is written on all tall large figures, *bik* on all flat large figures, *mur* on the tall small ones, and *cev* on the flat small ones. At the beginning of the experiment all blocks, well mixed as to color, size and shape, are scattered on a table in front of the subject. . . . The examiner turns up one of the blocks (the "sample"), shows and reads its name to the subject, and asks him to pick out all the blocks which he thinks might belong to the same kind. After the subject has done so . . . the examiner turns up one of the "wrongly" selected blocks, shows that this is a block of a different kind, and encourages the subject to continue trying. After each new attempt another of the wrongly placed blocks is turned up. As the number of the turned blocks increases, the subject by degrees obtains a basis for discovering to which characteristics of the blocks the nonsense words refer. As soon as he makes this discovery the . . . words . . . come to stand for definite kinds of objects (e.g., *lag* for large tall blocks, *bik* for large flat ones), and new concepts for which the language provides no names are thus built up. The subject is then able to complete the task of separating the four kinds of blocks indicated by the nonsense words. Thus the use of concepts has a definite functional value for the performance required by this test. Whether the subject actually uses conceptual thinking in trying to solve the problem . . . can be inferred from the nature of the groups he builds and from his procedure in building them: Nearly every step in his reasoning is reflected in his manipulations of the blocks. The first attack on the problem; the handling of the sample; the response to correction; the finding of the solution—all these stages of the experiment provide data that can serve as indicators of the subject's level of thinking.

In some important respects this procedure reverses Ach's experiments on concept formation. Ach begins by giving the subject a learning or practice period; he can handle the objects and read the nonsense words written on each before being told what the task will be. In our experiments, the problem is put to the subject from the start and remains the same throughout, but the clues to solution are introduced stepwise, with each new turning of a block. We decided on this sequence because we believe that facing the subject with the task is necessary in order to get the whole process started. The gradual introduction of the means of solution permits us to study the total process of concept formation in all its dynamic phases. The formation of the concept is followed by its transfer to other objects; the subject is induced to use the new terms in talking about objects other than the experimental blocks, and to define their meaning in a generalized fashion.

It is of a principal importance that such an organization of the experiment arrange the pyramid of concepts "upside down." The problem solving in our experiments follows the same path as it takes in real life, where the movement from the top of the pyramid to its bottom is no less important than the ascension from the concrete to the most abstract.

The real process of concept formation has nothing in common with Galton's composite photographs, where the concrete features gradually give way to an abstract "family portrait."[3]

Finally, the functional moment, mentioned by Ach, plays an important role. Rather than being taken as an isolated and static entity, the concept is studied in a live thinking process. The whole experiment can be broken down into a number of stages, each featuring a specific functional use of the concept. In the beginning comes the formation of concepts, then the application of an already formed concept to new objects, next the use of the concept in free associations, and finally the work of concepts in the formation of judgments and new concepts.

III

In the series of investigations of the process of concept formation begun in our laboratory by Sakharov and completed by us and our associates J. Kotelova and E. I. Pashkovskaja, more than three hundred people were studied—children, adolescents, and adults, including some with pathological disturbances of intellectual and linguistic activities.

The principal findings of our study may be summarized as follows: The development of the processes that eventually result in concept formation begins in earliest childhood, but the intellectual functions that in a specific combination form the psychological basis of the process of concept formation ripen, take shape, and develop only at puberty. Before that age, we find certain intellectual formations that perform functions similar to those of the genuine concepts to come. With regard to their composition, structure, and operation, these functional equivalents of concepts stand in the same relation to true concepts as the embryo to the fully formed organism. To equate the two is to ignore the lengthy developmental process between the earliest and the final stages.

It would not be an exaggeration to say that to equate the intellectual operations of three-year-olds with those of adolescents—as some psychologists do—means to use a sort of logic that would deny the existence of sexual maturation in puberty only because certain elements of sexuality are already present in infants.

Later on we shall discuss in detail the real concepts and their preconceptual equivalents. But right now we must focus on the process of concept formation in general. Our experimental study proved that it is a functional use of the word, or any other sign, as means of focusing one's attention, selecting distinctive features and analyzing and synthesizing them, that plays a central role in concept formation.

Concept formation is the result of such a complex activity, in which all basic intellectual functions take part. This process cannot, therefore, be reduced either to association, attention (G. E. Muller), imagery and judgment (K. Bühler), or determining tendencies (N. Ach). All these moments are indispensable, but they are insufficient without the use of a sign, or word. Words and other signs are those means that direct our mental operations, control their course, and channel them toward the solution of the problem confronting us.

None of the above-mentioned functions undergoes any substantial change in adolescence. These elementary functions continue their preadolescent development without any dramatic changes. But once they became involved in the process of concept formation, they appear in it in an entirely new form. They enter it not as independent entities, with their own logic of development, but as subordinated functions whose performance is mediated by word or sign. It is in this new role that these functions contribute to the process of problem solving, simultaneously entering into such new interrelations with each other that only can reveal their true functional psychological meaning.

We may say, therefore, that neither the growth of the number of associations, nor the strengthening of attention, nor the accumulation of images and representations, nor determining tendencies—that none of these processes, however advanced they might be, can lead to concept formation. Real concepts are impossible without words, and thinking in concepts does not exist beyond verbal thinking. That is why the central moment in concept formation, and its generative cause, is a specific use of words as functional "tools."

We have already mentioned that the presence of a problem to be solved through the formation of concepts cannot be considered as the cause of concept formation. It may trigger the process, but it cannot sustain its development. Goals as an explanatory principle fare no better than would a target as an explanatory principle for the ballistics of a cannon ball. Of course, the target enters into the equation of the movement, but only as one of its parameters. Similarly, the character of tasks and goals that may be achieved with the help of concept formation enter into the equation of concept formation.

Unlike the development of instincts, thinking and behavior of adolescents are prompted not from within but from without, by the social milieu. The tasks with which society confronts an adolescent as he enters the cultural, professional, and civic world of adults undoubtedly become an important factor in the emergence of conceptual thinking. If the milieu presents no such tasks to the adolescent, makes no new demands on him, and does not stimulate his intellect by providing a sequence of new goals, his thinking fails to reach the highest stages, or reaches them with great delay.

The cultural task per se, however, does not explain the developmental mechanism itself that results in concept formation. The investigator must aim to understand the intrinsic bonds between the external tasks and the developmental dynamics, and view concept formation as a function of the adolescent's total social and cultural growth, which affects not only the content but also the method of his thinking. The new significative use of the word, its use *as a means of concept formation,* is the immediate psychological cause of the radical change in the intellectual process that occurs on the threshold of adolescence.

No new *elementary* function, essentially different from those already present, appears at this age, but all existing functions are incorporated into a new structure, form a new synthesis, become parts of a new complex whole; the laws governing this whole also determine the destiny of each individual part. Learning to direct one's own mental processes with the aid of words or signs is an integral part of the process of concept formation. The ability to regulate one's actions by using auxiliary means reaches its full development only in adolescence.

Thorndike's hypothesis concerning the affinity between the basic mechanism of the higher intellectual processes and elementary association and concept formation turned out to be in contradiction to the experimental data of concept formation, which showed no sign of such an affinity. These latter data were collected in experiments with children and adults, and drawn from clinical cases.

The process of concept formation, like any other higher form of intellectual activity, is not a quantitative overgrowth of the lower associative activity, but a qualitatively new type. Unlike the lower forms, which are characterized by the *immediacy of intellectual processes, this new activity is mediated by signs.*

The structure of signification, which plays a formative role in all higher types of behavior, does not coincide with the associative structure of elementary processes. The quantitative growth of the associative connections would never lead to higher intellectual activity.

Thorndike's theory of the origin of intelligence emphasized that one and the same type of physiological connections stands behind elementary as well as higher mental functions. From this point of view, there is actually no difference between the intelligence of a child and the intelligence of an adolescent beyond the difference in the number of associative connections. As we have already mentioned, Thorndike's position turned out to be at odds with experimental data. A study of the ontogenetic development of concepts shows that the way from the lower to the higher forms of intelligence, far from being a simple quantitative growth, involves radical changes.

Speech itself is based on the relation between a sign and a structure of higher intellectual operations, rather than on purely associative connections. Phylogenetically as well, there is no reason to expect that the emergence of intelligence would be identified as a product of the

growth of associations. Studies by Köhler and Yerkes
support the contrary view, as does all our knowledge
about so-called "primitive people."

IV

Our investigation brought out that the ascent to concept
formation is made in three basic phases, each divided in
turn into several stages. In this and in the following six
sections, we shall describe these phases and their subdivi-
sions as they appear when studied by the method of
"double stimulation."

The young child takes the first step toward concept
formation when he puts together a number of objects in
an *unorganized congeries,* or "heap," in order to solve a
problem that we adults would normally solve by forming
a new concept. The heap, consisting of disparate objects
grouped together without any basis, reveals a diffuse,
undirected extension of the meaning of the sign (artificial
word) to inherently unrelated objects linked by chance in
the child's perception.

At that stage, word meaning denotes nothing more to
the child than a *vague syncretic conglomeration of individual
objects* that have somehow or other coalesced into an image in his mind. Because of its syncretic origin, that image is highly unstable.

In perception, in thinking, and in acting, the child
tends to merge the most diverse elements into one unarticulated image on the strength of some chance impression. Claparède gave the name "syncretism" to this
well-known trait of the child's thought. Pavel Blonsky
called it the "incoherent coherence" of the child's thinking.[4] We have described the phenomenon elsewhere as
the result of a tendency to compensate for the paucity of
well-apprehended objective relations by an overabun-
dance of subjective connections and to mistake these

subjective bonds for real bonds between things. These syncretic relations, and the heaps of objects assembled under one word meaning, also reflect objective bonds insofar as the latter coincide with the relations between the child's perceptions or impressions. Many words, therefore, have in part the same meaning to the child and to the adult, especially words referring to concrete objects in the child's habitual surroundings. The child's and the adult's meanings of a word often "meet," as it were, in the same concrete object, and this suffices to ensure mutual understanding.

The first phase of concept formation, which we have just outlined, subsumes three distinct stages. We were able to observe them in detail within the framework of the experimental study.

The first stage in the formation of syncretic heaps that represent to the child the meaning of a given artificial word is a manifestation of the *trial-and-error* stage in the development of thinking. The group is created at random, and each object added is a mere guess or trial; it is replaced by another object when the guess is proven wrong, i.e., when the experimenter turns the object and shows that it has a different name.

During the next stage, the composition of the group is determined largely by the spatial position of the experimental objects, i.e., by a purely syncretic *organization of the child's visual field*. The syncretic image or group is formed as a result of the single elements' contiguity in space or in time, or of their being brought into some other more complex relation by the child's immediate perception.

During the third stage of the first phase of concept formation, the syncretic image rests in a more complex base; it is composed of *elements taken from different groups or heaps that have already been formed by the child in the ways described above*. These newly combined elements have no intrinsic bonds with one another, so that the new formation has the same "incoherent coherence" as the first heaps. The sole difference is that in trying to give meaning to a new word, the child now goes through a two-step operation, but this more elaborate operation remains syncretic and results in no more order than the simple assembling of heaps.

V

The second major phase on the way to concept formation comprises many variations of a type of thinking that we shall call *thinking in complexes*. In a complex, individual objects are united in the child's mind not only by his subjective impressions but also by *bonds actually existing between these objects*. This is a new achievement, an ascent to a much higher level.

If the first phase of the child's development is characterized by syncretic images playing the role of "concepts," the second phase brings about complexes that have a functional equivalence with real concepts. In place of the "incoherent coherence" of syncretic thinking comes the grouping of objects that are actually related to each other.

When a child moves up to that level, he has partly overcome his egocentrism. He no longer mistakes connections between his own impressions for connections between things—a decisive step away from syncretism toward objective thinking. Thought in complexes is already coherent and objective thinking, although it does not reflect the relations between things in the same way as real conceptual thinking.

The difference between this second phase and the third one, which concludes the ontogenesis of concept formation, lies in the peculiarity of complex thinking. Complexes are formed according to rules that differ significantly from the rules of real concept formation.

Remains of complex thinking persist in the language of adults. Family names are perhaps the best example of this. Any family name, "Petrov," let us say, subsumes individuals in a manner closely resembling that of the child's complexes. The child at that stage of development thinks in family names, as it were; the universe of individual objects becomes organized for him by being grouped into separate, mutually related "families."

In a complex, the bonds between its components are *concrete and factual* rather than abstract and logical, just as we do not classify a person as belonging to the Petrov family because of any logical relation between him and other bearers of the name. The question is settled for us by facts.

The factual bonds underlying complexes are discovered through direct experience. A complex, therefore, is first and foremost a concrete grouping of objects connected by factual bonds. Since a complex is not formed on the plane of abstract logical thinking, the bonds that create it, as well as the bonds it helps to create, lack logical unity; they may be of many different kinds. *Any factually present* connection may lead to the inclusion of a given element into a complex. That is the main difference between a complex and a concept. While a concept groups objects according to one attribute, the bonds relating the elements of a complex to the whole and to one another may be as diverse as the contacts and relations of the elements are in reality.

In our investigation we observed five basic types of complexes, which succeed one another during this stage of development.

We call the first type of complex the *associative type*. It may be based on any bond the child notices between the sample object and some other blocks. In our experiment, the sample object, the one first given to the subject with its name visible, forms the nucleus of the group to be built. In building an associative complex, the child may add one block to the nuclear object because it is of the same color, another because it is similar to the nucleus in shape or in size, or in any other attribute that happens to strike him. Any bond between the nucleus and another object suffices to make the child include that object in the group and to designate it by the common "family name." The bond between the nucleus and the other object need not be a common trait, such as the same color or shape; a similarity, a contrast, or proximity in space may also establish the bond.

To the child at that stage, the word ceases to be the "proper name" of an individual object; it becomes the family name of a group of objects related to one another in many kinds of ways, just as the relationships in human families are many and different.

VI

Complex thinking of the second type consists in combining objects or the concrete impressions they make on the child into groups that most closely resemble *collections.* Objects are placed together on the basis of some one trait in which they differ and consequently complement one another.

In our experiments the child would pick out objects differing from the sample in color, form, size, or some other characteristic. He did not pick them at random; he chose them because they contrasted with and complemented the one attribute of the sample that he took to be the basis of grouping. The result was a collection of the colors or forms present in the experimental material, e.g., a group of blocks each of a different color.

Association by contrast, rather than by similarity, guides the child in compiling a collection. This form of thinking, however, is often combined with the associative form proper, described earlier, producing a collection based on mixed principles. The child fails to adhere throughout the process to the principle he originally accepted as the basis of collecting. He slips into the consideration of a different trait, so that the resulting group becomes a mixed collection, e.g., of both colors and shapes.

This long, persistent stage in the development of the child's thinking is rooted in his practical experience, in which collections of complementary things often form a set or a whole. Experience teaches the child certain forms of functional grouping: cup, saucer, and spoon; a place setting of knife, fork, spoon, and plate; the set of clothes he wears.

It is not surprising that in his verbal thinking he also forms complexes—collections that include objects that functionally complement each other. We shall see later that this form of complex thinking plays a particularly important role in the psychology of patients with neurological or mental problems. Even healthy adults, when speaking of dishes or clothes, usually have in mind sets of concrete objects rather than generalized concepts.

To recapitulate, the syncretic image leading to the formation of "heaps" is based on vague subjective bonds mistaken for actual bonds between objects: the associative complex, on similarities or other perceptually compelling ties between things; the collection complex, on relations between objects observed in practical experience. We might say that the collection complex is a *grouping of objects on the basis of their participation in the same practical operation*—of their functional cooperation.

VII

After the collection stage of thinking in complexes, we must place the *chain complex*—a dynamic, consecutive joining of individual links into a single chain, with meaning carried over from one link to the next. For instance, if the experimental sample is a yellow triangle, the child might pick out a few triangular blocks until his attention is caught by, let us say, the blue color of a block he has just added; he switches to selecting blue blocks of any shape—angular, circular, semicircular. This in turn is sufficient to change the criterion again; oblivious of color, the child begins to choose rounded blocks. The decisive attribute keeps changing during the entire process. There is no consistency in the type of the bonds or in the manner in which a link of the chain is joined with the one that precedes and the one that follows it. The original sample has no central significance. Each link, once included in a chain complex, is as important as the first and may become the magnet for a series of other objects.

The chain formation strikingly demonstrates the perceptually concrete, factual nature of complex thinking. An object included because of one of its attributes enters the complex not just as the carrier of that one trait but as an individual, with *all* its attributes. The single trait is not abstracted by the child from the rest and is not given a special role, as in a concept.

The chain complex gives us a chance to grasp the essential difference between complexes and concepts. In a complex, there is no hierarchical organization of the relations between different traits of the object. All attributes are functionally equal. There is a profound difference in what concerns the relations of the parts to the whole, and of one part to another, as these relations appear in complexes and in concepts.

In the chain complex, the structural center of the formation may be absent altogether. Two objects included in the complex may have nothing in common, and yet remain as parts of one and the same chain on the strength of sharing an attribute with still another of its elements.

Therefore, the chain complex may be considered the purest form of thinking in complexes. Unlike the associative complex, where elements are, after all, interconnected through one element—the nucleus of the complex—the chain complex has no nucleus. The "end" of the chain may have nothing in common with its "beginning." It is sufficient to have intermediate elements for "gluing" one element of the chain to another.

A complex does not rise above its elements as does a concept. The elements of a complex enter it as perceptually concrete wholes with all their attributes and connections. The complex merges with concrete objects that compose it. This fusion of the general and the particular, of the complex and its elements, this psychic amalgam, as Heinz Werner called it, is a distinctive feature of all complex thinking and of the chain complex in particular.[5]

VIII

Because the chain complex is factually inseparable from the group of concrete objects that form it, it often acquires a vague and floating quality. The type and nature of the bonds may change from link to link almost imperceptibly. Often a remote similarity is enough to create a bond. Attributes are sometimes considered similar, not because of genuine likeness, but because of a dim impression that they have something in common. This leads to the fourth type of complex observed in our experiments. It might be called the *diffuse complex.*

The diffuse complex is marked by the fluidity of the very attribute that unites its single elements. Perceptually concrete groups of objects or images are formed by means of diffuse, indeterminate bonds. To go with a yellow triangle, for example, a child would in our experiments pick out trapezoids as well as triangles, because they made him think of triangles with their tops cut off. Trapezoids would lead to squares, squares to hexagons, hexagons to semicircles, and finally to circles. Color as the basis of selection is equally floating and changeable. Yellow objects are apt to be followed by green ones; then green may change to blue, and blue to black.

Complexes resulting from this kind of thinking are so indefinite as to be in fact limitless. Like a biblical tribe that longed to multiply until it became countless like the stars in the sky or the sands of the sea, a diffuse complex in the child's mind is a kind of family that has limitless powers to expand by adding more and more individuals to the original group.

The child's generalizations in the nonpractical and nonperceptual areas of his thinking, which cannot be easily verified through perception or practical action, are the real-life parallel of the diffuse complexes observed in the experiments. It is well known that the child is capable of surprising transitions, of startling associations and generalizations, when his thought ventures beyond the boundaries of the small tangible world of his experience. Outside it he often constructs limitless complexes amazing in the universality of the bonds they encompass.

These limitless complexes, however, are built on the same principles as the circumscribed concrete complexes. In both, the child stays within the limits of concrete bonds between things, but insofar as the first kind of complex comprises objects outside the sphere of his practical cognition, these bonds are naturally based on dim, unreal, unstable attributes.

IX

To complete the picture of complex thinking, we must describe one more type of complex—the bridge, as it were, between complexes and the final, highest stage in the development of concept formation.

We call this type of complex the *pseudoconcept* because the generalization formed in the child's mind, although phenotypically resembling the adult concept, is psychologically very different from the concept proper; in its essence, it is still a complex.

More detailed study of the last type of complex reveals that phenotypical similarity between complexes and real concepts coexists in this case with genetic dissimilarity. Causal-dynamic relations that engender pseudoconcepts are essentially different from those giving birth to a concept proper. What we confront here is the appearance of a concept that conceals the inner structure of a complex.

In the experimental setting, the child produces a pseudoconcept every time he surrounds a sample with objects that could just as well have been assembled on the basis of an abstract concept. For instance, when the sample is a yellow triangle and the child picks out all the triangles in the experimental material, he could have been guided by the general idea or concept of a triangle. Experimental analysis shows, however, that in reality the child is guided by the concrete, visible likeness and has formed only an associative complex limited to a certain kind of perceptual bond. Although the results are identical, the process by which they are reached is not at all the same as in conceptual thinking.

We must consider this type of complex in some detail. It plays a dominant role in the child's real-life thinking, and it is important as a transitional link between thinking in complexes and true concept formation.[6]

X

Pseudoconcepts predominate over all other complexes in the preschool child's thinking for the simple reason that in real life *complexes corresponding to word meanings are not spontaneously developed by the child: The lines along which a complex develops are predetermined by the meaning a given word already has in the language of adults.*

Only under experimental conditions was the child, freed from the directing influences of well-established verbal connections, able to develop word meanings and to form complex generalizations according to his own preferences. This fact shows us the importance of experimental study, which alone can reveal the spontaneous activity of the child in mastering the language of adults. Experimental study shows us what the child's language and concept formation would look like if they were freed from the directing influence of the linguistic milieu.

One may argue that the subjunctive mood of our statement rather speaks against the experiment, because the child's speech, after all, is not free in its development. Experiment, however, reveals not only a hypothetical "free" development of the child's thinking, but also uncovers activities in forming generalizations usually hidden from view and driven into complicated channels by the influence of adult speech.

The linguistic milieu, with its stable, permanent words meanings, charts the way that the child's generalizations will take. But, constrained as it is, the child's thinking proceeds along this preordained path in the manner characteristic of the child's own stage of intellectual development. Adults, through their verbal communication with the child, are able to predetermine the path of the development of generalizations and its final point—a fully formed concept. But the adult cannot pass on to the child his mode of thinking. He merely supplies the ready-made meanings of the words, around which the child builds complexes. Such complexes are nothing but pseudoconcepts. They are similar to concepts in their appearance, but differ substantially in their essence.

It would be a mistake to perceive this double nature of the pseudoconcept as a sign of a schism existing in the child's thinking. Such a schism exists exclusively for the outside observer. For the child himself, there is only one perspective, that of a complex that coincides with an adult concept. More than once we observed how the child forms a complex with all the structural, functional, and genetic peculiarities of thinking in complexes, which in fact is identical in its content to a generalization that could have been formed by conceptual thinking. The outward similarity between the pseudoconcept and the real concept, which makes it very difficult to "unmask" this kind of complex, is a major obstacle in the genetic analysis of thought.

The functional equivalence of complex and concept, the coincidence, in practice, of many word meanings for the adult and the three-year-old child, the possibility of mutual understanding, and the apparent similarity of their thought processes have led to the false assumption that all the forms of adult intellectual activity are already present in embryo in the child's thinking and that no drastic change occurs at the age of puberty. It is easy to understand the origin of that misconception. The child learns very early a large number of words that mean the same to him and to the adult. The mutual understanding of adult and child creates the illusion that the end point in the development of word meaning coincides with the starting point, that the concept is provided ready-made from the beginning, and that no development takes place.

To find a borderline separating pseudoconcept from real concept is not easy, and this task is positively beyond the capacity of phenotypical analysis. Taken phenotypically, pseudoconcepts and concepts look alike, as a whale looks like a fish. But if we make our approach from the point of view of the "origin of species," a pseudoconcept would be classified as a complex with the same certainty with which we call a whale a mammal.

Thus, our analysis reveals an inner contradiction inherent in the pseudoconcept, which is indicated by its very name. This contradiction at one and the same time poses a great difficulty for the scientific investigation of concept formation and plays a major functional and genetic role as a decisive moment in the development of the child's thinking. This is a contradiction within such a form of thinking that functionally resembles the conceptual one and, because of that, in the course of communication with a child is not recognized by the adult as having the nature of a complex.

What we see here is the complex that, in practical terms, coincides with the concept, embracing the same set of objects. Such a complex is a "shadow" of the concept, its contour. As has been mentioned by one author, we see an image that is by no means a simple sign of a concept. It is rather a mental portrait or a short story about a concept. On the other hand, this is still a complex, i.e., a form of generalization that substantially differs from the real concept.

We have already discussed the nature of this contradiction. The child does not choose the meaning of his words. He is not free to form complexes at will. The meaning of the words is given to him in his conversations with adults. The child receives all the elements of his complexes in a ready-made form, from the speech of others. A set of things covered by one general name also comes pregrouped.

There is no spontaneity in the child's inclusion of a given word in one of the groups. Nor is he free when he applies a given word to a number of objects. He only follows the practice already established by adults. In a word, he does not create his own speech, but acquires the speech of adults. The latter fact explains everything, particularly the coincidence between the child's complexes and the concepts of adults. Complexes corresponding to word meanings were never invented by a child, but were found by him in ready-made generalizations and general names.

But, as we already mentioned, while coinciding in their final products, complexes and concepts are profoundly different in their intellectual, operational structure. This finding turns the pseudoconcept into a unique, ambivalent, and contradictory form of the child's thinking. If not for this unique character of pseudoconcepts, the child's complex thinking would become completely alien to adults (as it happens in experiment, when the child is freed from the fixed meanings of words). In such a case, mutual understanding would be impossible. Only functional equivalence of concepts and pseudoconcepts ensure a successful dialogue between the child and the adult.

This moment of mutual understanding, as was shown by Ach, plays a decisive role in turning words into concepts. Without such functional understanding, says Uznadze, no group of sounds would ever become a bearer of meaning, and no concept would ever come to being: "Obviously, even before it reaches the state of a mature concept, a word is able to substitute functionally for the concept, serving as a tool of mutual understanding between people" (Uznadze, 1966, p. 77).

The double nature of the pseudoconcept predetermines its specific genetic role. The pseudoconcept serves as a connecting link between thinking in complexes and thinking in concepts. It is dual in nature: a complex already carrying the germinating seed of a concept. Verbal communication with adults thus becomes a powerful factor in the development of the child's concepts. The transition from thinking in complexes to thinking in concepts passes unnoticed by the child because his pseudoconcepts already coincide in content with adult concepts. Thus, the child begins to operate with concepts, to practice conceptual thinking, before he is clearly aware of the nature of these operations.

The concept-in-itself and the concept-for-others are developed in the child earlier than the concept-for-myself. The concept-in-itself and the concept-for-others, which are already present in the pseudoconcept, are the basic genetic precondition for the development of real concepts. This peculiar genetic situation is not limited to the attainment of concepts; it is the rule rather than the exception in the intellectual development of the child.[7]

XI

We have now seen, with the clarity that only experimental analysis can give, the various stages and forms of complex thinking. This analysis permits us to uncover the very essence of the genetic process of concept formation in a schematic form, and thus gives us the key to understanding the process as it unfolds in real life. But an experimentally induced process of concept formation never mirrors the genetic development exactly as it occurs in life. The basic forms of concrete thinking that we have enumerated appear in reality in mixed states. The morphological analysis given so far must be followed by a functional and genetic analysis. We must try to connect the forms of complex thinking discovered in the experiment with the forms of thought found in the actual development of the child and check the two series of observations against each other.

The dialectical method never tried to set logical and historical forms of analysis in opposition. According to the well-known definition of Friedrich Engels, logical analysis is nothing but historical analysis freed from its historical *form* and from those accidents that obscure the lucidity of discourse. Logical inquiry starts at the very same point where historical development begins, and proceeds in the form of a theoretical reflection upon the unfolding of historical events. This reflection, however, takes each moment of development in its mature, classical form.

Applying this general methodological thesis to the subject of our inquiry, we find that the stages revealed in our experiments reflect the actual stages in the development of the child's thinking. Here the historical, i.e., developmental, perspective becomes a key to the logical interpretation of concept formation.

It has been mentioned that when the morphological analysis of psychological structures lacks its genetic counterpart, it becomes inadequate. With the growth of the complexity of psychological processes, the importance of the preceding developmental stages also grows. The greater the organization and differentiation of psychological structures, the more inadequate a pure morphological analysis becomes. Without genetic analysis and synthesis, without a study of early developmental stages, we would never be able to recognize those elementary forms that become bearers of the essential relations. Only the comparative analysis of subsequent developmental "cuts" may give us a step-by-step picture of the relations between different psychological structures.

Thus, development is a key to understanding the mature form. Arnold Gesell wrote that "the supreme genetic law appears to be this: All present growth hinges on past growth. Growth is not a simple function neatly determined by X units of inheritance plus Y units of environment, but is an historical complex which reflects at every stage the past which it incorporates. In other words we are led astray by an artificial dualism of heredity and environment, if it blinds us to the fact that growth is a continuous self-conditioning process, rather than a drama controlled, *ex machina*, by two forces" (Gesell, 1929, p. 357).

Experimental analysis of concept formation has led us to genetic and functional analysis. After the task of morphological classification of the complex form of thinking is achieved, we must focus on the comparison between the forms discovered in experiment and those occurring in actual child development. On the one hand, we must bring a historical, i.e., developmental, perspective to the experimental study; on the other hand, the actual development of the child's thinking should be elucidated with the help of experimental data. This alliance of experiment and genetic analysis, of "artifact" and reality, leads us from the morphology of complexes to a study of complexes in action.

XII

From our experiments we concluded that, at the complex stage, word meanings as perceived by the child refer to the same objects that the adult has in mind, which ensures understanding between child and adult, but that the child thinks the same thing in a different way, by means of different mental operations. We shall try to verify this proposition by comparing our observations with the data on the peculiarities of the child's thought, and of primitive thought in general, previously collected by psychological science.

If we observe what groups of objects the child links together in transferring the meanings of his first words, and how he goes about it, we discover a mixture of the two forms that we called in our experiments the associative complex and the syncretic image.

Let us borrow an illustration from Heinrich Idelberger, cited by Werner (1926, p. 206). On the 251st day of his life, a child applies the word *bow-wow* to a china figurine of a girl that usually stands on the sideboard and that he likes to play with. On the 307th day, he applies *bow-wow* to a dog barking in the yard, to the pictures of his grandparents, to a toy dog, and to a clock. On the 331st day, he applies it to a fur piece with an animal's head, noticing particularly the glass eyes, and to another fur stole without a head. On the 334th day, he applies it to a rubber doll that squeaks when pressed, and on the 396th, to his father's cufflinks. On the 433rd day, he utters the same word at the sight of pearl buttons on a dress and of a bath thermometer.

Werner analyzed this example and concluded that the diverse things called *bow-wow* may be catalogued as follows: first, dogs and toy dogs, and small oblong objects resembling the china doll, e.g., the rubber doll and the thermometer; second, the cufflinks, pearl buttons, and similar small objects. The criterial attribute is an oblong shape or a shiny surface resembling eyes.

Clearly, the child unites these concrete objects according to the principle of a complex. Such spontaneous complex formations make up the entire first chapter of the developmental history of children's words.

There is a well-known, frequently cited example of these shifts: a child's use of *quah* to designate first a duck swimming in a pond, then any liquid, including the milk in his bottle; when he happens to see a coin with an eagle on it, the coin also is called *quah*, and then any round, coinlike object. This is a typical chain complex—each new object included has some attribute in common with another element, but the attributes undergo endless changes.

Complex formation is also responsible for the peculiar phenomenon that one word may in different situations have different or even opposite meanings as long as there is some associative link between them. Thus, a child may say *before* for both before and after, or *tomorrow* for both tomorrow and yesterday. We have here a perfect analogy with some ancient languages—Hebrew, Chinese, Latin—in which one word also sometimes indicated opposites. The Romans, for instance, had one word for high and deep. Such a marriage of opposite meanings is possible only as a result of thinking in complexes.

XIII

There is another very interesting trait of primitive thought that shows us complex thinking in action and points up the difference between pseudoconcepts and concepts. This trait—which Levy-Bruhl was the first to note in primitive peoples, Alfred Storch in the insane, and Piaget in children—is usually called *participation*.[8] The term is applied to the relation of partial identity or close interdependence established by primitive thought between two objects or phenomena that actually have neither contiguity nor any other recognizable connection.

Levy-Bruhl (1918) quotes Karl von Steinen regarding a striking case of participation observed among the Bororo of Brazil, who pride themselves on being red parrots.[9] Von Steinen at first did not know what to make of such a categorical assertion, but finally decided that they really meant it. It was not merely a name they appropriated, or a family relationship they insisted upon—what they meant was identity of beings.

It seems to us that the phenomenon of participation has not yet received a sufficiently convincing psychological explanation, and this for two reasons: First, investigations have tended to focus on the contents of the phenomenon and to ignore the mental operations involved, i.e., to study the product rather than the process; second, no adequate attempts have been made to view the phenomenon in the context of the other bonds and relations formed by the primitive mind. Too often the extreme, the fantastic, like the Bororo notion that they are red parrots, attracts investigation at the expense of less spectacular phenomena. Yet careful analysis shows that even those connections that do not outwardly clash with our logic are formed by the primitive mind on the principles of complex thinking.

Since children of a certain age think in pseudoconcepts, and words designate to them complexes of concrete objects, their thinking must result in participation, i.e., in bonds unacceptable to adult logic. A particular thing may be included in different complexes on the strength of its different concrete attributes and consequently may have several names; which one is used depends on the complex activated at the time. In our experiments, we frequently observed instances of this kind of participation in which an object was included simultaneously in two or more complexes. Far from being an exception, participation is characteristic of complex thinking.

The phenomenon of participation among primitive peoples also has its roots in the complex character of their thinking. Primitive people think in complexes, and consequently the word in their languages does not function as a carrier of the concept, but rather as a family name for a group of concrete objects belonging together, not logically, but factually. Such thinking in complexes, as was shown by Werner, inevitably results in such an intertwining of them as to lead to participation. Werner's analysis convincingly shows that participation constitutes a definite historical stage in the development of relations between thought and language.[10]

Storch has shown that the same kind of thinking is characteristic of schizophrenics, who regress from conceptual thought to a more primitive level (Storch, 1924). Schizophrenics, as was mentioned by Bleuler, abandon concepts for the more primitive form of thinking in images and symbols. The use of concrete images instead of abstract concepts, according to Storch, is one of the most characteristic traits of primitive thought.[11]

Richard Thurnwald also emphasized that the use of syncretic images of natural events is a characteristic feature of the primitive mentality.[12]

Thus, the child, primitive man, and the insane, much as their thought processes may differ in other important respects, all manifest participation—a symptom of primitive complex thinking and of the function of words as family names.

We therefore believe that Levy-Bruhl's way of interpreting participation is incorrect. He approaches the Bororo statements about being red parrots from the point of view of our own logic when he assumes that to the primitive mind, too, such an assertion means identity of beings. But since words to the Bororo designate groups of objects, not concepts, their assertion has a different meaning: The word for parrot is the word for a complex that includes parrots and themselves. It does not imply identity any more than a family name shared by two related individuals implies that they are one and the same person.

XIV

The history of language clearly shows that complex thinking with all its peculiarities is the very foundation of linguistic development.

Modern linguistics distinguishes between the meaning of a word, or an expression, and its referent, i.e., the object it designates. There may be one meaning and different referents, or different meanings and one referent. Whether we say "the victor at Jena" or "the loser at Waterloo," we refer to the same person, yet the meaning of the two phrases differs. There is but one category of words—proper names—whose sole function is that of reference. Using this terminology, we might say that the child's and the adult's words coincide in their referents but not in their meanings.

Identity of referent combined with divergence of meaning is also found in the history of languages. A multitude of facts supports this thesis. The synonyms existing in every language are one good example. The Russian language has two words for moon, arrived at by different thought processes that are clearly reflected in their etymologies. One term derives from the Latin word connoting "caprice, inconstancy, fancy." It was obviously meant to stress the changing form that distinguishes the moon from the other celestial bodies. The originator of the second term, which means "measurer," had no doubt been impressed by the fact that time could be measured by lunar phases. Between languages, the same holds true. For instance, in Russian the word for tailor stems from an old word for a piece of cloth; in French and in German it means "one who cuts."

If we trace the history of a word in any language, we shall see, however surprising this may seem at first blush, that its meanings change just as in the child's thinking. In the example we have cited, *bow-wow* was applied to a series of objects totally disparate from the adult point of view. Similar transfers of meaning, indicative of complex thinking, are the rule rather than the exception in the development of a language. Russian has a term for day-and-night, *sutki*. Originally it meant a seam, the junction of two pieces of cloth, something woven together; then it was used for any junction, e.g., of two walls of a house, and hence a corner; it began to be used metaphorically for twilight, "where day and night meet"; then it came to mean the time from one twilight to the next, i.e., the 24-hour *sutki* of the present. Such diverse things as a seam, a corner, twilight, and 24 hours are drawn into one complex in the course of the development of a word, in the same way as the child incorporates different things into a group on the basis of concrete imagery.

What are the laws governing the formation of word families? More often than not, new phenomena or objects are named after inessential attributes, so that the name does not truly express the nature of the thing named. Because a name is never a concept when it first emerges, it is usually both too narrow and too broad. For instance, the Russian word for cow originally meant "horned," and the word for mouse, "thief." But there is much more to a cow than horns, and to a mouse than pilfering; thus their names are too narrow. On the other hand, they are too broad, since the same epithets may be applied—and actually are applied in some other languages—to a number of other creatures. The result is a ceaseless struggle within the developing language between conceptual thought and the heritage of primitive thinking in complexes. The complex-created name, based on one attribute, conflicts with the concept for which it has come to stand. In the contest between the concept and the image that gave birth to the name, the image gradually loses out; it fades from consciousness and from memory, and the original meaning of the word is eventually obliterated. Years ago all ink was black, and the Russian word for ink refers to its blackness. This does not prevent us today from speaking of red, green, or blue "blacking" without noticing the incongruity of the combination.

Transfers of names to new objects occur through contiguity or similarity, i.e., on the basis of concrete bonds typical of thinking in complexes. Words in the making in our own era present many examples of the process by which miscellaneous things are grouped together. When we speak of "the leg of a table," "the elbow of a road," "the neck of a bottle," and "a bottleneck," we are grouping things in a complexlike fashion. In these cases the visual and functional similarities mediating the transfer are quite clear. Transfer can be determined, however, by the most varied associations, and if it has occurred in the remote past, it is impossible to reconstruct the connections without knowing exactly the historical background of the event. It is concrete factual connections between things that is the basis of such transfer. Word appears here in their nominative function rather than their semantic function, and the whole process resembles that of complex thinking.

In the dialogue between child and adult, a somewhat similar process takes place—both of them may refer to the same object, but each will think of it in a fundamentally different framework. The child's framework is purely situational, with the word tied to something concrete, whereas the adult's framework is conceptual.

Alexander Potebnja suggested considering language as a device for human self-understanding.[13] If we look from this point of view at the role played by a child's language with respect to his thought, we shall find that his understanding of himself differs from his understanding of the adult. Mental acts based on the child's speech do not coincide with the mental acts of the adult, even if they are uttering one and the same word.

The primordial word by no means could be reduced to a mere sign of the concept. Such a word is rather a picture, image, mental sketch of the concept. It is a work of art indeed. That is why such a word has a "complex" character and may denote a number of objects belonging to one complex.

XV

Much can be learned about complex thinking from the speech of deaf-mute children, in whose case the main stimulus to the formation of pseudoconcepts is absent. Deprived of verbal communication with adults and left to determine for themselves what objects to group under a common name, they form their complexes freely, and the special characteristics of complex thinking appear in them in pure, clear-cut form.

In the sign language of deaf-mutes, touching a tooth may have three different meanings: "white," "stone," and "tooth." All three belong to one complex, whose further elucidation requires an additional pointing or imitative gesture to indicate the object meant in each case. The two functions of a word are, so to speak, physically separated. A deaf-mute touches his tooth and then, by pointing at its surface or by making a throwing gesture, tells us to what object he refers in a given case.

If we look at those forms of thinking that reveal themselves in our dreams, we would immediately recognize their complex character, with all its syncretism, condensation, and displacement of images. The mechanism of generalization realized in our dreams, observes Ernst Kretschmer, gives us a key to the correct understanding of the forms of primitive thinking.[14] It also helps to dispel a biased view according to which generalization exists only in a conceptual form.

Jaensch discovered in the field of purely eidetic imagery certain agglomerations or generalizations of images that look like concrete analogues of abstract concepts. He called this type of generalization a "fluxion." The adult constantly shifts from conceptual to concrete, complex thinking. The transitional, pseudoconceptual form of thought is not confined to the child's thinking; we too resort to it very often in our daily lives.

From the point of view of dialectical logic, concepts used in our everyday speech cannot be called concepts in the strict sense of this word. Rather, they should be called generalized representations of things. These representations occupy an intermediate position between complexes and pseudoconcepts, on the one hand, and real concepts on the other.

XVI

Our investigation led us to divide the process of concept formation into three major phases. We have described two of them, marked by the predominance of the syncretic image and of the complex, respectively, and we come now to the third phase. Like the second, it can be subdivided into several stages.

In reality, the new formations do not necessarily appear only after complex thinking has run the full course of its development. In a rudimentary shape, they can be observed long before the child begins to think in pseudoconcepts. Essentially, however, they belong in the third division of our schema of concept formation. If complex thinking is one root of concept formation, the forms we are about to describe are a second, independent root. They have a distinct genetic function, different from that of complexes, in the child's mental development.

The principal function of complexes is to establish bonds and relations. Complex thinking begins the unification of scattered impressions; by organizing discrete elements of experience into groups, it creates a basis for later generalizations.

But the advanced concept presupposes more than unification. To form such a concept it is also necessary *to abstract, to single out* elements, and to view the abstracted elements apart from the totality of the concrete experience in which they are embedded. In genuine concept formation, it is equally important to unite and to separate: Synthesis and analysis presuppose each other as in-halation presupposes exhalation (Goethe).

In the actual development of the child's thinking, the above-mentioned functions—generalization and abstraction—are closely intertwined. Only in scientific analysis do they appear as independent entities. But such an analysis is not an arbitrary one; it creates no new artifacts. The distinction between these two functions is rooted in their own psychological natures.

In our experiment, the first step toward abstraction was made when the child grouped together *maximally similar* objects, e.g., objects that were small *and* round, or red *and* flat. Since the test material contains no identical objects, even the maximally similar are dissimilar in some respects. It follows that in picking out these "best matches," the child must be paying more attention to some traits of an object than to others—giving them pref-erential treatment, so to speak. The attributes that, added up, make an object maximally similar to the sam-ple become the focus of attention and are thereby, in a sense, abstracted from the attributes to which the child attends less. This first attempt at abstraction is not obvi-ous as such, because the child abstracts a whole group of traits, without clearly distinguishing one from another; often the abstraction of such a group of attributes is based only on a vague, general impression of the objects' similarity.

Still, the global character of the child's perception has been breached. An object's attributes have been divided into two parts unequally attended to—a beginning of positive and negative abstraction (O. Külpe). An object no longer enters a complex *in toto,* with all its attributes—some are denied admission; if the object is impoverished thereby, the attributes that caused its inclusion in the complex acquire a sharper relief in the child's thinking.

XVII

During the next stage in the development of abstraction, the grouping of objects on the basis of maximum similarity is superseded by grouping on the basis of a single attribute—e.g., only round objects or only flat ones. Although the product is indistinguishable from the product of a concept, these formations, like pseudoconcepts, are only precursors of true concepts. Following the usage introduced by Karl Groos (1913), we shall call such formations *potential concepts*.[15]

Potential concepts, says Groos, can be viewed as a product of habit. In its most elementary form, the potential concept is an embodiment of a rule that situations having some features in common will produce similar impressions. Such a "concept" based on the rule of repetition should appear rather early in a child's development. But being a precursor of intellectual judgment, the potential concept by itself bears no sign of intelligence.

Potential concepts result from a series of isolating abstractions of such a primitive nature that they are present to some degree not only in very young children but even in animals. That is why we completely agree with Oswald Kroh when he points out that abstraction in the form of isolating abstraction appears very early, and not in adolescence, as many psychologists still believe.[16]

Actually, even hens can be trained to respond to one distinct attribute in different objects, such as color or shape. Groos was right when he refused to take the use of potential concepts as a sign of intellectual processes. Our elementary potential concepts, says Groos, are preintellectual formations. There is no necessity to assume any involvement of logical processes in order to account for the use of potential concepts. In particular, the relation between a word and what we call its "meaning" may take the form of a simple association, devoid of any real word meaning.

The first words of the child closely resemble potential concepts. These first words are (a) practically connected with a certain group of objects, and (b) appear as a product of isolating abstraction. The first words are potential concepts indeed—they have a potential to become concepts, but this potential is still idle in them.

Bühler pointed out that there is a certain analogy between the use of tools by chimpanzees and the use of words by children. Köhler's chimpanzees, once they learned to use a stick as a tool, used other long objects when they needed a stick and none was available. Similarly, once a child has associated a word with an object, he readily applies it to a new object that impresses him as similar in some way to the first.

Köhler observed, however, that it is a functional similarity rather than real likeness that allows different objects to substitute for a stick in the actions of chimpanzees.

The difference between Groos's and Köhler's potential concepts lies in their belonging to two different spheres of activity. Potential concepts, then, may be formed either in the sphere of perceptual thinking or in that of practical, action-bound thinking—on the basis of similar impressions in the first case, and on the basis of the similar functional roles in the second.

The latter are an important source of potential concepts. It is well known that until early school age, functional meanings play a very important role in the child's thinking. When asked to explain a word, a child will tell what the object the word designates can do, or—more often—what can be done with it. Even abstract concepts are often translated into the language of concrete action: "*Reasonable* means when I am hot and don't stand in a draft" (August Messer).[17]

Potential concepts already play a part in complex thinking, insofar as abstraction occurs also in complex formation. Associative complexes, for instance, presuppose the "abstraction" of one trait common to different units. But as long as complex thinking predominates, the abstracted trait is unstable, has no privileged position, and easily yields its temporary dominance to other traits. In potential concepts proper, a trait once abstracted is not easily lost again among the other traits. The concrete totality of traits has been destroyed through its abstraction, and the possibility of unifying the traits on a different basis opens up. Only the mastery of abstraction, combined with advanced complex thinking, enables the child to progress to the formation of genuine concepts. A concept emerges only when the abstracted traits are synthesized anew and the resulting abstract synthesis becomes the main instrument of thought. The decisive role in this process, as our experiments have shown, is played by the word, deliberately used to direct all the subprocesses of advanced concept formation.

It must be clear from this chapter that words also fulfill an important, though different function in the various stages of thinking in complexes. Therefore, we consider complex thinking a stage in the development of verbal thinking, unlike Volkelt, Werner, Kretschmer, and some others, who extend the term complex to include preverbal thinking and even thinking in animals.[18]

From our point of view, there is an essential difference between natural biologically grounded intelligence and historically developed human intelligence.

At the same time, the role played by the word in complex thinking by no means coincides with its role in conceptual thinking. On the contrary, the very difference between the complex and the concept lies in the different functional uses of the word. The word is a sign, and as such it may be used in different ways depending on what kind of intellectual operation it is involved in. From this difference in the intellectual operations with the word springs the difference between complex thinking and conceptual thinking.

XVIII

In our experimental study of the intellectual processes of adolescents, we observed how the primitive syncretic and complex forms of thinking gradually subside, potential concepts are used less and less, and true concepts begin to be formed—seldom at first, then with increasing frequency.

It would be erroneous, however, to imagine that this transition from complexes to concepts is a mechanical process in which the higher developmental stage completely supersedes the lower one. The developmental scene turns out to be much more complex. Different genetic forms coexist in thinking, just as different rock formations coexist in the earth's crust. Such a structure is not an exception, but rather a rule of behavior. We know fairly well that human actions do not belong necessarily to the highest and the most advanced level of development. Developmentally late forms coexist in behavior with younger formations.

The same is true for the ontogenetic development of the child's thinking. Even after the adolescent has learned to produce concepts, he does not abandon the more elementary forms; they continue for a long time to operate, indeed to dominate, in many areas of his thinking. As we have mentioned earlier, even adults often resort to complex thinking. Moreover, even conceptual thinking in adolescents and adults, insofar as it is involved in solving daily problems, does not advance beyond the level of pseudoconcepts. Possessing all characteristics of conceptuality, such thinking, viewed from the dialecticological perspective, remains complex.

Adolescence, therefore, is less a period of completion than one of crisis and transition.

The transitional character of adolescent thinking becomes especially evident when we observe the actual functioning of the newly acquired concepts. Experiments specially devised to study the adolescent's operations with concepts bring out, in the first place, a striking discrepancy between his ability to form concepts and his ability to define them.

The adolescent will form and use a concept quite correctly in a concrete situation, but will find it strangely difficult to express that concept in words, and the verbal definition will, in most cases, be much narrower than might have been expected from the way he used the concept. The same discrepancy occurs also in adult thinking, even at very advanced levels. This confirms the assumption that concepts evolve in ways differing from deliberate conscious elaboration of experience in logical terms. Analysis of reality with the help of concepts precedes analysis of the concepts themselves.

The adolescent encounters another obstacle when he tries to apply a concept that he has formed in a specific situation to a new set of objects or circumstances, where the attributes synthesized in the concept appear in configurations differing from the original one. (An example would be the application to everyday objects of the new concept "small and tall," evolved on test blocks.) Still, the adolescent is usually able to achieve such a transfer at a fairly early stage of development.

Much more difficult than the transfer itself is the task of defining a concept when it is no longer rooted in the original situation and must be formulated on a purely abstract plane, without reference to any concrete situa-

tion or impressions. In our experiments, the child or adolescent who had solved the problem or concept formation
correctly very often descended to a more primitive level
of thought in giving a verbal definition of the concept
and began simply to enumerate the various objects to
which the concept applied in the particular setting. In
this case, he operated with the name as with a concept,
but defined it as a complex—a form of thought vacillat-
ing between complex and concept, and typical of that
transitional age.

The greatest difficulty of all is the application of a concept, finally grasped and formulated on the abstract level,
to new concrete situations that must be viewed in these
abstract terms—a kind of transfer usually mastered only
toward the end of the adolescent period. The transition
from the abstract to the concrete proves just as arduous
for the youth as the earlier transition from the concrete
to the abstract. Our experiments leave no doubt that on
this point, at any rate, the description of concept formation given by traditional psychology, which simply reproduced the schema of formal logic, is totally unrelated to
reality.

According to the classical school, concept formation is
achieved by the same process as the "family portrait" in
Galton's composite photographs. These are made by taking pictures of different members of a family on the same
plate, so that the "family" traits common to several people stand out with an extraordinary vividness, while the
differing personal traits of individuals are blurred by the
superimposition. A similar intensification of traits shared
by a number of objects is supposed to occur in concept
formation; according to traditional theory, the sum of
these traits *is* the concept. In reality, as some psychologists noted long ago, and as our experiments show, the
path by which adolescents arrive at concept formation
never conforms to this logical schema. When the process

of concept formation is seen in all its complexity, it appears as a *movement* of thought within the pyramid of concepts, constantly alternating between two directions: from the particular to the general, and from the general to the particular (Peter Vogel).[19]

Lately Karl Bühler has suggested a model that presupposes two major roots of concept formation. The first of them is the association of a number of the child's representations into groups. The second, genetic, root of concept formation is seen in the function of judgment. The concept appears to be a product of an intellectual act, i.e., of a well-formed judgment. Bühler points out that a child's words designating concepts very rarely reproduce judgments corresponding to these concepts. Thus, judgment appears as the most elementary act. Representations and judgments then interact in the course of concept formation—which means that concept formation is carried out from both sides, from the concrete and from the general almost simultaneously.

The first words of a child already play the role of generalizations. The word "flower" appears in a child's vocabulary much earlier than the names of concrete flowers. And even if by some accident the child learns the word "rose" prior to that of "flower," he uses "rose" as a general name, calling all flowers he sees "rose."

We must say that while the observation that the child's first words are generalizations is correct, at the same time it creates the wrong impression that abstract concepts appear as early as the first words-generalizations. Charlotte Bühler, for example, constructed a theory according to which adolescents use, in principle, the same mental operations as three-year-olds.

We, in our turn, would like to emphasize that the use of words-generalizations does not presuppose an early mastery of abstract thinking. As we have already shown in concept-formation experiments and through observations of the education process, mental operations of the child and those of the adult are quite different. Though the child and the adult may use one and the same word in referring to one and the same object, their mental operations are quite different. The early use of words, which in adult thinking stand for concepts, does not imply that the child has already mastered the skill of abstract reasoning.

We do not agree with Karl Bühler in what concerns the role of the child's judgment in concept formation. The concept, indeed, appears as an integral part of a larger whole, which is judgment or statement. When a child answers to a word-stimulus "house", saying "big," and to "tree," saying "with apples," he confirms this rule.

Like a word that exists only in the phrase, and like a sentence that appears in the child's speech earlier than a separate word, judgment appears in the child prior to the concept. That is why association alone cannot engender a concept.

Our experiments confirmed Bühler's view on the role associations and judgments play in concept formation, and yet we disagree with his conclusion that these two forms are the real roots of concept formation.

Bühler ignores the role of the word in the complexes that precede concepts. He tried to derive concepts from the natural working out of impressions, overlooking the historical and verbal character of complex formation. Bühler made no distinction between natural complexes represented by eidetic "concepts" (Jaensch) and complexes engendered by highly developed verbal thinking. Speaking about judgments, Bühler also ignored the distinction between the biological and the historical forms of thinking, between natural and cultural elements, and between verbal and nonverbal forms.

From our point of view, the processes leading to concept formation develop along two main lines. The first is complex formation: The child unites diverse objects in groups under a common "family name"; this process passes through various stages. The second line of development is the formation of "potential concepts," based on singling out certain common attributes. In both, the use of the word is an integral part of the developing processes, and the word maintains its guiding function in the formation of genuine concepts, to which these processes lead.

6

The Development of Scientific Concepts in Childhood: The Design of a Working Hypothesis

I

To devise successful methods of instructing the school-child in systematic knowledge, it is necessary to understand the development of scientific concepts in the child's mind. No less important than this practical aspect of the problem is its theoretical significance for psychological science. Yet our knowledge of the entire subject is surprisingly scanty.

The study to be discussed in this chapter appears as a pioneering attempt to investigate systematically the development of scientific and spontaneous concepts in childhood. This investigation, carried out by Zhozephina Shif, was designed to test experimentally our working hypothesis concerning the specificity of the development of scientific concepts in comparison with spontaneous concepts.[1] We assumed that concepts, i.e., word meanings, cannot be assimilated by the child in a ready-made form, but have to undergo a certain development. We also suggested that it would be incorrect to apply the results obtained in a study of spontaneous concepts to scientific concepts. To test this hypothesis, we developed an experimental procedure that included structurally similar tasks containing either scientific or everyday-life material.

The experiment included making up stories from a series of pictures that showed the beginning of an action, its continuation, and its end, and completing fragments of sentences ending in *because* or *although*. These tests were complemented by clinical discussion, during which we tried to identify the level of the child's conscious comprehension of the causal relations.

Material for one series of tests was taken from social science courses of the second and fourth grades. The second series used simple situations of daily life, such as "The boy went to the movies because . . . ," "The girl cannot yet read, although . . . ," "He fell off his bicycle because . . ." Supplementary methods of study included testing the child's scholastic achievements, and observations made during lessons. The children we studied were primary school students. [The first-graders were, on average, seven-year-olds.]

Analysis of the data compared separately for each age group in the following table shows that as long as the curriculum supplies the necessary material, the *development of scientific concepts runs ahead of the development of spontaneous concepts.*

Correct completions of sentence fragments

	Second grade (%)	Fourth grade (%)
Fragments ending in *because*		
Scientific concepts	79.7	81.8
Spontaneous concepts	59.0	81.3
Fragments ending in *although*		
Scientific concepts	21.3	79.5
Spontaneous concepts	16.2	65.5

The data available indicated that the level of conscious comprehension of the material is higher in the case of scientific concepts. Accumulation of knowledge supports a steady growth of scientific reasoning, which in its turn favorably influences the development of spontaneous thinking. Thus, systematic learning plays a leading role in the development of schoolchildren.

We know that adversative relations [*but, although*] appear later than causal relations in the child's thinking, and one may see that in the adversative category, fourth-graders perform no better than second-graders in the causal category.

These findings led us to a hypothesis of two different paths in the development of two different forms of reasoning. In the case of scientific thinking, the primary role is played by *initial verbal definition*, which being applied systematically, gradually comes down to concrete phenomena. The development of spontaneous concepts knows no systematicity and goes from the phenomena upward toward generalizations.

The scientific concepts evolve under the conditions of systematic cooperation between the child and the teacher. Development and maturation of the child's higher mental functions are products of this cooperation. Our study shows that the developmental progress reveals itself in the growing *relativity* of causal thinking, and in the achievement of a certain *freedom* of thinking in scientific concepts. Scientific concepts develop earlier than spontaneous concepts because they benefit from the systematicity of instruction and cooperation. This early maturity of scientific concepts gives them the role of a propaedeutic guide in the development of spontaneous concepts.

The weak aspect of the child's use of spontaneous concepts lies in the child's inability to use these concepts freely and voluntarily and to form abstractions. The difficulty with scientific concepts lies in their *verbalism*, i.e., in their excessive abstractness and detachment from reality. At the same time, the very nature of scientific concepts prompts their deliberate use, the latter being their advantage over the spontaneous concepts. At about the fourth grade, verbalism gives way to concretization, which in turn favorably influences the development of spontaneous concepts. Both forms of reasoning reach, at that moment, approximately the same level of development.

What happens in the mind of the child to the scientific concepts he is taught at school? What is the relation between the assimilation of information and the internal development of a scientific concept in the child's consciousness?

Contemporary child psychology has two answers to these questions. One school of thought believes that scientific concepts have no inward history, i.e., do not undergo development, but are absorbed ready-made through a process of understanding and assimilation. Most educational theories and methods are still based on this view. It is, nevertheless, a view that fails to stand up under scrutiny, either theoretically or in its practical applications. As we know from investigations of the process of concept formation, a concept is more than the sum of certain associative bonds formed by memory, more than a mere mental habit; it is a complex and genuine act of thought that cannot be taught by drilling, but can be accomplished only when the child's mental development itself has reached the requisite level. At any age, a concept embodied in a word represents an act of generalization. But word meanings evolve. When a new word has been learned by the child, its development is barely starting; the word at first is a generalization of the most primitive type; as the child's intellect develops, it is replaced by generalizations of a higher and higher type—a process that leads in the end to the formation of true concepts. The development of concepts, or word meanings, presupposes the development of many intellectual functions: deliberate attention, logical memory, abstraction, the ability to compare and to differentiate. These complex psychological processes cannot be mastered through the initial learning alone.

Practical experience also shows that direct teaching of concepts is impossible and fruitless. A teacher who tries to do this usually accomplishes nothing but empty verbalism, a parrotlike repetition of words by the child, simulating a knowledge of the corresponding concepts but actually covering up a vacuum.

Leo Tolstoy, with his profound understanding of the nature of word and meaning, realized more clearly than most other educators the impossibility of simply relaying a concept from teacher to pupil. He tells of his attempts to teach literary language to peasant children by first "translating" their own vocabulary into the language of folk tales, then translating the language of tales into literary Russian. He found that one could not teach children literary language by artificial explanations, compulsive memorizing, and repetition, as one teaches a foreign language. Tolstoy writes, "We have to admit that we attempted several times . . . to do this, and always met with an invincible distaste on the part of the children, which shows that we were on the wrong track. These experiments have left me with the certainty that it is quite impossible to explain the meaning of a word. . . . When you explain any word, the word 'impression,' for instance, you put in its place another equally incomprehensible word, or a whole series of words, with the connection between them as incomprehensible as the word itself" (Tolstoy, 1903, p. 143).

In this categorical statement, correct and false ideas are present in equal amounts. It is correct, and any teacher will confirm this, that the major problem is an absence of appropriate concepts in the child: "It is not a word, that is difficult to comprehend, but the concept denoted by this word, which the child does not understand. The word is almost always at hand when the concept is ready. Also, the relation of the word to thought, and the formation of new concepts, is such a delicate, complex and mysterious process that any interference results in awkwardness that hinders the process of development" (Tolstoy, 1903, p. 143).

It is true that concepts and word meanings evolve, and that this is a complex and delicate process. But Tolstoy is wrong when he suggests abandoning any attempt to direct the acquisition of concepts and calls for natural unhindered development. Suggesting this, he divorces the process of development from that of learning and instruction, particularly because his formulation is so categorical.

At the same time, Tolstoy himself understood that it is only rough interference that hinders the development, while more subtle and roundabout methods may have a positive effect: "When he has heard or read an unknown word in an otherwise comprehensible sentence, and another time in another sentence, he begins to have a hazy idea of the new concept; sooner or later he will . . . feel the need to use that word—and once he has used it, the word and the concept are his. . . . But to give the pupil new concepts deliberately . . . is, I am convinced, as impossible and futile as teaching a child to walk by the laws of equilibrium" (Tolstoy, 1903, p. 143).

Thus, Tolstoy shows that he is aware of the existence of many other ways through which concepts can be acquired, and that these ways should not be necessarily scholastic. But he still overemphasizes the role of spontaneity, of chance, and of obscure feelings. He overplays the inner workings of concept formation, and underplays learning and instruction.

Leaving aside what is wrong in Tolstoy's position, we

would like to subscribe to his idea, which is correct, that the path from the first encounter with a new concept to the point where the concept and the corresponding word are fully appropriated by the child is long and complex.

Our experimental study proved that it is not only possible to teach children to use concepts, but that such "interference" may influence favorably the development of concepts that have been formed by the student himself. But the same study shows that to introduce a new concept means just to start the process of its appropriation. Deliberate introduction of new concepts does not preclude spontaneous development, but rather charts the new paths for it.

It must be taken into account that when Tolstoy writes about learning, what he actually means is the learning of Russian literary language. This subject does not presuppose, necessarily, a systematic learning of scientific concepts. It is rather an acquisition of new concepts and words that will be woven into the existing texture of the child's concepts. Examples given by Tolstoy confirm this; for example, he discusses how to explain and interpret such words as "impression" and "tool"—words that do not require a rigorous system for their comprehension. Here lies the difference between our study—which is aimed at an investigation of the systematic learning of scientific concepts—and Tolstoy's studies. This difference poses a question as to what extent Tolstoy's observations are applicable to the process of scientific-concept formation.

Noting the fact that scientific and spontaneous concepts differ, we do not venture, at this moment, to foretell its importance. This problem will become a subject of discussion later in this chapter. What we would like to emphasize now is that the very distinction between scientific and spontaneous concepts hardly can be called a commonplace in contemporary psychology, and must be defended in the first place.

As we have mentioned earlier, contemporary psychology offered two answers to the problem of the development of scientific concepts in schoolchildren. The first answer, which we have already discussed and dismissed, denies such a development altogether.

The second conception of the evolution of scientific concepts does not deny the existence of a developmental process in the schoolchild's mind; it holds, however, that this process does not differ in any essential from the development of the concepts formed by the child in his everyday experience and that it is pointless to consider the two processes separately. What is the basis for this view?

The literature in this field shows that in studying concept formation in childhood, most investigators have used everyday concepts formed by children without systematic instruction. The laws based on these data are assumed to apply also to the child's scientific concepts, and no checking of this assumption is deemed necessary. Only a few of the more perspicacious modern students of the child's thought question the legitimacy of such an extension. Piaget draws a sharp line between the child's ideas of reality developed mainly through his own mental efforts and those that were decisively influenced by adults; he designates the first group as *spontaneous*, the second as *nonspontaneous*, and admits that the latter may deserve independent investigation. In this respect, he goes farther and deeper than any of the other students of children's concepts.

Piaget found that certain characteristics are shared by spontaneous and nonspontaneous concepts: (1) both of them resist suggestion; (2) both have deep roots in the child's thinking; (3) both appear in more or less similar forms in children of the same age; (4) both have a long life in the child's mind and die out gradually, unlike the "suggested concepts," which disappear instantly; (5) both reveal themselves in the first correct answers of the child. These characteristics shared by both types of concepts serve as a demarcation line separating them from those concepts and answers that are suggested to a child.

These are correct observations and they could lead to recognition of nonspontaneous concepts as deserving of special study. At the same time, there are errors in Piaget's reasoning that detract from the value of his views. We shall focus on three of his major errors, which are intricately interconnected. The first of them stems from Piaget's belief that spontaneous concepts alone can truly enlighten us as to the special qualities of the child's thought. From this point of view, nonspontaneous concepts merely reflect the assimilation of adult thought by children, but tell nothing about the development of their own reasoning. Piaget finds himself in disagreement with his own correct observation that the child, while assimilating adult concepts, stamps them with characteristics of his own mentality. Piaget, however, tends to apply this observation exclusively to spontaneous concepts.

The second error is just an extension of the first. Since spontaneous concepts alone are perceived as characteristic of child thought, Piaget attempts to present spontaneous and nonspontaneous concepts as firmly divided and self-contained entities whose interaction is impossible. He fails to see the interaction between these two types of concepts and the bonds uniting them into a total system. These errors lead to yet another.

On the one hand, Piaget emphasized that it is spontaneous concepts that reflect the characteristic quality of the child's thinking; on the other hand, it is one of the basic tenets of Piaget's theory that progressive socialization of thinking is the very essence of the child's mental development. But if Piaget's views on the nature of non-spontaneous concepts were correct, it would follow that such an important factor in the socialization of thought as school learning is unrelated to the inner developmental processes. It would look as if the inner development of the child's thought had no relation to socialization, while socialization had no relevance for the development of the child's concepts. This inconsistency is the weak spot in Piaget's theory, both theoretically and practically.

Theoretically, socialization of thought is seen by Piaget as a mechanical abolition of the characteristics of the child's thought, their gradual withering away. All that is new in development comes from without, replacing the child's own modes of thought. These characteristically infantile modes of reasoning include the solipsism of early infancy and egocentrism of childhood, which already shows certain signs of compromise between extreme child egocentricity and rational, conceptual thinking of adults. The entire process of development appears as mechanical displacement of one mentality by the other. The child's own thinking plays no constructive role in this process, being simply gradually replaced by an adult mode of reasoning. Throughout childhood, there is a ceaseless conflict between two mutually antagonistic forms of thinking, with a series of compromises at each successive developmental level, until adult thought wins out.

This theoretical position leaves no alternative other than antagonism for the relation between development and learning. All nonspontaneous concepts learned from adults must be in sharp opposition to those developed by the child himself. Throughout the history of the child's development runs a "warfare" between spontaneous and nonspontaneous, systematically learned, concepts. Each stage in this development is characterized by a measure of quantitative prevalence of one of the types of reasoning. In schoolchildren of eleven to twelve, the nonspontaneous concepts completely replace the spontaneous, and with this, according to Piaget, intellectual development reaches its port of arrival. The real culmination of the developmental process, i.e., the formation of mature, scientific concepts in adolescence, simply has no place in Piaget's model. The real content of development, according to Piaget, lies in continuous confrontation between two antagonistic forms of thinking; the development of this confrontation is marked by a series of compromises, which can be measured in terms of the diminishing power of the child's egocentrism.

In what concerns the practical applications, the above-mentioned contradiction results in the impossibility of applying data obtained in a study of spontaneous concepts to nonspontaneous concepts. What we face here is a vicious circle: on the one hand, it was emphasized that nonspontaneous concepts have nothing to reveal about a child's mental development; on the other hand, each time one confronts an educational problem, one attempts to apply the principles of the development of spontaneous concepts to the process of learning in school. This vicious circle became particularly evident in Piaget's paper "Child Psychology and History Instruction" (1933). In this paper Piaget claims that the best way to formulate a method of teaching history is to study the child's spontaneous concepts—even if at the first glance they seem to be naive and unimportant. But in the very same paper Piaget comes to the conclusion that the child's thought is devoid of objectivity, critical approach, understanding of relations, and stability—in a word, those characteristics essential for mastering historical material. Consequently, on the one hand, a study of spontaneous concepts is regarded as a foundation of teaching; on the other hand, spontaneous concepts are shown to be of no value in rendering systematic knowledge. Piaget "resolves" this contradiction by suggesting a principle of antagonism between development and learning. It seems that when he says that nothing is more important for effective teaching than a thorough knowledge of the spontaneous thought of children, he means that the child's thought must be known as any enemy must be known in order to be fought successfully.[2]

We shall counter these erroneous premises with the premise that the development of nonspontaneous concepts must possess all the traits peculiar to the child's thought at each developmental level because these concepts are not simply acquired by rote but evolve with the aid of strenuous mental activity on the part of the child himself. We believe that the two processes—the development of spontaneous and of nonspontaneous concepts—are related and constantly influence each other. They are parts of a single process: the development of concept formation, which is affected by varying external and internal conditions but is essentially a unitary process, not a conflict of antagonistic, mutually exclusive forms of thinking. Instruction is one of the principal sources of the schoolchild's concepts and is also a powerful force in directing their evolution; it determines the fate of his total mental development. If so, the results of the psychological study of children's concepts can be applied to the problems of teaching in a manner very different from that envisioned by Piaget.

Before discussing these premises in detail, we want to set forth our own reasons for differentiating between spontaneous and nonspontaneous—in particular, scientific—concepts and for subjecting the latter to special study.

1. First, we know from simple observation that spontaneous and scientific concepts evolve under entirely different inner and outer conditions. The relation of the child's experience to scientific concepts differs greatly from its

relation to spontaneous concepts. Scientific concepts that originate in classroom instruction could not but differ from the concepts evolving in everyday life. Even the motives prompting the child to form the two kinds of concepts are not the same. The mind faces different problems when assimilating concepts at school and when left to its own devices. One may conclude that since scientific and spontaneous concepts differ in their relation to the child's experience, and in the child's attitude toward their objects, they may be expected to follow differing developmental paths from inception to final form.

Empirical data suggest that the strong and weak aspects of scientific and spontaneous concepts are different—the strong side of one indicates the weak side of the other, and vice versa. A simple example suffices to show this. When asked to define the concept "brother," a student turns out to be more confused than when asked to define the Archimedean law. The understanding of "brother" is deeply rooted in the child's experience and passes a number of stages before arriving at the definition made in conceptual form. Such a development does not start in a classroom and does not involve a teacher's explanations. At the same time, almost all empirical content of the concept "brother" is already assimilated by the child. The concept of "Archimedean law," on the contrary, does not evoke such a repercussion in the child's own experience.

2. Here we are going to discuss the theoretical aspect. We shall start with a premise used by Piaget, namely, that child speech is an original formation, and does not copy the speech of adults. In this presupposition, Piaget followed Stern, but extended Stern's idea to the child's thought, claiming that the child's thought is even more original and idiosyncratic than his language.

But if this premise is true, then one must admit that more complex forms of the child's reasoning, i.e., those associated with scientific concepts, will, most probably, be even more original and idiosyncratic than those associated with spontaneous concepts. It is hard to imagine that scientific concepts could be assimilated by the child in an unaltered, ready-made form. This becomes obvious if only one agrees that scientific concepts, like spontaneous concepts, just start their development, rather than finish it, at a moment when the child learns the term or word meaning denoting the new concept. This developmental principle is equally applicable to both groups of concepts, but each group has its own scenario for the beginning and development of concepts. The latter thought may become more clear if one compares it with the difference between learning a native language and a foreign language. The analogy with learning different languages goes beyond a superficial similarity, for it reveals psychological relations that are actually akin to those existing between scientific and spontaneous concepts.

It is well known that to learn a foreign language at school and to develop one's native language involve two entirely different processes. While learning a foreign language, we use word meanings that are already well developed in the native language, and only translate them; the advanced knowledge of one's own language also plays an important role in the study of the foreign one, as well as those inner and outer relations that are characteristic only in the study of a foreign language. And yet, in spite of all these differences, the acquisition of the foreign and the native languages belongs to one general class of the processes of speech development. One may also add to this class the acquisition of written language, which has many idiosyncratic features that cannot be derived from either one of the previously mentioned types of speech development. At the same time, all three of these processes are intricately interconnected. The acquisition of a foreign language differs from the acquisition of the native one precisely because it uses the semantics of the native language as its foundation.

The reciprocal dependence is less known and less appreciated. But Goethe clearly saw it when he wrote that he who knows no foreign language does not truly know his own. Experimental studies fully endorse this. It has been shown that a child's understanding of his native language is enhanced by learning a foreign one. The child becomes more conscious and deliberate in using words as tools of his thought and expressive means for his ideas. One may say that the knowledge of the foreign language stands to that of the native one in the same way as knowledge of algebra stands to knowledge of arithmetic, enhancing it and turning it into a concrete application of the general algebraic laws. The child's approach to language becomes more abstract and generalized. As algebra liberates the child from the domination of concrete figures and elevates him to the level of generalizations, the acquisition of foreign language—in its own peculiar way—liberates him from the dependence on concrete linguistic forms and expressions.

There are serious grounds for believing that similar relations do exist between spontaneous and scientific concepts. First of all, the development of concepts, both spontaneous and scientific, belongs to the semantic aspect of speech development; from the psychological point of view, the development of concepts and the development of word meanings are but two forms of one and the same process, which imprints its characteristic signature on both. Further, the external and internal conditions for the development of scientific concepts and the acquisition of a foreign language mostly coincide, differing in a similar way from the conditions for the development of spontaneous concepts and the acquisition of the native language. The demarcation line is drawn here between spontaneous development and systematic instruction. In a certain sense, one may call the development of one's native language a spontaneous process, and the acquisition of the foreign a nonspontaneous process.

Scientific and spontaneous concepts reveal different attitudes toward the object of study and different ways of its representation in the consciousness. The process of acquiring scientific concepts reaches far beyond the immediate experience of the child, using this experience in the same way as the semantics of the native language is used in learning a foreign language. In learning a new language, one does not return to the immediate world of objects and does not repeat past linguistic developments, but uses instead the native language as a mediator between the world of objects and the new language. Similarly, the acquisition of scientific concepts is carried out with the mediation provided by already acquired concepts.

3. The singling out of scientific concepts as an object of study also has a heuristic value. At present, psychology has only two ways of studying concept formation. One deals with the child's real concepts, but uses methods—such as verbal definition—that do not penetrate below the surface; the other permits incomparably deeper psychological analysis, but only through studying the formation of artificially devised experimental concepts. An urgent methodological problem confronting us is to find ways of studying *real* concepts in *depth*—to find a method that could utilize the results already obtained by the two methods used so far. The most promising approach to the problem would seem to be the study of scientific concepts, which are real concepts, yet are formed under our eyes almost in the fashion of artificial concepts.

4. Finally, the study of scientific concepts as such has important implications for education and instruction. These concepts are not absorbed ready-made, and in-

struction and learning play a leading role in their acquisition. To uncover the complex relation between instruction and the development of scientific concepts is an important practical task.

These were the considerations that guided us in separating scientific from everyday concepts and subjecting them to comparative study. To illustrate the kind of question we tried to answer, let us take the concept "brother"—a typical everyday concept, which Piaget used so skillfully to establish a whole series of peculiarities of the child's thought—and compare it with the concept "exploitation," to which the child is introduced in his social science classes. Is their development the same, or is it different? Does "exploitation" merely repeat the developmental course of "brother," or is it, psychologically, a concept of a different type? We submit that the two concepts must differ in their development as well as in their functioning and that these two variants of the process of concept formation must influence each other's evolution.

II

To study the relation between the development of scientific and that of everday concepts, we need a yardstick for comparing them. To construct a measuring device, we must know the typical characteristics of everyday concepts at school age and the direction of their development during that period.

Piaget demonstrated that the schoolchild's concepts are marked primarily by his lack of conscious awareness of relations, though he handles relations correctly in a spontaneous, unreflective way. Piaget asked seven- to eight-year-olds the meaning of the word *because* in the sentence, "I won't go to school tomorrow because I am sick." Most of the children answered, "It means that he is sick"; others said, "It means that he won't go to school." A child is unable to realize that the question does not refer to the separate facts of sickness and of school absence but to their connection. Yet he certainly grasps the meaning of the sentence. Spontaneously, he uses *because* correctly, but he does not know how to use it deliberately. Thus, he cannot supply a correct ending to the sentence, "The man fell off his bicycle because. . . ." Often he will substitute a consequence ("because he broke his arm") for the cause. The child's thought is nondeliberate and unconscious of itself. How, then, does the child eventually reach awareness and mastery of his own thoughts? To explain the process, Piaget cites two psychological laws.

One is the law of awareness, formulated by Claparède, who proved by very interesting experiments that awareness of difference precedes awareness of likeness. The child quite naturally responds in similar ways to objects that are alike and has no need to become aware of his mode of response, while dissimilarity creates a state of maladaptation that leads to awareness. Claparède's law states that the more smoothly we use a relation in action, the less conscious we are of it; we become aware of what we are doing in proportion to the difficulty we experience in adapting to a situation.

Piaget uses Claparède's law to explain the development of thinking that takes place between the seventh year and the twelfth year. During that period, the child's mental operations repeatedly come in conflict with adult thinking. He suffers failures and defeats because of the deficiencies of his logic, and these painful experiences create the need to become aware of his concepts.

Realizing that need is not a sufficient explanation for any developmental change, Piaget supplements Claparède's law by the law of shift, or displacement. To become conscious of a mental operation means to transfer it from the plane of action to that of language, i.e., to re-create it in the imagination so that it can be expressed in words. This change is neither quick nor smooth. The law states that mastering an operation on the higher plane of verbal thought presents the same difficulties as the earlier mastering of that operation on the plane of action. This accounts for the slow progress.

First of all, it was Piaget himself who mentioned that Claparède's law of awareness has a limited explanatory power. And actually, to say that awareness appears as a result of a child's need to become aware of something amounts to a claim that wings originate in a bird's need to fly. In what concerns scientific epistemology, such an explanation seems antiquated. It also endows the need with the ability to create apparatus necessary for its satisfaction, while robbing consciousness of its developmental aspect and portraying it as a preformed entity.

Claparède's findings may have a different explanation. Our own experimental studies suggest that the child becomes aware of differences earlier than of likenesses, not because differences lead to malfunctioning, but because awareness of similarity requires a more advanced structure of generalization and conceptualization than awareness of dissimilarity. In analyzing the development of concepts of difference and likeness, we found that consciousness of likeness presupposes the formation of a generalization, or of a concept, embracing the objects that are alike; consciousness of difference requires no such generalization—it may come about in other ways. The fact that the developmental sequence of these two concepts reverses the sequence of the earlier behavioral handling of similarity and difference is not unique. Our experiments established, for instance, that the child responds to pictorially represented action earlier than to the representation of an object, but becomes fully conscious of the object earlier than of action.

Identical pictures were shown two groups of preschool children of similar age and developmental level. One group was asked to act out the picture—which would indicate the degree of their immediate grasp of its content; the other group was asked to tell about it in words, a task requiring a measure of conceptually mediated understanding. It was found that the "actors" rendered the sense of the represented action situation, while the narrators enumerated separate objects.

One may question the applicability of Claparède's law of consciousness to the problems discussed by Piaget. Piaget uses Claparède's findings to account for the development of concepts in children between seven and twelve. That period is characterized by series of failures of the child's logic in its confrontation with the logic of adults. The child's thought bumps into the wall of its own inadequacy, and the resultant "bruises"—as it was wisely observed by J. J. Rousseau—become its best teachers. Such collisions are a powerful stimulus, evoking awareness, which, in its turn, magically reveals to a child a chamber of conscious and voluntary concepts.

But one must inquire whether that series of failures is the sole "teacher" of the child. Is it possible for the inadequacy of the child's thought to be the only real source of higher forms of generalization known as concepts? It suffices to formulate these questions in a clear-cut way, and one cannot but admit that the answer is negative. As one cannot derive awareness from the need of awareness, one also cannot derive the development of thought from the failure of thought.

The second law used by Piaget, the law of shift, is an example of the widespread genetic theory according to which certain events or patterns observed in the early stages of a developmental process will recur in its advanced stages. The traits that do recur often blind the observer to significant differences caused by the fact that the later processes take place on a higher developmental level. We can dispense with discussing the principle of repetition as such, since we are concerned merely with its explanatory value in respect to the growth of awareness. The law of shift, like the law of awareness, may at best answer the question why the schoolchild is not conscious of his concepts; it cannot explain how consciousness is achieved. We must look for another hypothesis to account for that decisive event in the child's mental development.

According to Piaget, the schoolchild's lack of awareness is a residue of his waning egocentrism, which still retains its influence in the sphere of verbal thought just beginning to form at that time. Consciousness is achieved when mature socialized thinking crowds out the residual egocentrism from the level of verbal thought.

But such a model of development does not require any laws, for if awareness of concepts is initially lacking, and if it is true that when awareness comes, it comes in a ready-made form from the world of adults, then one needs no specific laws of the child's psyche in order to account for such a development. This model does not stand up in the face of either theory or facts. The lack of conscious use of concepts by schoolchildren cannot be explained with the help of the notion of egocentrism, because it is precisely during the early school age that the higher intellectual functions, whose main features are reflective awareness and deliberate control, come to the fore in the developmental process.

The central issue of development during school age is the transition from primitive remembering and involuntary attention to the higher mental processes of voluntary attention and logical memory. Attention, previously involuntary, becomes increasingly dependent on the child's own thinking; mechanical memory changes to logical memory guided by meaning, and can now be deliberately used by the child. One may say that both attention and memory become "logical" and voluntary, since the control of a function is a counterpart of one's consciousness of this function. Intellectualization of a function and voluntary control of it are just two moments of one and the same process of the formation of higher mental functions.

Nevertheless, the fact established by Piaget cannot be denied: The schoolchild, though growing steadily in awareness and mastery of such functions as memory and attention, is not aware of his conceptual operations. All the basic functions become "intellectual," except the intelligence itself.

To resolve this seeming paradox, we must turn to basic laws governing psychological development. Elsewhere we have already discussed the role played by functional interactions in mental development.[3] It was shown and proved experimentally that mental development does not coincide with the development of separate psychological functions, but rather depends on changing relations between them. The development of each function, in turn, depends upon the progress in the development of the interfunctional system. Consciousness evolving as a real whole changes its inner structure with each step forward. The fate of each functional ingredient of consciousness thus depends upon the development of the entire system.

The idea that consciousness is a holistic system is as old as scientific psychology itself. And yet, while accepting this idea, the old psychology, but often the new one as well, proceeded in a direction contrary to the very essence of this thesis. Accepting that interfunctional relations are important, such psychology nevertheless attempted to study consciousness as if it were a sum of its functional moments. This approach also spread from general to developmental psychology, and the development of the child's consciousness appeared as a product of changes occurring in separate mental functions. Functional aspects of consciousness were dogmatically placed before consciousness as a system.

To understand how such paradoxical transformation of the initial idea might happen, one must be able to expose the tacit premises of traditional psychology. These premises include (1) the unchangeable character of interfunctional relations; (2) the constancy of the interfunctional component, which, therefore, could be "bracketed" and actually ignored in a study of a concrete mental function; and (3) the idea that the development of consciousness may be viewed as a product of the development of separate functions. The latter functions, although interconnected, develop autonomously because their interrelations are presumed to be constant.

All these premises are essentially incorrect. First of all, the interfunctional relations, far from being unchangeable, undergo a considerable development. Moreover, this development, i.e., *changes in the functional composition of consciousness, are the real subject of mental development.*

What served as a postulate in the old psychology—the interconnectedness of mental functions—must become a problem in the new one. The changing interfunctional relations thus must become a central issue in the study of consciousness. It is this new approach that must be used in tackling the problem of lack of consciousness and deliberate control in schoolchildren. The general law of development says that awareness and deliberate control appear only during a very advanced stage in the development of a mental function, after it has been used and practiced unconsciously and spontaneously. In order to subject a function to intellectual and volitional control, we must first possess it.

The stage of undifferentiated functions in infancy is followed by the differentiation and development of perception in early childhood and the development of memory in the preschooler, to mention only the outstanding aspects of mental development at each age. Attention, which is a correlate of the structuring of what is perceived and remembered, participates in this development. Consequently, the child about to enter school possesses, in a fairly mature form, the functions he must next learn to subject to conscious control. But concepts—or rather preconcepts, as they should be called at that stage—are barely beginning to evolve from complexes at that time, and it would indeed be a miracle if the child were able to become conscious of them and to govern them, during the same period. For this to be possible, consciousness would not merely have to take possession of its single functions, but to create them.

Before continuing, we want to clarify the term *consciousness* as we use it in speaking of nonconscious functions becoming conscious. In the works of Piaget and Claparède, two different meanings of the concept of unconsciousness coexist, causing serious confusion. One of these meanings is borrowed from general psychology, the other from the works of Freud. When Piaget speaks about the unconsciousness of the child's thought, he does not imply that the child is completely unaware of his own thinking. What Piaget means is that the child does not have a complete conscious control over his own reasoning. According to Piaget's developmental model, the child's thought reflects the changing equilibrium between egocentrism, which is connected with a certain deficit of conscious control, and socialization. This model implies that the child's thought is not fully conscious; it contains conscious as well as unconscious elements.

But the unconscious as "the not yet conscious" differs essentially from the Freudian "unconscious" resulting from repression, which is a late development, an effect of a relatively high differentiation of consciousness. That is why the nonconscious is not something partly conscious and partly unconscious; it is not a degree of awareness, but the other direction in the activity of consciousness.

The activity of consciousness can take different directions; it may illuminate only a few aspects of a thought or an act. I have just tied a knot—I have done so consciously, yet I cannot explain how I did it, because my awareness was centered on the knot rather than on my own motions, the *how* of my action. When the latter becomes the object of my awareness, I shall have become fully conscious. We use *consciousness* to denote awareness of the activity of the mind—the consciousness of being conscious. A preschool child who, in response to the question, "Do you know your name?" tells his name, lacks this self-reflective awareness: He knows his name but is not conscious of knowing it.

Piaget's studies showed that introspection begins to develop only during the school years. This process has a good deal in common with the development of external perception and observation in the transition from infancy to early childhood, when the child passes from primitive wordless perception to perception of objects guided by and expressed in words—perception in terms of meaning. Similarly, the schoolchild passes from unformulated to verbalized introspection; he perceives his own psychic processes as meaningful. But perception in terms of meaning always implies a degree of generalization. Consequently, the transition to verbalized self-observation denotes a beginning process of generalization of the inner forms of activity. The shift to a new type of inner perception means also a shift to a higher type of inner activity, since a new way of seeing things opens up new possibilities for handling them. A chessplayer's moves are determined by what he sees on the board; when his perception of the game changes, his strategy will also change. In perceiving some of our acts in a generalizing fashion, we isolate them from our total mental activity and are thus enabled to focus on this process as such and to enter into a new relation to it. In this way, becoming conscious of our operations and viewing each as a process of a certain *kind*—such as remembering or imagining—leads to their mastery.

School instruction induces the generalizing kind of perception and thus plays a decisive role in making the child conscious of his own mental processes. Scientific concepts, with their hierarchical system of interrelation, seem to be the medium within which awareness and mastery first develop, to be transferred later to other concepts and other areas of thought. Reflective consciousness comes to the child through the portals of scientific concepts.

Piaget's characterization of the child's spontaneous concepts as nonconscious and nonsystematic tends to confirm our thesis. The implication that *spontaneous,* when applied to concepts, is a synonym of *nonconscious* is obvious throughout his writings, and the basis for this is easily seen. In operating with spontaneous concepts, the child is not conscious of them because his attention is always centered on the object to which the concept refers, never on the act of thought itself. Piaget's view that spontaneous concepts exist for the child outside any systematic context is equally clear. According to him, if we wish to discover and explore the child's own spontaneous idea hidden behind the nonspontaneous concept he voices, we must begin by freeing it from all ties to a system. This approach resulted in the kind of answers expressing the child's nonmediated attitude toward objects that fill all the books of Piaget.

To us it seems obvious that a concept can become subject to conscious and deliberate control only when it is a part of a system. If consciousness means generalization, generalization, in turn, means the formation of a superordinate concept (*Oberbegriff-übergeordneter Begriff*) that includes the given concept as a particular case. A superordinate concept implies the existence of a series of subordinate concepts, and it also presupposes a hierarchy of concepts of different levels of generality. Thus, the given concept is placed within a system of relations of generality.

It was Piaget himself who showed that the child's thought is unsystematic, that it lacks coherence and deduction, that the child is insensitive to contradictions and juxtaposes statements when one must synthesize them. Later, we shall return to phenomena discovered by Piaget and shall show that they belong exclusively to the sphere of unsystematic reasoning. These phenomena are relevant when the concepts involved lack system.

But at this moment, we are more concerned to show that systematicity and consciousness do not come from outside, displacing the child's spontaneous concepts, but that, on the contrary, they presuppose the existence of rich and relatively mature representations. Without the latter, the child would have nothing to systematize. Systematic reasoning, being initially acquired in the sphere of scientific concepts, later transfers its structural organization into spontaneous concepts, remodeling them "from above." The interdependence between spontaneous and scientific concepts stems from the special relations existing between the scientific concept and the object. In the scientific concepts that the child acquires in school, the relation to an object is mediated from the start by some other concept. Thus, the very notion of scientific concept implies a certain position in relation to other concepts, i.e., a place within a system of concepts. It is our contention that the rudiments of systematization first enter the child's mind by way of his contact with scientific concepts and are then transferred to everyday concepts, changing their psychological structure from the top down.

The specific character of scientific concepts was thoroughly defined by Marx, who wrote that "if the appearance and essence of things were similar, there would be no need to have science." Scientific concepts would be unnecessary if they were reflecting mere appearances of objects, as empirical concepts do. The scientific concept, thus, stands in a different relation to the object, in a relation achievable only in conceptual form, which, in its turn, is possible only through a system of concepts. From this point of view, any real concept must be taken only together with its system of relations that determine its measure of generality. A concept is like a living cell that must be viewed only together with its offshoots penetrating into surrounding tissue. It becomes clear that logically the distinction between spontaneous and nonspontaneous concepts coincides with the distinction between empirical and scientific concepts.

The following example may illustrate the function of varying degrees of generality in the emergence of a system: A child learns the word *flower,* and shortly afterwards the word *rose;* for a long time the concept "flower," though more widely applicable than "rose," cannot be said to be more general for the child. It does not include and subordinate "rose"—the two are interchangeable and juxtaposed. When "flower" becomes generalized, the relation of "flower" and "rose," as well as of "flower" and other subordinate concepts, also changes in the child's mind. A system is taking shape.

Let us now return to the beginning of our discussion, i.e., to Piaget's question: Where does consciousness come from? We have shown that, contrary to Piaget's belief, the deficit of awareness cannot be derived from the child's egocentrism. It is, rather, a product of the unsystematicity of spontaneous concepts. The conscious use of concepts is achievable through their systematization based on the relations of generality between concepts. The conscious use of concepts simultaneously implies that concepts can be controlled voluntarily. Piaget's inability to resolve the problem of consciousness stems from his adherence to spontaneous concepts, viewed by him as the only legitimate products of the child's thought. Rejecting the notion of a conceptual system, Piaget made the resolution of the problem of consciousness impossible.

III

The interrelation of scientific and spontaneous concepts is a special case within a much broader subject: the relation of school instruction to the mental development of the child. Several theories concerning this relation have been advanced in the past, and the question remains one of the major preoccupations of Soviet psychology. We shall review three attempts to answer it, in order to place our own study within the broader context.

The first and still most widely held theory considers instruction and development to be mutually independent. Development is seen as a process of maturation subject to natural laws, and instruction as the utilization of the opportunities created by development. Typical of this school of thought are its attempts to separate with great care the products of development from those of instruction, supposedly to find them in their pure form. No investigator has yet been able to achieve this. The blame is usually laid on inadequate methods, and the failures are compensated for by redoubled speculative analyses. These efforts to divide the child's intellectual equipment into two categories may go hand in hand with the notion that development can run its normal course and reach a high level without any assistance from instruction—that even children who never attend school can develop the highest forms of thinking accessible to human beings. More often, however, this theory is modified to take into account a relation that obviously exists between development and instruction: The former creates the potentialities; the latter realizes them. Education is seen as a kind of superstructure erected over maturation; or, to change the metaphor, education is related to development as consumption to production. A one-sided relation is thus conceded: Learning depends on development, but the course of development is not affected by learning.

This theory rests on the simple observation that any instruction demands a certain degree of maturity of certain functions: One cannot teach a one-year-old to read, or a three-year-old to write. The analysis of learning is thus reduced to determining the developmental level that various functions must reach for instruction to become feasible. When the child's memory has progressed enough to enable him to memorize the alphabet, when his attention can be held by a boring task, when his thinking has matured to the point where he can grasp the connection between sign and sound—then instruction in writing may begin. According to this variant of the first theory, instruction hobbles behind development. Development must complete certain cycles before instruction can begin.

The truth of this last statement is obvious; a necessary minimum level does exist. Nevertheless, this one-sided view results in a series of misconceptions. Suppose the child's memory, attention, and thinking have developed to the point where he can be taught writing and arithmetic; does the study of writing and arithmetic do anything to his memory, attention, and thinking, or does it not? Traditional psychology answers thus: Yes insofar as they exercise these functions; but the process of development as such does not change; nothing new happens in the mental growth of the child; he has learned to write—that is all.

This view, characteristic of old-fashioned educational theory, particularly that of Meumann, also colors the writings of Piaget, who believes that the child's thinking goes through certain phases and stages regardless of any instruction received. Instruction remains an extraneous factor. The gauge of the child's mental development is not what he has learned and understands, but the manner in which he thinks on subjects about which he has no knowledge. Piaget selects questions that in principle cannot be answered with the help of knowledge acquired through instruction. Here, the separation—indeed, the opposition—of instruction and development is carried to its extreme.

The second theory concerning development and instruction identifies the two processes. Originally expounded by James, it bases both processes on association and habit formation, thus rendering instruction synonymous with development. This view enjoys a certain revival at present, with Thorndike as its chief protagonist. Reflexology, which has translated associationism into the language of physiology, sees the intellectual development of the child as a gradual accumulation of conditional reflexes; and learning is viewed in exactly the same way. Since instruction and development are identical, no question of any concrete relation between them can arise.

The third school of thought, represented by Gestalt psychology, tries to reconcile the two foregoing theories while avoiding their pitfalls. Although this eclecticism results in a somewhat inconsistent approach, a certain synthesis of the two opposite views is achieved. Koffka states that all development has two aspects, maturation and learning. Although this means accepting in a less extreme form both of the older points of view, the new theory represents an improvement on the two others, in three ways.

First, Koffka admits some interdependence between the two aspects of development. On the basis of a number of facts, he demonstrates that maturation of an organ is contingent on its functioning, which improves through learning and practice. Maturation, in turn, provides new opportunities for learning. But Koffka merely postulates mutual influence without examining its nature in detail. Second, this theory introduces a new conception of the educational process itself as the formation of new structures and the perfecting of old ones. Instruction is thus accorded a meaningful structural role. A basic characteristic of any structure is its independence from its original substance—it can be transferred to other media. Once a child has formed a certain structure, or learned a certain operation, he will be able to apply it in other areas. We have given him a pennyworth of instruction, and he has gained a small fortune in development. The third point in which this theory compares favorably with the older ones is its view of the temporal relation between instruction and development. Since instruction given in one area can transform and reorganize other areas of the child's thought, it may not only follow maturing or keep in step with it but also precede it and further its progress. The admission that different temporal sequences are equally possible and important is a contribution by the eclectic theory that should not be underestimated.

This theory brings us face to face with an old issue reappearing in a new guise: the almost forgotten theory of formal discipline, usually associated with the name of Johannes Herbart.[4] It maintained that instruction in certain subjects develops the mental faculties in general, besides importing knowledge of the subject and special skills. This genuinely sound idea, however, led to the most reactionary forms of schooling, such as the Russian and German "classical gymnasiums." The curriculum of the gymnasiums stresses Greek and Latin as sources of "formal discipline," while in so-called real schools this role was assigned to mathematics. This system was eventually discarded, partially because the concept of "formal discipline" remained poorly elaborated, but mostly because it did not meet the practical aims of modern Western education.

Within psychology itself, Thorndike, in a series of investigations, did his best to discredit formal discipline and to prove that instruction had no long-term effects on development. His criticism is convincing insofar as it applies to the ridiculous exaggerations of the doctrine of formal discipline, but it does not touch its valuable kernel.

Thorndike approaches the problem of formal discipline from the position of the influence of everything on everything. He asks whether a study of the multiplication table helps to make a judicious choice of spouse. From the correct observation that not all forms of instruction are connected with all forms of development, he incorrectly infers that such an influence does not exist at all.

In his effort to disprove Herbart's conception, Thorndike experimented with the narrowest, most specialized, and most elementary functions. From the point of view of a theory that reduces all learning to the formation of associative bonds, the choice of activity would make little difference. In some experiments he gave his subjects practice in distinguishing between the relative lengths of lines and then tried to establish whether this practice increased their ability to distinguish between sizes of angles. Naturally, he found that it did not. The influence of instruction on development had been postulated by the theory of formal discipline only in relation to such subjects as mathematics and languages, which involve vast complexes of psychic functions. The ability to gauge the lengths of lines may not affect the ability to distinguish between angles, but the study of the native language— with its attendant sharpening of concepts—may still have some bearing on the study of arithmetic. Thorndike's work merely makes it appear likely that there are two kinds of instruction: the narrowly specialized training in some skill, such as typing, involving habit formation and exercise and more often found in trade schools for adults; and the kind of instruction given schoolchildren, which activates large areas of consciousness. The idea of formal discipline may have little to do with the first kind, but may well prove to be valid for the second. It stands to reason that in the higher processes emerging during the cultural development of the child, formal discipline must play a role that it does not play in the more elementary processes: All the higher functions have in common awareness, abstraction, and control. In line with Thorndike's theoretical conceptions, the qualitative differences between the lower and the higher functions are ignored in his studies of the transfer of training.

In formulating our own tentative theory of the relation between instruction and development, we take our departure from four series of investigations.[5] Their common purpose was to uncover these complex interrelations in certain definite areas of school instruction: reading and writing, grammar, arithmetic, natural science, and social science. The specific inquiries concerned such topics as the mastering of the decimal system in relation to the development of the concept of number; the child's awareness of his operations in solving mathematical problems; and the processes of constructing and solving problems by first-graders. Much interesting material came to light on the development of oral language and written language during school age, the consecutive levels of understanding of figurative meaning, the influence of mastering grammatical structures on the course of mental development, and the understanding of relations in the study of social science and natural science. The investigations focused on the level of maturity of psychic functions at the beginning of schooling and the influence of schooling on their development; on the temporal sequence of instruction and development; and on the "formal discipline" function of the various subjects of instruction. We shall discuss these issues in succession.

1. In our first series of studies, we examined the level of development of the psychic functions requisite for learning the basic school subjects—reading and writing, arithmetic, and natural science. We found that at the beginning of instruction, these functions could not be considered mature, even in the children who proved able to master the curriculum very successfully. Written language is a good illustration. Why does writing come so hard to the schoolchild that at certain periods there is a lag of as much as six or eight years between his "linguistic age" in speaking and in writing? This used to be explained by the novelty of writing: As a new function, it must repeat the developmental stages of speech; therefore the writing of an eight-year-old must resemble the speech of a two-year-old. This explanation is patently insufficient. A two-year-old uses few words and a simple syntax because his vocabulary is small and his knowledge of more complex sentence structures nonexistent; but the schoolchild possesses the vocabulary and the grammatical forms for writing, since they are the same as for oral speech. Nor can the difficulties of mastering the mechanics of writing account for the tremendous lag between the schoolchild's oral language and written language.

Our investigation has shown that the development of writing does not repeat the developmental history of speaking. Written speech is a separate linguistic function, differing from oral speech in both structure and mode of functioning. Even its minimal development requires a high level of abstraction. It is speech in thought and image only, lacking the musical, expressive, intonational qualities of oral speech. In learning to write, the child must disengage himself from the sensory aspect of speech and replace words by images of words. Speech that is merely imagined and that requires symbolization of the sound image in written signs (i.e., a second degree of symbolization) naturally must be as much harder than oral speech for the child as algebra is harder than arithmetic. Our studies show that it is the abstract quality of written language that is the main stumbling block, not the underdevelopment of small muscles or any other mechanical obstacles.

Writing is also speech without an interlocutor, addressed to an absent or an imaginary person or to no one in particular—a situation new and strange to the child. Written speech is monologous; it is a conversation with a blank sheet of paper. Thus, writing requires a double abstraction: abstraction from the sound of speech and abstraction from the interlocutor. But just as learning algebraic formulas does not repeat the process of acquiring arithmetic skills, the development of writing does not repeat the development of oral speech.

Our studies show that the child has little motivation to learn writing when we begin to teach it. He feels no need for it and has only a vague idea of its usefulness. In conversation, every sentence is prompted by a motive. Desire or need lead to request, question to answer, bewilderment to explanation. The changing motives of the interlocutors determine at every moment the turn oral speech will take. It does not have to be consciously directed—the dynamic situation takes care of that. The motives for writing are more abstract, more intellectualized, further removed from immediate needs. In written speech, we are obliged to create the situation, to represent it to ourselves. This demands detachment from the actual situation.

Writing also requires deliberate analytical action on the part of the child. In speaking, he is hardly conscious of the sounds he pronounces and quite unconscious of the mental operations he performs. In writing, he must take cognizance of the sound structure of each word, dissect it, and reproduce it in alphabetical symbols, which he must have studied and memorized before. In the same deliberate way, he must put words in a certain sequence to form a sentence. Written language demands conscious work because its relation to inner speech is different from that of oral speech: The latter precedes inner speech in the course of development, while written speech follows inner speech and presupposes its existence (the act of writing implying a translation from inner speech). J. H. Jackson and Henry Head even claimed that written speech is a key to inner speech.[6]

But the grammar of thought is not the same in the two cases. One might even say that the syntax of inner speech is the exact opposite of the syntax of written speech, with oral speech standing in the middle.

Inner speech is condensed, abbreviated speech. Written speech is deployed to its fullest extent, more complete than oral speech. Inner speech is almost entirely predicative because the situation, the subject of thought, is always known to the thinker. Written speech, on the contrary, must explain the situation fully in order to be intelligible. The change from maximally compact inner speech to maximally detailed written speech requires what might be called deliberate semantics—deliberate structuring of the web of meaning.

Written speech is considerably more conscious, and it is produced more deliberately than oral speech. Wundt even assumed that the main difference between the development of oral speech and the development of writing lies in this deliberate and conventional character of written speech. He thought that the cuneiform alphabet, for example, is a consciously elaborated system of conventionally accepted signs, while the corresponding oral speech is a product of unconscious development.

In our study, we found in ontogenetic material the same type of difference that Wundt sought in historical or phylogenetic data. Consciousness and volitional control characterize the child's written speech from the very beginning of its development. Signs of writing and methods of their use are acquired consciously. Writing, in its turn, enhances the intellectuality of the child's actions. It brings awareness to speech. Moreover, the motives of writing are more abstract and more detached from immediate needs.

We may conclude that (a) the essential difference between written and oral speech reflects the difference between two types of activity, one of which is spontaneous, involuntary, and nonconscious, while the other is abstract, voluntary, and conscious; (b) the psychological functions on which written speech is based have not even begun to develop in the proper sense when instruction in writing starts. It must build on barely emerging, immature processes.

Similar results were obtained in the fields of arithmetic, grammar, and natural science. In every case, the requisite functions are immature when instruction begins. We shall briefly discuss the case of grammar, which presents some special features.

Grammar is a subject that seems to be of little practical use. Unlike other school subjects, it does not give the child new skills. He conjugates and declines before he enters school. The opinion has even been voiced that school instruction in grammar could be dispensed with. We can only reply that our analysis clearly showed the study of grammar to be of paramount importance for the mental development of the child.

The child does have a command of the grammar of his native tongue long before he enters school, but it is unconscious, acquired in a purely structural way, like the phonetic composition of words. If you ask a young child to produce a combination of sounds, for example *sk,* you will find that its deliberate articulation is too hard for him; yet within a structure, as in the word *Moscow,* he pronounces the same sounds with ease. The same is true of grammar. The child will use the correct case or tense within a sentence, but cannot decline or conjugate a word on request. He may not acquire new grammatical or syntactic forms in school, but, thanks to instruction in grammar and writing, he does become aware of what he is doing and learns to use his skills consciously. Just as the child realizes for the first time in learning to write that the word *Moscow* consists of the sounds *m-o-s-k-ow* and learns to pronounce each one separately, he also learns to construct sentences, to do consciously what he has been doing unconsciously in speaking. Grammar and writing help the child to rise to a higher level of speech development.

Thus our investigation shows that the development of the psychological foundations of instruction in basic subjects does not precede instruction, but unfolds in a continuous interaction with the contributions of instruction.

2. Our second series of investigations centered on the temporal relation between the processes of instruction and the development of the corresponding psychological functions. We found that instruction usually precedes development. The child acquires certain habits and skills in a given area before he learns to apply them consciously and deliberately. There is never complete parallelism between the course of instruction and the development of the corresponding functions.

Instruction has its own sequences and organization, it follows a curriculum and a timetable, and its rules cannot be expected to coincide with the inner laws of the developmental processes it calls to life. On the basis of our studies, we tried to plot curves of the progress of instruction and of the participating psychological functions; far from coinciding, these curves showed an exceedingly complex relation.

For example, the different steps in learning arithmetic may be of unequal value for mental development. It often happens that three or four steps in instruction add little to the child's understanding of arithmetic, and then, with the fifth step, something clicks; the child has grasped a general principle, and his developmental curve rises markedly. For this particular child, the fifth operation was decisive, but this cannot be a general rule. The turning points at which a general principle becomes clear to the child cannot be set in advance by the curriculum.

Development and instruction have different "rhythms." These two processes are interconnected, but each of them has its own measure. The acquisition of the rules of inflection of nouns cannot simply coincide in time with the conscious mastering of one's speech. The child is not taught at school the decimal system as such; he is taught to write figures, to add and to multiply, to solve problems, and out of all this, at a certain moment, some general concept of the decimal system does emerge.

We are thus coming to the following conclusion: When the child learns some operation of arithmetic or some scientific concept, the development of that operation or concept has only begun; the curve of development does not coincide with the curve of school instruction; by and large, instruction precedes development.

3. Our third series of investigation resembles Thorndike's studies of the transfer of training, except that we experimented with subjects of school instruction and

with the higher rather than the elementary functions, i.e., with subjects and functions that could be expected to be meaningfully related.

We found that intellectual development, far from following Thorndike's atomistic model, is not compartmentalized according to topics of instruction. Its course is much more unitary, and the different school subjects interact in contributing to it. While the processes of instruction follow their own logical order, they awaken and direct a system of processes in the child's mind that is hidden from direct observation and subject to its own developmental laws. To uncover these developmental processes stimulated by instruction is one of the basic tasks of the psychological study of learning.

Specifically, our experiments brought out the following interrelated facts: the psychological prerequisites for instruction in different school subjects are to a large extent the same; instruction in a given subject influences the development of the higher functions far beyond the confines of that particular subject; the main psychic functions involved in studying various subjects are interdependent—their common bases are consciousness and deliberate mastery, the principal contributions of the school years. It follows from these findings that all the basic school subjects act as formal discipline, each facilitating the learning of the others; the psychological functions stimulated by them develop in one complex process.

4. In the fourth series of studies, we attacked a problem that has not received sufficient attention in the past, but that we consider of focal importance for the study of learning and development.

Most of the psychological investigations concerned with school learning measured the level of mental development of the child by making him solve certain standardized problems. The problems he was able to solve by himself were supposed to indicate the level of his mental development at the particular time. But in this way, only the completed part of the child's development can be measured, which is far from the whole story. We tried a different approach. Having found that the mental age of two children was, let us say, eight, we gave each of them harder problems than he could manage on his own and provided some slight assistance: the first step in a solution, a leading question, or some other form of help. We discovered that one child could, in cooperation, solve problems designed for twelve-year-olds, while the other could not go beyond problems intended for nine-year-olds. The discrepancy between a child's actual mental age and the level he reaches in solving problems with assistance indicates the zone of his proximal development; in our example, this zone is four for the first child and one for the second. Can we truly say that their mental development is the same? Experience has shown that the child with the larger zone of proximal development will do much better in school. *This measure gives a more helpful clue than mental age does to the dynamics of intellectual progress.*[7]

Psychologists today cannot share the layman's belief that imitation is a mechanical activity and that anyone can imitate almost anything if shown how. To imitate, it is necessary to possess the means of stepping from something one knows to something new. With assistance, every child can do more than he can by himself—though only within the limits set by the state of his development.

If imitative ability had no limits, any child would be able to solve any problem with an adult's assistance. But this is not the case. The child is most successful in solving problems that are closer to those solved independently; then the difficulties grow until, at a certain level of complexity, the child fails, whatever assistance is provided.

The ease with which he is able to move from independent to assisted problem solving is the best indicator of the dynamic of his development.

Köhler found that a chimpanzee can imitate only those intelligent acts of other apes that it could have performed on its own. Persistent training, it is true, can induce it to perform much more complicated actions, but these are carried out mechanically and have all the earmarks of meaningless habits rather than of insightful solutions. The cleverest animal is incapable of intellectual development through imitation. It can be drilled to perform specific acts, but the new habits do not result in new general abilities.

Comparative psychology has identified a number of symptoms that may help to distinguish intelligent, conscious imitation from automatic copying. In the first case, the solution comes instantly in the form of insight not requiring repetition. Such a solution pertains to all characteristics of intellectual action. It involves understanding the field structure and relations between objects. On the contrary, drill imitation is carried out through repeating trial-and-error series, which show no sign of conscious comprehension and do not include understanding the field structure. In this sense, it can be said that animals are unteachable.

In the child's development, on the contrary, imitation and instruction play a major role. They bring out the specifically human qualities of the mind and lead the child to new developmental levels. In learning to speak, as in learning school subjects, imitation is indispensable. What the child can do in cooperation today he can do alone tomorrow. Therefore the only good kind of instruction is that which marches ahead of development and leads it; it must be aimed not so much at the ripe as at the ripening functions. It remains necessary to determine the lowest threshold at which instruction in, say, arithmetic may begin, since a certain minimal ripeness of functions is required. But we must consider the upper threshold as well; instruction must be oriented toward the future, not the past.

For a time, our schools favored the "complex" system of instruction, which was believed to be adapted to the child's ways of thinking. In offering the child problems he was able to handle without help, this method failed to utilize the zone of proximal development and to lead the child to what he could not yet do. Instruction was oriented to the child's weakness rather than his strength, thus encouraging him to remain at the preschool stage of development.

For each subject of instruction, there is a period when its influence is most fruitful because the child is most receptive to it. It has been called the *sensitive period* by Montessori and other educators. The term is used also in biology, for the periods in ontogenetic development when the organism is particularly responsive to influences of certain kinds. During that period an influence that has little effect earlier or later may radically affect the course of development. But the existence of an optimal time for instruction in a given subject cannot be explained in purely biological terms, at least not for such complex processes as written speech. Our investigation demonstrated the social and cultural nature of the development of the higher functions during these periods, i.e., its dependence on cooperation with adults and on instruction. Montessori's data, however, retain their significance. She found, for instance, that if a child is taught to write early, at four-and-a-half or five years of age, he responds by "explosive writing," an abundant and imaginative use of written speech that is never duplicated by children a few years older. This is a striking example of the strong influence that instruction can have when the corresponding functions have not yet fully matured.

The existence of sensitive periods for all subjects of instruction is fully supported by the data of our studies. The school years as a whole are the optimal period for instruction in operations that require awareness and deliberate control; instruction in these operations maximally furthers the development of the higher psychological functions while they are maturing. This applies also to the development of the scientific concepts to which school instruction introduces the child.

IV

In order to be able to make a comparative analysis of spontaneous and scientific concepts, one must design two structurally identical tasks addressing scientific and spontaneous concepts, respectively. Our experiments that used such tasks [described at the beginning of this chapter] revealed that the developments of these two conceptual systems are by no means identical. Analysis of the data showed that as long as the curriculum supplies the necessary material, the *development of scientific concepts runs ahead of the development of spontaneous concepts* (see the table in section I of this chapter).

How are we to explain the fact that problems involving scientific concepts are solved correctly more often than similar problems involving everyday concepts? We can at once dismiss the notion that the child is helped by factual information acquired at school and lacks experience in everyday matters. Our tests, like Piaget's, dealt entirely with things and relations familiar to the child and often spontaneously mentioned by him in conversation. No one would assume that a child knows less about bicycles, children, or school than about the class struggle, exploitation, or the Paris Commune. The advantage of familiarity is all on the side of the everyday concepts.

The child must find it hard to solve problems involving

life situations because he lacks awareness of his concepts and therefore cannot operate with them at will as the task demands. A child of eight or nine uses *because* correctly in spontaneous conversation; he would never say that a boy fell and broke his leg *because* he was taken to the hospital. Yet that is the sort of thing he comes up with in experiments until the concept "because" becomes fully conscious. On the other hand, he correctly finishes sentences on social science subjects: "Planned economy is possible in the U.S.S.R. because there is no private property—all land, factories, and plants belong to the workers and peasants." Why is he capable of performing the operation in this case? Because the teacher, working with the pupil, has explained, supplied information, questioned, corrected, and made the pupil explain. The child's concepts have been formed in the process of instruction, in collaboration with an adult. In finishing the sentence, he makes use of the fruits of that collaboration, this time independently. The adult's help, invisibly present, enables the child to solve such problems earlier than everyday problems.

At the same age level (second grade), *although* sentences present a different picture: Scientific concepts are not ahead of everyday ones. We know that adversative relations appear later than causal relations in the child's spontaneous thinking. A child of that age can learn to use *because* consciously, since by then he has already mastered its spontaneous use. Not having mastered *although* in the same way, he naturally cannot use it deliberately in his "scientific" thinking; hence, the percentage of successes is equally low in both test series.

Our data show quick progress in the solution of problems involving everyday concepts: In the fourth grade, *because* fragments are completed correctly with equal frequency for everyday and for scientific material. This bears out our assumption that mastering a higher level in the realm of scientific concepts also raises the level of spontaneous concepts. Once the child has achieved consciousness and control in one kind of concepts, all of the previously formed concepts are reconstructed accordingly.

The relation between scientific and spontaneous concepts in the adversative category presents in the fourth grade a picture very similar to that of the causal category in the second grade. The percentage of correct solutions for tasks involving scientific concepts surpasses the percentage for those involving everyday concepts. If the dynamics are the same for both categories, everyday concepts may be expected to rise sharply in the next stage of development and finally to catch up with scientific concepts. Starting two years later, the whole process of the development of "although" would duplicate that of "because."

We believe that our data warrant the assumption that from the very beginning, the child's scientific and his spontaneous concepts—for instance, "exploitation" and "brother"—*develop in reverse directions*: Starting far apart, they move to meet each other. This is the key point of our hypothesis.

The child becomes conscious of his spontaneous concepts relatively late; the ability to define them in words, to operate with them at will, appears long after he has acquired the concepts. He has the concept (i.e., knows the object to which the concept refers), but is not conscious of his own act of thought. The development of a scientific concept, on the other hand, usually *begins* with its verbal definition and its use in nonspontaneous operations—with working on the concept itself. It starts its life in the child's mind at the level that his spontaneous concepts reach only later.

A child's everyday concept, such as "brother," is

saturated with experience. Yet, when he is asked to solve an abstract problem about a brother's brother, as in Piaget's experiments, he becomes confused. On the other hand, though he can correctly answer questions about "slavery," "exploitation," or "civil war," these concepts are schematic and lack the rich content derived from personal experience.

For example, when asked about revolution, a third-grader, who already learned at school about the Russian revolutions of 1905 and 1917, answers, "Revolution is a war of the exploited against the exploiters" or "This is a civil war, citizens of one country fight each other." One finds a sign of the development of consciousness and the class criterion in these answers. But the conscious understanding of subject still differs here essentially, in terms of penetration and comprehension, from the understanding of adults.

Another example. After the student explained that "those peasants who were the property of a landowner we call serfs," he was asked about the life of the gentry in the epoch of serfdom. He answered, "They lived very well. Everything was very rich. Ten-story house, many rooms, and all beautiful. Electric arcs burned." This oversimplified development of the concept of serfdom looks more like an image than a scientific concept. At the same time, when asked to define the concept of "brother," the child turns out to be completely captured by the logic of actual situations, and cannot approach this concept as an abstract one.

One might say that *the development of the child's spontaneous concepts proceeds upward, and the development of his scientific concepts downward,* to a more elementary and concrete level. This is a consequence of the different ways in which the two kinds of concepts emerge. The inception of a spontaneous concept can usually be traced to a face-to-face meeting with a concrete situation, while a scientific concept involves from the first a "mediated" attitude toward its object.

Though scientific and spontaneous concepts develop in reverse directions, the two processes are closely connected. The development of a spontaneous concept must have reached a certain level for the child to be able to absorb a related scientific concept. For example, historical concepts can begin to develop only when the child's everyday concept of the past is sufficiently differentiated—when his own life and the life of those around him can be fitted into the elementary generalization "in the past and now"; his geographic and sociological concepts must grow out of the simple schema "here and elsewhere." In working its slow way upward, an everyday concept clears a path for the scientific concept and its downward development. It creates a series of structures necessary for the evolution of a concept's more primitive, elementary aspects, which give it body and vitality. Scientific concepts, in turn, supply structures for the upward development of the child's spontaneous concepts toward consciousness and deliberate use. Scientific concepts grow downward through spontaneous concepts; spontaneous concepts grow upward through scientific concepts.

The strength of scientific concepts lies in their conscious and deliberate character. Spontaneous concepts, on the contrary, are strong in what concerns the situational, empirical, and practical. These two conceptual systems, developing "from above" and "from below," reveal their real nature in the interrelations between actual development and the zone of proximal development.

Spontaneous concepts that confront a deficit of conscious and volitional control find this control in the zone of proximal development, in the cooperation of the child with adults. That is why it is essential first to bring spontaneous concepts up to a certain level of development that would guarantee that the scientific concepts are actually just above the spontaneous ones.[8]

The influence of scientific concepts on the mental development of the child is analogous to the effect of learning a foreign language, a process that is conscious and deliberate from the start. In one's native language, the primitive aspects of speech are acquired before the more complex ones. The latter presuppose some awareness of phonetic, grammatical, and syntactic forms. With a foreign language, the higher forms develop before spontaneous, fluent speech. The intellectualistic theories of language, such as Stern's, which place a full grasp of the relation between sign and meaning at the very beginning of linguistic development, contain a measure of truth in the case of a foreign language. The child's strong points in a foreign language are his weak points in his native language, and vice versa. In his own language, the child conjugates and declines correctly, but without realizing it. He cannot tell the gender, the case, or the tense of the word he is using. In a foreign language, he distinguishes between masculine and feminine genders and is conscious of grammatical forms from the beginning.

Of phonetics, the same is true. Faultlessly articulating his native speech, the child is unconscious of the sounds he pronounces, and in learning to spell, he has great difficulty in dividing a word into its constituent sounds. In a foreign language, he does this easily, and his writing does not lag behind his speech. It is the pronunciation, the "spontaneous phonetics," that he finds hard to master. Easy, spontaneous speech with a quick and sure command of grammatical structures comes to him only as the crowning achievement of long, arduous study.

Success in learning a foreign language is contingent on a certain degree of maturity in the native language. The child can transfer to the new language the system of meanings he already possesses in his own. The reverse is also true—a foreign language facilitates mastering the higher forms of the native language. The child learns to see his language as one particular system among many, to view its phenomena under more general categories, and this leads to awareness of his linguistic operations.

There are three reasons why we returned to the analogy between the study of a foreign language and the acquisition of scientific concepts. First of all, experimental evidence yielded by our studies disproved the theory of shift, or displacement, which stated that the later stage repeats the course of the earlier one, including the recurrence of difficulties already overcome on the lower plane. All our evidence supports the hypothesis that analogous systems develop in reverse directions at the higher and the lower levels, each system influencing the other and benefiting from the strong points of the other. Thus, the development of analogous systems obeys the law of the zone of proximal development. The fact that there is indeed a similarity between the study of a foreign language and the acquisition of scientific concepts supports this developmental model.

Second, it is of particular importance that the suggested analogy is not a result of formal coincidence, but reflects an essential affinity between both processes. These two processes simply represent two aspects of one and the same process of the development of verbal thought.

However, while in the study of a foreign language attention centers on the exterior, phonetic, and physical aspects of verbal thought, in the development of scientific concepts it centers on semantics. And since physical and semantic aspects of speech develop along their own independent lines, our analogy cannot be a complete one. The two developmental processes follow separate, though similar, paths.

Third, there is the mediative role played by the native language and by spontaneous concepts. A foreign word is not related to its object immediately, but through the meanings already established in the native language; similarly a scientific concept relates to its object only in a mediated way, through previously established concepts. Moreover, the mediative role prompts semantic development of native speech and cognitive development of spontaneous concepts.

But there is also an important difference between these two processes. In the case of language study, the native language serves as an already established system of meanings. In the acquisition of scientific concepts, the *system* must be built simultaneously with their development. The concept of system organization thus becomes a crucial one.

We can now turn to the interrelation of concepts in a system—the focal problem of our analysis.

Concepts do not lie in the child's mind like peas in a bag, without any bonds between them. If that were the case, no intellectual operation requiring coordination of thoughts would be possible, nor would any general conception of the world. Not even separate concepts as such could exist; their very nature presupposes a system.

The study of the child's concepts at each age level shows that the degree of generality (plant, flower, rose) is the basic psychological variable according to which they can be meaningfully ordered. If every concept is a generalization, then the relation between concepts is a *relation of generality*. The logical aspect of that relation has been studied much more fully than its genetic and psychological aspects. Our study attempts to fill this gap.

It is well known that the child does not follow in his development the logical way from the particular to more general. He first learns the idea of a "flower" and only subsequently that of a "rose." We compared the degree of generality achieved by the child in his real-life concepts with the structures of generalization—syncretism, complex, preconcept, and concept proper—revealed in concept-formation experiments. We discovered that *the degree of a concept's generality does not coincide with the stages in the development of the structure of generalization.* First of all, concepts of differing degrees of generality may occur in one and the same generalizational structure. For instance, the ideas "flower" and "rose" may both be present at the stage of complex thinking. Correspondingly, concepts of equal generality may appear within different structures of generalization, e.g., "flower" may apply to any and all flowers at the complex stage as well as in conceptual thinking. We found, however, that in spite of this lack of complete correspondence, each phase, or generalizational structure, has as its counterpart a specific level of generality, a specific relation of superordinate and subordinate concepts, a typical combination of the concrete and the abstract. The term *flower,* it is true, may be equally general at the level of complex and of concept, but only in relation to the objects to which it refers. Equal generality here does not imply identity of all the psychological processes involved in the use of this term. Thus, in complex thinking the relation of "flower" to "rose" is not superordination; the wider and the narrower concepts coexist on the same plane.

In our experiments, a mute child learned without much difficulty the words *table, chair, bureau, couch, shelves,* and so on. The term *furniture,* however, proved too hard to grasp. The same child, having successfully learned *shirt, hat, coat, pants,* etc., could not rise above the level of this series and master *clothes.* We found that at a certain level of development, the child is incapable of moving "vertically" from one word meaning to another, i.e., of understanding their relations of generality. All his concepts are on one level, refer directly to objects, and are delimited from one another in the same way that the objects themselves are delimited: Verbal thought is no more than a dependent component of perceptual, object-determined thought. Hence, this stage must be considered an early, presyncretic stage in the development of word meaning. The appearance of the first generalized concept, such as "furniture" or "clothes," is as significant a symptom of progress as the first meaningful word.

The higher levels in the development of word meanings are governed by the law of equivalence of concepts, according to which *any concept can be formulated in terms of other concepts in a countless number of ways.* We shall illustrate the schema underlying this law by an analogy not ideally accurate, but close enough to serve its purpose.

If we imagine the totality of concepts as distributed over the surface of a globe, the location of every concept may be defined by means of a system of coordinates, corresponding to longitude and latitude in geography. One of these coordinates will indicate the location of a concept between the extremes of maximally generalized abstract conceptualization and the immediate sensory grasp of an object—i.e., its degree of concreteness and abstraction. The second coordinate will represent the objective reference of the concept, the locus within reality to which it applies. Two concepts applying to different areas of reality but comparable in degree of abstractness—e.g., plants and animals—could be conceived of as varying in latitude but having the same longitude.

The "longitude" of concepts will, thus, be the characteristic of thought processes, while the "latitude" will be the characteristic of their objective reference. These two parameters must be sufficient to provide exhaustive information on the nature of a concept. The "coordinates" of the concept determine all relations of the given concept to other, i.e., to its coordinate, superordinate, and subordinate concepts. This position of a concept within the total system of concepts may be called its *measure of generality*.

Of course, the geographic analogy is neither complete nor entirely accurate. For example, a more general concept necessarily applies to a broader area of content, which should be represented by a line, not a point, and which thus requires a number of coordinates for its identification.

The manifold mutual relations of concepts on which the law of equivalence is based are determined by their respective measures of generality. Let us take two extreme examples: the child's early (presyncretic) words, lacking any variation in degree of generality, and the concepts of numbers developed through the study of arithmetic. In the first case, obviously, every concept can be expressed only through itself, never through other concepts. In the second case, any number may be expressed in countless ways, because of the infinity of numbers and because the concept of any number contains also all of its relations to all other numbers. "One," for instance, may be expressed as "1,000 minus 999" or, in general, as the difference between any two consecutive numbers, or as any number divided by itself, and in a myriad of other ways. This is a pure example of equivalence of concepts. *Insofar as equivalence depends on the relations of generality between concepts, and these are specific for every generalizational structure, the latter determines the equivalence of concepts possible within its sphere.*

The measure of generality provides a starting point both in functioning and in experiencing concepts. When some concept, for example, "mammals," is named, we experience the following—our thought is placed at a certain position in the intersection of coordinates that provide an orienting point for further movement. Each separate concept appearing in our consciousness brings with it an entire system of predispositions. Thus, the isolated concept appears as a figure against the background of the corresponding relations of generality. And we choose among all the possible ways existing in this background the one that will become a path for our thought. That is why the measure of generality determines not only the equivalence of concepts but also all of the intellectual operations possible with a given concept. All intellectual operations—comparisons, judgments, conclusions—require some movement within the net of coordinates we have outlined. Developmental changes in the structure of generalization cause changes also in these operations. For example, as higher levels of generality and equivalence of concepts are reached, it becomes easier for a child to remember thoughts independently of words. A young child must reproduce the exact words in which a meaning was conveyed to him. A schoolchild can already render a relatively complex meaning in his own words; thus his intellectual freedom increases. In pathological disturbances of conceptual thinking, the measure of generality of concepts is distorted, the balance between the abstract and the concrete is upset, and the relation to other concepts becomes unstable. The mental act through which both the object and the object's relation to the concept are grasped loses its unity, and thought begins to run along broken, capricious, illogical lines.

One goal of our study of the child's real concepts was to find reliable indices of their structure of generalization. Only with their help could the genetic schema yielded by our experimental studies of artificial concepts be profitably applied to the child's developing real concepts. Such an index was finally discovered in the concept's measure of generality, which varies on the different levels of development, from syncretic formations to concepts proper. Analysis of the child's real concepts also helped us to determine how concepts differ at the various levels in their relation to the object and to word meaning, and in the intellectual operations they make possible.

Furthermore, the investigation of real concepts complemented the experimental study by making it clear that every new stage in the development of generalization is built on generalizations of the preceding level; the products of the intellectual activity of the earlier phases are not lost.[9] The inner bond between the consecutive phases could not be uncovered in our experiments because the subject had to discard, after each wrong solution, the generalizations he had formed and start all over again. Also, the nature of the experimental objects did not permit their conceptualization in hierarchical terms.

The investigation of real concepts filled these gaps. The preschooler's ideas (which have the structure of complexes) were found to result, not from grouping images of individual objects, but from the elaboration of generalizations predominant during an earlier phase. At a higher level, we found an analogous relation between old and new formations in the development of concepts of arithmetic and algebra. The rise from preconcepts (which the schoolchild's concepts of arithmetic usually are) to true concepts, such as the algebraic concepts of adolescents, is achieved by generalizing the generalizations of the earlier level. At the earlier stage certain aspects of objects had been abstracted and generalized into ideas of numbers. Algebraic concepts represent abstractions and generalizations of certain aspects of numbers, not objects, and thus signify a new departure—a new, higher plane of thought.

The new, higher concepts, in turn, transform the meaning of the lower. The adolescent who has mastered algebraic concepts has gained a vantage point from which he sees concepts of arithmetic in a broader perspective. We saw this especially clearly in experimenting with shifts from the decimal to other numerical systems. As long as the child operates with the decimal system without having become conscious of it as such, he has not mastered the system, but is, on the contrary, bound by it. When he becomes able to view it as a particular instance of the wider concept of a scale of notation, he can operate deliberately with this or any other numerical system. The ability to shift at will from one system to another (e.g., to "translate" from the decimal system into one that is based on five) is the criterion of this new level of consciousness, since it indicates the existence of a general concept of a system of numeration.

A study of real-life concepts was able to shed some light on how concepts develop within a given form of generalization. The principle of generalization of generalizations is valid here, but it does not produce drastic changes. The relations of generality do not undergo here such radical transformations as in the case of the transition from one structure of generality to another.

It also became clear that the child advancing toward the higher level of generalization does not restructure all of his earlier concepts separately, which indeed would be a Sisyphean labor. Once a new structure has been incorporated into his thinking—usually through concepts recently acquired in school—it gradually spreads to the older concepts as they are drawn into the intellectual operation of the higher type. The work of the child's thought embodied in earlier generalizations is not wasted; it is superseded, i.e., saved as a necessary premise for the higher intellectual activity.

Our investigation of children's real-life concepts throws a new light on another important issue in the theory of thought. The Würzburg school demonstrated that the course of thought and the connection between concepts are not governed by associations. Karl Bühler showed that retention and reproduction of thoughts fol-

low the connections between meanings, rather than associations. However, specific factors determining the
development of thought remained obscure. Gestalt psychology substituted the principle of structure for that of
association. But this new principle also has it weak points.
First of all, it failed to distinguish thought proper from
perceptual images, memory, and all other functions subject to structural laws. Thus, it failed to explain why it
happens that in thought we see such types of connections
that are absent in perception and memory. Gestalt psychology repeated the pattern of associationism in reducing all functions to one level. In a certain sense, that was a
step backward in comparison with the Würzburg studies
that asserted a special status for cognitive processes.

Second, the reduction of a thought to the structural
laws of perception and memory precludes the very possibility of a correct approach to higher mental functions.
As we have shown, each new stage in the development of
concepts brings with it a new, higher form of generalization. The autonomous speech of children does not reveal
any real relations of generality between concepts. Connections on that level are dominated by the structures of
perception. Later developments, however, lead to real
thinking, i.e., thinking in concepts. Such a transition cannot be satisfactorily explained in the framework of Gestalt psychology.

In order to understand such a transition, one must
turn from a study of concepts as isolated entities to a
study of the "fabric" made of concepts. One will then
discover that the connections between concepts are
neither associative nor structural, but are based on the
principle of the relations of generality. This point can be il-
lustrated by Max Wertheimer's study of productive
thinking.[10] Wertheimer demonstrated that reasoning
associated with formal logical syllogisms does not belong
to a sphere of productive thinking. Really productive

thought is based on "insight," i.e., instant transfiguration of the field of thought. The problem X that is a subject of our thought must be transferred from the structure A within which it was first apprehended to the entirely different context of structure B, in which alone X could be solved. But to transfer an object or thought from structure A to structure B, one must transcend the given structural bonds, and this, as our studies show, requires shifting to a plane of greater generality, to a concept subsuming and governing both A and B. We know that each structure of generalization has a corresponding system of relations of generality. This means that each structure of generalization presupposes its own class of possible logical operations. And this is one of the basic laws of the psychology of concept formation, the law that reaffirms the unity of the structural and functional aspects of thinking.

We can now reaffirm on a sound basis of data that the *absence of a system* is the cardinal psychological difference distinguishing spontaneous from scientific concepts. It could be shown that all the peculiarities of the child's thought described by Piaget (such as syncretism, juxtaposition, and insensitivity to contradiction) stem from the absence of a system in the child's spontaneous concepts—a consequence of undeveloped relations of generality. For example, to be disturbed by a contradiction, the child would have to view the contradictory statements in the light of some general principle, i.e., within a system. But when a child in Piaget's experiments says of one object that it dissolved in water because it was small, and of another that it dissolved because it was big, he merely makes empirical statements of facts that follow the logic of perceptions. No generalization of the kind "Smallness leads to dissolution" is present in his mind, and hence the two statements are not felt to be contradictory. It is this lack of distance from the immediate experience—and not syncretism viewed as a compromise between the logic of dreams and reality—that accounts for the peculiarities of the child's thought. Therefore, these peculiarities do not appear in the child's scientific concepts, which from their very inception carry within them relations of generality, i.e., some rudiments of a system. The formal discipline of scientific concepts gradually transforms the structure of the child's spontaneous concepts and helps organize them into a system: this furthers the child's ascent to higher developmental levels.[11]

Our disagreement with Piaget centers on one point only, but an important point. He assumes that development and instruction are entirely separate, incommensurate processes, that the function of instruction is merely to introduce adult ways of thinking, which conflict with the child's own and eventually supplant them. Such a position stems from the old psychological tradition of separating the structural from the functional aspects of development. In the beginning, to study intelligence meant studying the content of thought. The difference between highly developed intelligence and elementary intelligence was sought in the relative number of mental representations and their connections serving these two forms of intellectual activity. Mental operations themselves were considered to be uniform and universal. Edward Thorndike's work on the measurement of intelligence remains a grandiose attempt to prove that mental development is a continuous process of quantitative growth. He saw such a development as a ladder of improvement that directly connects the "mentality" of a worm with that of a college student (Thorndike, 1901).

Reacting to this position, its critics rushed to the opposite extreme. They paid no attention at all to mental representations and focused their studies on mental acts and operations. The Würzburg school went so far as to deny the role of images and objects of reasoning altogether.

Intelligence appeared in the works of the Würzburg psychologists as a purely spiritual power enabling the individual to comprehend abstract relations. It is true that the Würzburg studies enriched our knowledge of the variety of intellectual operations. But at the same time, the problem of reflection and conceptualization of reality in thinking was practically abandoned.

Now we are faced with the necessity of returning to that problem. It became clear that the functioning of intelligence depends on the structure of thought. Piaget's works are but the most explicit expression of the concern with the structural aspect of thought. But even Piaget was unable to fill the gap between the structural and functional approaches. And because of that, development is presented in his theory apart from instruction. But if one takes—as we attempted to do in our work—both aspects, i.e., structure *and* function, and if one works with the assumption that "what" functions determines to a certain extent "how" it functions, then one would be able to see that the problem of development and instruction does have a solution. When word meaning is considered as belonging to a certain structural type, then a corresponding group of operations could be recognized as feasible in the framework of this structure, while another group of operations will be feasible only within another structure.

Studying child thought apart from the influence of instruction, as Piaget did, excludes a very important source of change and bars the researcher from posing the question of the interaction of development and instruction peculiar to each age level. Our own approach focuses on this interaction. Having found many complex inner ties between spontaneous and scientific concepts, we hope that future comparative investigations will further clarify their interdependence, and we anticipate an extension of the study of development and instruction to lower age levels. Instruction, after all, does not begin in school. A future investigator may well find that the child's spontaneous concepts are a product of preschool instruction, just as scientific concepts are a product of school instruction.

V

Apart from theoretical conclusions, our comparative study of scientific and everyday concepts yielded some important methodological results. The methods we worked out for use in this study permit us to bridge the gap between the investigations of experimental concepts and real concepts. The information gathered on the mental processes of the schoolchild studying social science, schematic and rudimentary as it is, has suggested some possible improvements in the teaching of that subject.

In retrospect, we are aware of some omissions and of some methodological defects, perhaps inevitable in a first approach to a new field. We did not study experimentally and in detail the nature of the schoolchild's everyday concepts. This leaves us without the data needed to describe the total course of psychological development during school age; hence, our criticism of Piaget's basic theses is insufficiently buttressed by reliable, systematically obtained facts.

The study of scientific concepts was conducted in one category only—social science concepts—and the particular concepts selected for study do not form or suggest a system inherent in the logic of the subject. While we learned a good deal about the development of scientific concepts compared with spontaneous concepts, we learned little about the regularities specific to the development of sociological concepts as such. Future studies should include concepts from various fields of school instruction, each set matched against a set of everyday concepts drawn from a similar area of experience.

Last but not least, the conceptual structures that we studied were not sufficiently differentiated. For example, in using sentence fragments ending in *because,* we did not separate the various types of causal relations (empirical, psychological, logical) as Piaget did in his studies. Had we done that, we might have been able to make a finer distinction among the test performances of schoolchildren of different ages.

These very flaws, however, help in mapping the course of future investigations. The present study is merely a first, very modest step in exploring a new and highly promising area in the psychology of the child's thought.

It remains to be said that the actual development of our working hypothesis and our experimental studies differs from their presentation in this chapter. The course of actual investigation never coincides with its final published record. For example, our working hypothesis was not complete at the moment when we started our experiments. Hypothesis and experiment—these two poles of one dynamic whole, as Kurt Lewin called them—developed and grew side by side, promoting each other. The fact that theoretical hypothesis and experimental data following their own paths have led to one and the same conclusion seem to be the best proof of the feasibility and fruitfulness of our approach.

7

Thought and Word

The word I forgot
Which once I wished to say
And voiceless thought
Returns to shadows' chamber.

Osip Mandelstam[1]

I

We began our study with an attempt to discover the relation between thought and speech at the earliest stages of phylogenetic and ontogenetic development. We found no specific interdependence between the genetic roots of thought and word. It became plain that the inner relations we were looking for were not a prerequisite for, but rather a product of, the historical development of human consciousness.

In animals, even in anthropoids whose speech is phonetically like human speech and whose intellect is akin to man's, speech and thinking are not interrelated. A prelinguistic period in thought and a preintellectual period in speech undoubtedly exist also in the development of the child. Thought and word are not connected by a primary bond. A connection originates, changes, and grows in the course of the evolution of thinking and speech.

It would be wrong, however, to regard thought and speech as two unrelated processes, either parallel or crossing at certain points and mechanically influencing each other. The absence of a primary bond does not mean that a connection between them can be formed only in a mechanical way. The futility of most of the earlier investigations was largely due to the assumption that thought and word were isolated, independent elements, and verbal thought the fruit of their external union.

The method of analysis based on this conception was bound to fail. It sought to explain the properties of verbal thought by breaking it up into its component elements, thought and word, neither of which, taken separately, possesses the properties of the whole. This method is not true analysis, helpful in solving concrete problems. It leads, rather, to generalization. We compared it to the analysis of water into hydrogen and oxygen—which can result only in findings applicable to all water existing in nature, from the Pacific Ocean to a raindrop. Similarly, the statement that verbal thought is composed of intellectual processes and speech functions proper applies to all verbal thought and all its manifestations and explains none of the specific problems facing the student of verbal thought.

We tried a new approach and replaced analysis into elements [*elementy*] by analysis into units [*edinitsy*]. Units are products of analysis that correspond to specific aspects of the phenomena under investigation. At the same time, unlike elements, units are capable of retaining and expressing the essence of that whole being analyzed. The unit of our analysis will thus contain in the most fundamental and elementary form those properties that belong to verbal thinking as a whole.[2]

We found this unit of verbal thought in word meaning. Word meaning is an elementary "cell" that cannot be further analyzed and that represents the most elementary form of the unity between thought and word.

The meaning of a word represents such a close amalgam of thought and language that it is hard to tell whether it is a phenomenon of speech or a phenomenon of thought. A word without meaning is an empty sound; meaning, therefore, is a criterion of "word," its indispensable component. It would seem, then, that it may be regarded as a phenomenon of speech. But from the point of view of psychology, the meaning of every word is a generalization or a concept. And since generalizations and concepts are undeniably acts of thought, we may regard meaning as a phenomenon of thinking. It does not follow, however, that meaning formally belongs in two different spheres of psychic life. Word meaning is a phenomenon of thought only insofar as thought is embodied in speech, and of speech only insofar as speech is connected with thought and illuminated by it. It is a phenomenon of verbal thought, or meaningful speech—a union of word and thought.

Our experimental investigations fully confirm this basic thesis. They not only proved that the concrete study of the development of verbal thought is made possible by the use of word meaning as the analytical unit, but they also led to a further thesis, which we consider the major result of our study and which issues directly from the first: the thesis that word meanings develop. This insight must replace the postulate of the immutability of word meanings.

From the point of view of the old schools of psychology, the bond between word and meaning is an associative bond, established through the repeated simultaneous perception of a certain sound and a certain object. A word calls to mind its content as the overcoat of a friend reminds us of that friend, or a house of its inhabitants. The association between word and meaning may grow stronger or weaker, be enriched by linkage with other objects of a similar kind, spread over a wider field, or become more limited (i.e., it may undergo quantitative and external changes), but it cannot change its psychological nature. To do that, it would have to cease being an association. From that point of view, any development in word meanings is inexplicable and impossible—an implication that handicapped linguistics as well as psychology. Once having committed itself to the association theory, semantics persisted in treating word meaning as an association between a word's sound and its content. All words, from the most concrete to the most abstract, appeared to be formed in the same manner in regard to meaning, and to contain nothing peculiar to speech as such; a word made us think of its meaning just as any object might remind us of another. It is hardly surprising that semantics did not even pose the larger question of the development of word meanings. Development was reduced to changes in the associative connections between single words and single objects: A word might denote at first one object and then become associated with another, just as an overcoat, having changed owners, might remind us first of one person and later of another. Linguistics did not realize that in the historical evolution of language the very structure of meaning and its psychological nature also change. From primitive generalizations, verbal thought rises to the most abstract concepts. It is not merely the content of a word that changes, but the way in which reality is generalized and reflected in a word.

Association theory is equally inadequate in explaining the development of word meanings in childhood. Here, too, it can account only for the purely external, quantitative changes in the bonds uniting word and meaning, for their enrichment and strengthening, but not for the fundamental structural and psychological changes that can and do occur in the development of language in children.

Oddly enough, the fact that associationism in general had been abandoned for some time did not seem to affect the interpretation of word and meaning. The Würzburg school, whose main object was to prove the impossibility of reducing thinking to a mere play of associations and to demonstrate the existence of specific laws governing the flow of thought, did not revise the association theory of word and meaning, or even recognize the need for such a revision. It freed thought from the fetters of sensation and imagery and from the laws of association, and turned it into a purely spiritual act. By so doing, it went back to the prescientific concepts of St. Augustine and Descartes and finally reached extreme subjective idealism.

Oswald Kulpe not only subscribed to Descartes's "cogito ergo sum," but also claimed that "the world exists in forms that we establish and define" (Kulpe, 1914, p. 81). The psychology of thought was moving toward the ideas of Plato, as was admitted by Kulpe himself. Speech, at the same time, was left at the mercy of association. Even after the work of the Würzburg school, the connection between a word and its meaning was still considered a simple associative bond. The word was seen as the external concomitant of thought, its attire only, having no influence on its inner life. Thought and speech had never been as widely separated as during the Würzburg period. The overthrow of the association theory in the field of thought actually increased its sway in the field of speech.

The work of other psychologists further reinforced this trend. Otto Selz continued to investigate thought without considering its relation to speech and came to the conclusion that man's productive thinking and the mental operations of chimpanzees were identical in nature—

so completely did he ignore the influence of words on thought.[3]

Even Ach, who made a special study of word meaning and who tried to overcome associationism in his theory of concepts, did not go beyond assuming the presence of "determining tendencies" operative, along with associations, in the process of concept formation. Hence, the conclusions he reached did not change the old understanding of word meaning. By identifying concept with meaning, he did not allow for development and changes in concepts. Once established, the meaning of a word was set forever; its development was completed. The same principles were taught by the very psychologists whom Ach attacked. To both sides, the starting point was also the end of the development of a concept; the disagreement concerned only the way in which the formation of word meanings began.

In Gestalt psychology, the situation was not very different. This school was more consistent than others in trying to surmount the general principle of associationism. Not satisfied with a partial solution of the problem, it tried to liberate thinking *and* speech from the rule of association and to put both under the laws of structure formation. Surprisingly, even this most progressive of modern psychological schools made no progress in the theory of thought and speech.

For one thing, it retained the complete separation of these two functions. In the light of Gestalt psychology, the relation between thought and word appears as a simple analogy, a reduction of both to a common structural denominator. The formation of the first meaningful words of a child is seen as similar to the intellectual operations of chimpanzees in Köhler's experiments. Words enter into the structure of things and acquire a certain functional meaning, in much the same way as the stick, to the chimpanzee, becomes part of the structure of obtaining the fruit and acquires the functional meaning of tool. The connection between word and meaning is no longer regarded as a matter of simple association, but as a matter of structure. That seems like a step forward. But if we look more closely at the new approach, it is easy to see that the step forward is an illusion and that we are still standing in the same place. The principle of structure is applied to all relations between things in the same sweeping, undifferentiated way as the principle of association was before it. It remains impossible to deal with the specific relations between word and meaning. They are from the outset accepted as identical in principle with any and all other relations between things. All cats are as gray in the dusk of Gestalt psychology, as in the earlier fogs of universal associationism.

While Ach sought to overcome associationism with the "determining tendency," Gestalt psychology combated it with the principle of structure—retaining, however, the two fundamental errors of the older theory: the assumption of the identical nature of all connections and the assumption that word meanings do not change. The old and the new psychologies both assume that the development of a word's meaning is finished as soon as it emerges. The new trends in psychology brought progress in all branches except in the study of thought and speech. Here the new principles resemble the old ones like twins.

If Gestalt psychology is at a standstill in the field of speech, it has made a big step backward in the field of thought. The Würzburg school at least recognized that thought had laws of its own. Gestalt psychology denies their existence. By reducing to a common structural denominator the perceptions of domestic fowl, the mental operations of chimpanzees, the first meaningful words of the child, and the conceptual thinking of the adult, it obliterates every distinction between the most elementary perception and the highest forms of thought.

This critical survey may be summed up as follows: All the psychological schools and trends overlook the cardinal point that every thought is a generalization; and they all study word and meaning without any reference to development. As long as these two conditions persist in the successive trends, there cannot be much difference in the treatment of the problem.

II

The discovery that word meanings evolve leads the study of thought and speech out of a blind alley. Word meanings are dynamic rather than static formations. They change as the child develops; they change also with the various ways in which thought functions.

If word meanings change in their inner nature, then the relation of thought to word also changes. To understand the dynamics of that relation, we must supplement the genetic approach of our main study by functional analysis and examine the role of word meaning in the process of thought.

Let us consider the process of verbal thinking from the first dim stirring of a thought to its formulation. What we want to show now is not how meanings develop over long periods of time, but the way they function in the live process of verbal thought. On the basis of such a functional analysis, we shall be able to show also that each stage in the development of word meaning has its own particular relation between thought and speech. Since functional problems are most readily solved by examining the highest form of a given activity, we shall, for a while, put aside the problem of development and consider the relations between thought and word in the mature mind.

As soon as we start approaching these relations, the most complex and grand panorama opens before our eyes. Its intricate architectonics surpasses the richest imagination of research schemas. The words of Lev Tolstoy proved to be correct: "The relation of word to thought, and the creation of new concepts is a complex, delicate, and enigmatic process unfolding in our soul" (Tolstoy, 1903, p. 143).

The leading idea in the following discussion can be reduced to this formula: The relation of thought to word is not a thing but a process, a continual movement back and forth from thought to word and from word to thought. In that process, the relation of thought to word undergoes changes that themselves may be regarded as development in the functional sense. Thought is not merely expressed in words; it comes into existence through them. Every thought tends to connect something with something else, to establish a relation between things. Every thought moves, grows and develops, fulfills a function, solves a problem. This flow of thought occurs as an inner movement through a series of planes. An analysis of the interaction of thought and word must begin with an investigation of the different phases and planes a thought traverses before it is embodied in words.

The first thing such a study reveals is the need to distinguish between two planes of speech. Both the inner, meaningful, semantic aspect of speech and the external, phonetic aspect, though forming a true unity, have their own laws of movement. The unity of speech is a complex, not a homogeneous, unity. A number of facts in the linguistic development of the child indicate independent movement in the phonetic and the semantic spheres. We shall point out two of the most important of these facts.

In mastering external speech, the child starts from one word, then connects two or three words; a little later, he advances from simple sentences to more complicated ones, and finally to coherent speech made up of series of such sentences; in other words, he proceeds from a part to the whole. In regard to meaning, on the other hand, the first word of the child is a whole sentence. Semantically, the child starts from the whole, from a meaningful complex, and only later begins to master the separate semantic units, the meanings of words, and to divide his formerly undifferentiated thought into those units. The external and the semantic aspects of speech develop in opposite directions—one from the particular to the whole, from word to sentence, and the other from the whole to the particular, from sentence to word.

This in itself suffices to show how important it is to distinguish between the vocal and the semantic aspects of speech. Since they move in opposite directions, their development does not coincide; but that does not mean that they are independent of each other. On the contrary, their difference is the first stage of a close union. In fact, our example reveals their inner relatedness as clearly as it does their distinction. A child's thought, precisely because it is born as a dim, amorphous whole, must find expression in a single word. As his thought becomes more differentiated, the child is less apt to express it in single words, but constructs a composite whole. Conversely, progress in speech to the differentiated whole of a sentence helps the child's thoughts to progress from a homogeneous whole to well-defined parts. Thought and word are not cut from one pattern. In a sense, there are more differences than likenesses between them. The structure of speech does not simply mirror the structure of thought; that is why words cannot be put on by thought like a ready-made garment. Thought undergoes many changes as it turns into speech. It does not merely find expression in speech; it finds its reality and form.

The semantic and the phonetic developmental processes are essentially one, precisely because of their opposite directions.

The second, equally important, fact emerges at a later period of development. Piaget demonstrated that the child uses subordinate clauses with *because, although,* etc., long before he grasps the structures of meaning corresponding to these syntactic forms. Grammar precedes logic. Here, too, as in our previous example, the discrepancy does not exclude union, but is, in fact, necessary for union.

In adults, the divergence between the semantic and the phonetic aspects of speech is even more striking. Modern, psychologically oriented linguistics is familiar with this phenomenon, especially in regard to grammatical and psychological subject and predicate. For example, in the sentence "The clock fell," emphasis and meaning may change in different situations. Suppose I notice that the clock has stopped and ask how this happened. The answer is, "The clock fell." Grammatical and psychological subject coincide: "The clock" is the first idea in my consciousness; "fell" is what is said about the clock. But if I hear a crash in the next room and inquire what happened, and get the same answer, subject and predicate are psychologically reversed. I knew something had fallen—that is what we are talking about. "The clock" completes the idea. The sentence could be changed to "What has fallen is the clock"; then the grammatical and the psychological subjects would coincide. In the prologue to his play *Duke Ernst von Schwaben,* Uhland says, "Grim scenes will pass before you." Psychologically, "will pass" is the subject. The spectator knows he will see events unfold; the additional idea, the predicate, is "grim scenes." Uhland meant, "What will pass before your eyes is a tragedy."

Anaysis shows that any part of a sentence may become

a psychological predicate, the carrier of topical emphasis. The grammatical category, according to Hermann Paul, is a petrified form of the psychological one.[4] To revive it, one makes a logical emphasis that reveals its semantic meaning. Paul shows that entirely different meanings may lie hidden behind one and the same grammatical structure. Accord between syntactical organization and psychological organization is not as prevalent as we tend to assume—rather, it is a requirement that is seldom met. Not only the subject and predicate, but grammatical gender, number, case, tense, degree, etc., have their psychological doubles. A spontaneous utterance, wrong from the point of view of grammar, may have charm and esthetic value. Alexander Pushkin's lines

As rose lips without a smile,
Without error in the grammar
I Russian language will despise. . . .

bear a more serious message than is usually assumed. Absolute correctness is achieved only in mathematics. It seems that Descartes was the first who recognized in mathematics a form of thought that, although originating in language, goes beyond it. Our daily speech constantly fluctuates between the ideals of mathematical harmony and imaginative harmony.

We shall illustrate the interdependence of the semantic and the grammatical aspects of language by citing two examples that show that changes in formal structure can entail far-reaching changes in meaning.

In translating the fable "The Grasshopper and the Ant," Krylov substituted a dragonfly for La Fontaine's grasshopper. In French, *grasshopper* is feminine and therefore well suited to symbolize a lighthearted, carefree attitude. The nuance would be lost in a literal translation, since in Russian *grasshopper* is masculine. When he settled for *dragonfly,* which is feminine in Russian, Krylov disregarded the literal meaning in favor of the grammatical form required to render La Fontaine's thought.

Tiutchev did the same in his translation of Heine's poem about a fir and a palm. In German *fir* is masculine and *palm* feminine, and the poem suggests the love of a man for a woman. In Russian, both trees are feminine. To retain the implication, Tiutchev replaced the fir by a masculine cedar. Lermontov, in his more literal translation of the same poem, deprived it of these poetic overtones and gave it an essentially different meaning, more abstract and generalized. One grammatical detail may, on occasion, change the whole purport of what is said.

Behind words, there is the independent grammar of thought, the syntax of word meanings. The simplest utterance, far from reflecting a constant, rigid correspondence between sound and meaning, is really a process. Verbal expressions cannot emerge fully formed, but must develop gradually. This complex process of transition from meaning to sound must itself be developed and perfected. The child must learn to distinguish between semantics and phonetics and understand the nature of the difference. At first, he uses verbal forms and meanings without being conscious of them as separate. The word, to the child, is an integral part of the object it denotes. Such a conception seems to be characteristic of primitive linguistic consciousness. Wilhelm von Humboldt retells the anecdotal story about the rustic who said he wasn't surprised that savants with all their instruments could figure out the size of stars and their course—what baffled him was how they found out their names. Simple experiments show that preschool children "explain" the names of objects by their attributes. According to them, an animal is called "cow" because it has horns, "calf" because its horns are still small, "dog" because it is small and has no horns; an object is called "car" because it is not an animal. When asked whether one could interchange the names of objects, for instance, call a cow "ink," and ink "cow," children will answer no, "because ink is used for writing, and the cow gives milk." An exchange of names would mean an exchange of characteristic features, so inseparable is the connection between them in the child's mind. In one experiment, the children were told that in a game a dog would be called "cow." Here is a typical sample of questions and answers:

"Does a cow have horns?"
"Yes."
"But don't you remember that the cow is really a dog? Come now, does a dog have horns?"
"Sure, if it is a cow, if it's called cow, it has horns. That kind of dog has got to have little horns."

We can see how difficult it is for children to separate the name of an object from its attributes, which cling to the name when it is transferred like possessions following their owner.

The fusion of the two planes of speech, semantic and vocal, begins to break down as the child grows older, and the distance between them gradually increases. Each stage in the development of word meanings has its own specific interrelation of the two planes. A child's ability to communicate through language is directly related to the differentiation of word meanings in his speech and consciousness.

To understand this, we must remember a basic characteristic of the structure of word meanings. In the semantic structure of a word, we distinguish between referent and meaning; correspondingly, we distinguish a word's nominative function from its significative function. When we compare these structural and functional relations at the earliest, middle, and advanced stages of development, we find the following genetic regularity: In the beginning, only the nominative function exists; and semantically, only the objective reference; signification independent of naming, and meaning independent of reference, appear later and develop along the paths we have attempted to trace and describe.

Only when this development is completed does the child become fully able to formulate his own thought and to understand the speech of others. Until then, his usuage of words coincides with that of adults in its objective reference, but not in its meaning.

III

We must probe still deeper and explore the plane of inner speech lying beyond the semantic plane. We shall discuss here some of the data of the special investigation we have made of it. The relation of thought and word cannot be understood in all its complexity without a clear understanding of the psychological nature of inner speech. Yet, of all the problems connected with thought and language, this is perhaps the most complicated, beset as it is with terminology and other misunderstandings.

The term *inner speech,* or *endophasy,* has been applied to various phenomena, and authors argue about different things that they call by the same name. Originally, inner speech seems to have been understood as verbal memory. An example would be the silent recital of a poem known by heart. In that case, inner speech differs from vocal speech only as the idea or image of an object differs from the real object. It was in this sense that inner speech was understood by the French authors who tried to find out how words were reproduced in memory—whether as auditory, visual, motor, or synthetic images. We shall see that word memory is indeed one of the constituent elements of inner speech, but not all of it.

In a second interpretation, inner speech is seen as truncated external speech—as "speech minus sound" (Müller) or "subvocal speech" (Watson). Ivan Sechenov called it a reflex arrested after it traveled two-thirds of its way. Vladimir Bekhterev defined it as a speech reflex inhibited in its motor part.[5] All these definitions may serve as subordinate moments in the scientific interpretation of inner speech, but taken in themselves they are grossly inadequate.

The third definition is, on the contrary, too broad. To Kurt Goldstein, the term covers everything that precedes the motor act of speaking, including Wundt's "motives of speech" and the indefinable, nonsensory and nonmotor specific speech experience—i.e., the whole interior aspect of any speech activity.[6] It is hard to accept the equation of inner speech with an inarticulate inner experience in which the separate identifiable structural planes are dissolved without trace. This central experience is common to all linguistic activity, and for this reason alone Goldstein's interpretation does not fit that specific, unique function that alone deserves the name of inner speech. Logically developed, Goldstein's view must lead to the thesis that inner speech is not speech at all, but rather an intellectual and affective-volitional activity, since it includes the motives of speech and the thought that is expressed in words.

To get a true picture of inner speech, one must start from the assumption that it is a specific formation, with its own laws and complex relations to the other forms of speech activity. Before we can study its relation to thought, on the one hand, and to speech, on the other hand, we must determine its special characteristics and function.

Inner speech is speech for oneself; external speech is for others. It would be surprising indeed if such a basic difference in function did not affect the structure of the two kinds of speech. That is why Jackson and Head were most probably wrong when they claimed that the difference between these two kinds of speech is just in degree but not in nature. Absence of vocalization per se is only a consequence of the specific character of inner speech, which is neither an antecedent of external speech nor its reproduction in memory, but is, in a sense, the opposite of external speech. The latter is the turning of thoughts into words, their materialization and objectification. With inner speech, the process is reversed, going from outside to inside. Overt speech sublimates into thoughts. Consequently, the structures of these two kinds of speech must differ.

The area of inner speech is one of the most difficult to investigate. It remained almost inaccessible to experiments until ways were found to apply the genetic method of experimentation. Piaget was the first to pay attention to the child's egocentric speech and to see its theoretical significance, but he remained blind to the most important trait of egocentric speech—its genetic connection with inner speech—and this warped his interpretation of its function and structure. We made that relation the central problem of our study, and thus were able to investigate the nature of inner speech with unusual completeness. A number of considerations and observations led us to conclude that egocentric speech is a stage of development preceding inner speech: Both fulfill intellectual functions; their structures are similar; egocentric speech disappears at school age, when inner speech begins to develop. From all this we infer that one changes into the other.

If this transformation does take place, then egocentric speech provides the key to the study of inner speech. One advantage of approaching inner speech through egocentric speech is its accessibility to experimentation and observation. It is still vocalized, audible speech, i.e., external in its mode of expression, but at the same time it is inner speech in function and structure. To study an internal process, it is necessary to externalize it experimentally, by connecting it with some outer activity; only then is objective functional analysis possible. Egocentric speech is, in fact, a natural experiment of this type.

This method has another great advantage: Since egocentric speech can be studied at the time when some of its characteristics are waning and new ones forming, we are able to judge which traits are essential to inner speech and which are only temporary, and thus to determine the goal of this movement from egocentric speech to inner speech—i.e., the nature of inner speech.

Before we go on to the results obtained by this method, we shall briefly discuss the nature of egocentric speech, stressing the differences between our theory and Piaget's. Piaget contends that the child's egocentric speech is a direct expression of the egocentrism of his thought, which in turn is a compromise between the primary autism of his thinking and its gradual socialization. As the child grows older, autism recedes and socialization progresses, leading to the waning of egocentrism in his thinking and speech.

In Piaget's conception, the child in his egocentric speech does not adapt himself to the thinking of adults. His thought remains entirely egocentric; this makes his talk incomprehensible to others. Egocentric speech has no function in the child's realistic thinking or activity—it merely accompanies them. And since it is an expression of egocentric thought, it disappears together with the child's egocentrism. From its climax at the beginning of the child's development, egocentric speech drops to zero on the threshold of school age. Its history is one of involution rather than evolution. One may say about egocentric speech what Ferenz List said about the infant prodigy, that his entire future lies in the past.

In our conception, egocentric speech is a phenomenon of the transition from interpsychic to intrapsychic functioning, i.e., from the social, collective activity of the child to his more individualized activity—a pattern of development common to all the higher psychological functions. Speech for oneself originates through differentiation from speech for others. Since the main course of the child's development is one of gradual individualization, this tendency is reflected in the function and structure of his speech.

Our experimental results indicate that the function of egocentric speech is similar to that of inner speech: It does not merely accompany the child's activity; it serves mental orientation, conscious understanding; it helps in overcoming difficulties; it is speech for oneself, intimately and usefully connected with the child's thinking. Its fate is very different from that described by Piaget. Egocentric speech develops along a rising, not a declining, curve; it goes through an evolution, not an involution. In the end, it becomes inner speech.

Our hypothesis has several advantages over Piaget's: It explains the function and development of egocentric speech and, in particular, its sudden increase when the child faces difficulties that demand consciousness and reflection—a fact uncovered by our experiments and that Piaget's theory cannot explain. But the greatest advantage of our theory is that it supplies a satisfying answer to a paradoxical situation described by Piaget himself. To Piaget, the quantitative drop in egocentric speech as the child grows older means the withering of that form of speech. If that were so, its structural peculiarities might also be expected to decline; it is hard to believe that the process would affect only its quantity, and not its inner structure. The child's thought becomes infinitely less egocentric between the ages of three and seven. If the characteristics of egocentric speech that make it incomprehensible to others are indeed rooted in egocentrism, they should become less apparent as that form of speech becomes less frequent; egocentric speech should approach social speech and become more and more intelligible. Yet what are the facts? Is the talk of a three-year-old harder to follow than that of a seven-year-old? Our investigation established that the traits of egocentric speech that make for inscrutability are at their lowest point at three and at their peak at seven. They develop in a direction opposite to the frequency of egocentric speech. While the latter keeps falling and reaches zero at school age, the structural characteristics become more and more pronounced.

This throws a new light on the quantitative decrease in egocentric speech, which is the cornerstone of Piaget's thesis.

What does this decrease mean? The structural peculiarities of speech for oneself and its differentiation from external speech increase with age. What is it, then, that diminishes? Only one of its aspects: vocalization. Does this mean that egocentric speech as a whole is dying out? We believe that it does not, for how then could we explain the growth of the functional and structural traits of egocentric speech? On the other hand, their growth is perfectly compatible with the decrease of vocalization—indeed, clarifies its meaning. Its rapid dwindling and the equally rapid growth of the other characteristics are contradictory in appearance only.

To explain this, let us start from an undeniable, experimentally established fact. The structural and functional qualities of egocentric speech become more marked as the child develops. At three, the difference between egocentric speech and social speech equals zero; at seven, we have speech that in structure and function is totally unlike social speech. A differentiation of the two speech functions has taken place. This is a fact—and facts are notoriously hard to refute.

Once we accept this, everything else falls into place. If the developing structural and functional peculiarities of egocentric speech progressively isolate it from external speech, then its vocal aspect must fade away; and this is exactly what happens between three and seven years. With the progressive isolation of speech for oneself, its vocalization becomes unnecessary and meaningless and, because of its growing structural peculiarities, also impossible. Speech for oneself cannot find expression in external speech. The more independent and autonomous egocentric speech becomes, the poorer it grows in its external manifestations. In the end, it separates itself entirely from speech for others, ceases to be vocalized, and thus appears to die out.

But this is only an illusion. To interpret the sinking coefficient of egocentric speech as an indication that this kind of speech is dying out is like saying that the child stops counting when he ceases to use his fingers and starts adding in his head. In reality, behind the symptoms of dissolution lies a progressive development, the birth of a new speech form.

The decreasing vocalization of egocentric speech denotes a developing abstraction from sound, the child's new faculty to "think words" instead of pronouncing them. This is the positive meaning of the sinking coefficient of egocentric speech. The downward curve indicates development toward inner speech.

We can see that all the known facts about the functional, structural, and genetic characteristics of egocentric speech point to one thing: It develops in the direction of inner speech. Its developmental history can be understood only as a gradual unfolding of the traits of inner speech.

We believe that this corroborates our hypothesis about the origin and nature of egocentric speech. To turn our hypothesis into a certainty, we must devise an experiment capable of showing which of the two interpretations is correct. What are the data for this critical experiment?

Let us restate the theories between which we must decide. Piaget believes that egocentric speech stems from the insufficient socialization of speech and that its only development is decrease and eventual death. Its culmination lies in the past. Inner speech is something new brought in from the outside along with socialization. We believe that egocentric speech stems from the insufficient individualization of primary social speech. Its culmination lies in the future. It develops into inner speech.

To obtain evidence for one or the other view, we must place the child alternately in experimental situations encouraging social speech and in situations discouraging it, and see how these changes affect egocentric speech. We consider this an *experimentum crucis* for the following reasons.

If the child's egocentric talk results from the egocentrism of his thinking and its insufficient socialization, then any weakening of the social elements in the experimental setup, any factor contributing to the child's isolation from the group, must lead to a sudden increase in egocentric speech. But if the latter results from an insufficient differentiation of speech for oneself from speech for others, then the same changes must cause it to decrease.

We took as the starting point of our experiment three of Piaget's own observations: (1) Egocentric speech occurs only in the presence of other children engaged in the same activity, and not when the child is alone; i.e., it is a collective monologue. (2) The child is under the illusion that his egocentric talk, directed to nobody, is understood by those who surround him. (3) Egocentric speech has the character of external speech: It is not inaudible or whispered. These are certainly not chance peculiarities. From the child's own point of view, egocentric speech is not yet separated from social speech. It occurs under the subjective and objective conditions of social speech and may be considered a correlate of the insufficient isolation of the child's individual consciousness from the social whole.

Our position regarding these observations of Piaget can hardly be called biased, for Abraham Grünbaum came to the same conclusion as we do, making no counterexperiments, but just interpreting Piaget's own data.[7]

For a superficial observer—explains Grünbaum—the child appears to be deep in his thoughts, but this is an erroneous impression, stemming from an erroneous expectation. Three-year-olds do not have a logical outlook, and this absence of a logical attitude is incorrectly taken as a sign of the child's egocentrism. Three- to five-year-olds while playing together often speak only to themselves. What looks like a conversation turns out to be a collective monologue. But even such a monologue, being the most spectacular example of child "egocentrism," actually reveals the social engagement of the child's psyche. A collective monologue does not require either a purposive isolation or autism. Children who are participants of the collective monologue do believe that they communicate with each other. They believe that their thoughts, even those that are poorly expressed or unarticulated, belong to all participants. This, according to Grünbaum, points to the insufficient separation of the child's individual psyche from the social whole.

And yet it is experiment, and not interpretations, that can resolve the problem of inner speech and egocentrism. In our first series of experiments,[8] we tried to destroy the illusion of being understood. After measuring the child's coefficient of egocentric speech in a situation similar to that of Piaget's experiments, we put him into a new situation: either with deaf-mute children or with children speaking a foreign language. In all other respects the setup remained the same. The coefficient of egocentric speech dropped to zero in the majority of cases, and in the rest to one-eighth of the previous figure, on the average. This proves that the illusion of being understood is not a mere epiphenomenon of egocentric speech, but is functionally connected with it. Our results must seem paradoxical from the point of view of Piaget's theory: The weaker the child's contact is with the group—the less the social situation forces him to adjust his thoughts to others and to use social speech—the more freely should the egocentrism of his thinking and speech manifest itself. But from the point of view of our hypothesis, the meaning of these findings is clear: Egocentric speech, springing from the lack of differentiation of speech for oneself from speech for others, disappears when the feeling of being understood, essential for social speech, is absent.

In the second series of experiments, the variable factor was the possibility of collective monologue. Having measured the child's coefficient of egocentric speech in a situation permitting collective monologue, we put him into a situation excluding it—in a group of children who were strangers to him or by himself at a separate table in a corner of the room; or working quite alone (even the experimenter left the room). The results of this series agreed with the first results. The exclusion of the group monologue caused a drop in the coefficient of egocentric speech, though not such a striking one as in the first case—seldom to zero, and, on the average, to one-sixth of the original figure. The different methods of precluding collective monologue were not equally effective in reducing the coefficient of egocentric speech. The trend, however, was obvious in all the variations of the experiment. The exclusion of the collective factor, instead of giving full freedom to egocentric speech, depressed it. Our hypothesis was once more confirmed.

In the third series of experiments, the variable factor was the vocal quality of egocentric speech. Just outside the laboratory where the experiment was in progress, an orchestra played so loudly, or so much noise was made, that it drowned out not only the voices of others but the child's own; in a variant of the experiment, the child was expressly forbidden to talk loudly and allowed to talk only in whispers. Once again the coefficient of egocentric speech went down, the relation to the original figure being 5:1. Again the different methods were not equally effective, but the basic trend was invariably present.

The purpose of all three series of experiments was to eliminate those characteristics of egocentric speech that bring it close to social speech. We found that this always led to the dwindling of egocentric speech. It is logical, then, to assume that egocentric speech is a form developing out of social speech and not yet separated from it in its manifestation, though already distinct in function and structure.

The disagreement between us and Piaget on this point will be made quite clear by the following example: I am sitting at my desk talking to a person who is behind me and whom I cannot see; he leaves the room without my noticing it, and I continue to talk, under the illusion that he listens and understands. Outwardly, I am talking with myself and for myself, but psychologically my speech is social. From the point of view of Piaget's theory, the opposite happens in the case of the child: His egocentric talk is for and with himself; it only has the appearance of social speech, just as my speech gave the false impression of being egocentric. From our point of view, the whole situation is much more complicated than that: Subjectively, the child's egocentric speech already has its own peculiar function—to that extent, it is independent from social speech; yet its independence is not complete because it is not felt as inner speech and is not distinguished by the child from speech for others. Objectively, also, it is different from social speech, but again not entirely, because it functions only within social situations. Both subjectively and objectively, egocentric speech represents a transition from speech for others to speech for oneself. It already has the function of inner speech, but remains similar to social speech in its expression.[9]

The investigation of egocentric speech has paved the way to the understanding of inner speech, which we shall examine next.

IV

Our experiments convinced us that inner speech must be regarded, not as speech minus sound, but as an entirely separate speech function. Its main characteristic trait is its peculiar syntax. Compared with external speech, inner speech appears disconnected and incomplete.

It is not a new observation. All students of inner speech, even those who approached it from behavioristic standpoint, have noted this trait. But they usually did not venture to explore it. Even purely phenotypical analysis remained incomplete. The method of genetic analysis permits us to go beyond a mere description. Watson hypothesized that the abbreviated character of soundless speech stems from the same mechanism that produces "shortcuts" in the acquisition of sensory-motor skills. We think, however, that even if recorded in full with the help of some supersensitive phonograph, the inner speech would remain abbreviated and incoherent. The only way to investigate such speech is to trace its development from its very origin as a social function to its mature form, which is as an instrument of individual thought.

Observing the evolution of the child's egocentric speech step by step, we may discover that it becomes more and more peculiar and ultimately becomes inner speech. We applied the genetic method and found that as egocentric speech develops, it shows a tendency toward an altogether specific form of abbreviation, namely: omitting the subject of a sentence and all words connected with it, while preserving the predicate. This tendency toward predication appears in all our experiments with such regularity that we must assume it to be the basic form of syntax of inner speech.

It may help us to understand this tendency if we recall certain situations in which external speech shows a similar structure. Pure predication occurs in external speech in two cases: either as an answer or when the subject of the sentence is known beforehand to all concerned. The answer to "Would you like a cup of tea?" is never "No, I don't want a cup of tea," but a simple "No." Obviously, such a sentence is possible only because its subject is tacitly understood by both parties. To "Has your brother read this book?" no one ever replies, "Yes, my brother has read this book." The answer is a short "Yes," or "Yes, he has." Now let us imagine that several people are waiting for a bus. No one will say, on seeing the bus approach, "The bus for which we are waiting is coming." The sentence is likely to be an abbreviated "Coming," or some such expression, because the subject is plain from the situation. Quite frequently, shortened sentences cause confusion. The listener may relate the sentence to a subject foremost in his own mind, not the one meant by the speaker. If the thoughts of two people coincide, perfect understanding can be achieved through the use of mere predicates, but if they are thinking about different things they are bound to misunderstand each other.

Very good examples of the condensation of external speech and its reduction to predicates are found in the novels of Tolstoy, who quite often dealt with the psychology of understanding: "No one heard clearly what he said, but Kitty understood him. She understood because her mind incessantly watched for his needs" (*Anna Karenina,* part V, chapter 18). We might say that her thoughts, following the thoughts of the dying man, contained the subject to which his word, understood by no one else, referred. But perhaps the most striking example is the declaration of love between Kitty and Levin by means of initial letters (*Anna Karenina,* part IV, chapter 13):

"I have long wished to ask you something."
"Please do."
"This," he said, and wrote the initial letters: *W y a: i c n b, d y m t o n.* These letters meant: "When you answered: it can not be, did you mean then or never?" It seemed impossible that she would be able to understand the complicated sentence.

"I understand," she said, blushing.

"What word is that?" he asked, pointing to the *n* which stood for "never."

"The word is 'never,' " she said, "but that is not true." He quickly erased what he had written, handed her the chalk, and rose. She wrote: *I c n a o t.*

His face brightened suddenly: he had understood. It meant: "I could not answer otherwise then."

She wrote the initial letters: *s t y m f a f w h.* This meant: "So that you might forget and forgive what happened."

He seized the chalk with tense, trembling fingers, broke it, and wrote the initial letters of the following: "I have nothing to forget and forgive. I never ceased loving you."

"I understand," she whispered. He sat down and wrote a long sentence. She understood it all and, without asking him whether she was right, took the chalk and answered at once.

For a long time he could not make out what she had written, and he kept looking up into her eyes. His mind was dazed with happiness. He was quite unable to fill in the words she had meant; but in her lovely, radiantly happy eyes he read all that he needed to know. And he wrote down three letters. Before he had finished writing, she was already reading under his hand, and she finished the sentence herself and wrote the answer, "Yes." Everything had been said in their conversation: that she loved him, and would tell her father and mother that he would call in the morning.

This example has an extraordinary psychological interest because, like the whole episode between Kitty and Levin, it was taken by Tolstoy from his own life. In just this way, Tolstoy told his future wife of his love for her. These examples show clearly that when the thoughts of the speakers are the same, the role of speech is reduced to a minimum. Tolstoy points out elsewhere that between people who live in close psychological contact, such communication by means of abbreviated speech is the rule rather than the exception: "Now Levin was used to expressing his thought fully without troubling to put it into exact words: He knew that his wife, in such moments filled with love, as this one, would understand what he wanted to say from a mere hint, and she did" (*Anna Karenina*, part VI, chapter 3).

Lev Jakubinsky and Evgeni Polivanov absolutely correctly emphasized that shared apperception by communicating parties is a necessary precondition of normal dialogue.[10] If we were to communicate in an absolutely formal manner, we would use many more words than we usually use to convey our thoughts. In a word, it is natural that we talk by hints.

A simplified syntax, condensation, and a greatly reduced number of words characterize the tendency to predication that appears in external speech when the partners know what is going on. In complete contrast to this kind of understanding are the comical mix-ups resulting from people's thoughts going in different directions. The confusion to which this may lead is well rendered in this little poem of Pushkin:

Before the judge who's deaf two deaf men bow.
One deaf man cries: "He led away my cow."
"Beg pardon," says the other in reply,
"That meadow was my father's land in days gone by."
The judge decides: "For you to fight each other is a shame.
Nor one nor t'other, but the girl's to blame."

Kitty's conversation with Levin and the judgment of the deaf are extreme cases, the two poles, in fact, of external speech. One exemplifies the mutual understanding that can be achieved through utterly abbreviated speech when the subject is the same in two minds; the other, the total misunderstanding, even with full speech, when people's thoughts wander in different directions. It is not only the deaf who cannot understand one another, but any two people who give a different meaning to the same word or who hold divergent views. As Tolstoy noted, those who are accustomed to solitary, independent thinking do not easily grasp another's thought and are very partial to their own; but people in close contact apprehend one another's complicated meanings by "laconic and clear" communication in the fewest words.

V

Having examined abbreviation in external speech, we can now return enriched to the same phenomenon in inner speech, where it is not an exception but the rule. It will be instructive to compare abbreviation in oral speech, inner speech, and written speech. Communication in writing relies on the formal meanings of words and requires a much greater number of words than oral speech to convey the same idea. It is addressed to an absent person who rarely has in mind the same subject as the writer. Therefore it must be fully deployed; syntactic differentiation is at a maximum; and expressions are used that would seem unnatural in conversation. Griboedov's "He talks like writing" refers to the droll effect of elaborate constructions in daily speech.

The multifunctional nature of language, which has recently attracted the close attention of linguists, had already been pointed out by Humboldt in relation to poetry and prose—two forms very different in function and also in the means they use.[11] Poetry, according to Humboldt, is inseparable from music, while prose depends entirely on language and is dominated by thought. Consequently, each has its own diction, grammar, and syntax. This is a conception of primary importance, although neither Humboldt nor Potebnja, who further developed his thought, fully realized its implications. They distinguished only between poetry and prose, and within the latter between the exchange of ideas and ordinary conversation, i.e., the mere exchange of news or conventional chatter. There are other important functional distinctions in speech. One of them is the distinction between dialogue and monologue. Written speech and inner speech represent the monologue; oral speech, in most cases, the dialogue.

Dialogue always presupposes in the partners sufficient knowledge of the subject to permit abbreviated speech and, under certain conditions, purely predicative sentences. It also presupposes that each person can see his partners, their facial expressions and gestures, and hear the tone of their voices. Only situations like that can produce speech that is, as Gabriel Tarde put it, "a mere supplement to the exchange of glances." We have already discussed abbreviation and shall consider here only its auditory aspect, using a classical example from Dostoevsky's *The Diary of a Writer* to show how much intonation helps the subtly differentiated understanding of a word's meaning.

Dostoevsky relates a conversation of drunks that entirely consisted of one unprintable word (*The Diary of a Writer*, for 1873):

One Sunday night I happened to walk for some fifteen paces next to a group of six drunken young workmen, and I suddenly realized that all thoughts, feelings, and even a whole chain of reasoning could be expressed by that one noun, which is moreover extremely short. One young fellow said it harshly and forcefully, to express his utter contempt for whatever it was they had all been talking about. Another answered with the same noun but in a quite different tone and sense— doubting that the negative attitude of the first one was warranted. A third suddenly became incensed with the first and roughly intruded on the conversation, excitedly shouting the same noun, this time as a curse and obscenity. Here the second fellow interfered again, angry at the third, the aggressor, and restraining him, in the sense of "Now why do you have to butt in, we were discussing things quietly and here you come and start swearing." And he told this whole thought in one word, the same venerable word, except that he also raised his hand and put it on the third fellow's shoulder. All at once a fourth, the youngest of the group, who had kept silent till then, probably having suddenly found a solution to the original difficulty which had started the argument, raised his hand in a transport of joy and shouted . . . Eureka, do you think? Found it? Found it? No, not Eureka at all; nor did he find anything; he repeated the same unprintable noun, one word, merely one word, but with ecstasy, in a shriek of delight—which was apparently too strong, because the sixth and the oldest, a glum-looking fellow, did not like it and cut the infantile joy of the other one short, addressing him in a sullen, exhortative bass and repeating . . . yes, still the same noun, forbidden in the presence of ladies but which this time clearly meant "What are you yelling yourself hoarse for?" So, without uttering a single other word, they repeated that one beloved word six times in a row, one after another, and understood one another completely.

Here we see one more source of the abbreviation of oral speech, i.e., the modulation of voice that reveals psychological context within which a word is to be understood. In Dostoevsky's story it was contemptuous negation in one case, doubt in another, anger in the third. We have discovered so far two factors of abbreviation. One is connected with shared apperception by the persons involved in dialogue; the other occurs when the idea can be rendered by inflection, and when it really becomes possible to convey all thoughts, feelings, and even an entire chain of reasoning by one word.

In written speech, as tone of voice and knowledge of subject are excluded, we are obliged to use many more words, and to use them more exactly. Written speech is the most elaborate form of speech.

Some linguists, particularly Lev Scherba, consider dialogue the natural form of oral speech, the one in which language fully reveals its nature, and monologue to a great extent artificial. Psychological investigation leaves no doubt that monologue is indeed the higher, more complicated form, and of later historical development. At present, however, we are interested in comparing them only in regard to the tendency toward abbreviation.

The speed of oral speech is unfavorable to a complicated process of formulation—it does not leave time for deliberation and choice. Dialogue implies immediate unpremeditated utterance. It consists of replies, repartee; it is a chain of reactions. Monologue, by comparison, is a complex formation; the linguistic elaboration can be attended to leisurely and consciously.

In written speech, lacking situational and expressive supports, communication must be achieved only through words and their combinations; this requires the speech activity to take complicated forms—hence the use of first drafts. The evolution from the draft to the final copy reflects our mental process. Planning has an important part in written speech, even when we do not actually write out a draft. Usually we say to ourselves what we are going to write; this is also a draft, though in thought only. As we tried to show in the preceding chapter, this mental draft is inner speech. Since inner speech functions as a draft not only in written speech but also in oral speech, we shall now compare both these forms with inner speech in respect to the tendency toward abbreviation and predication.

This tendency, never found in written speech and only sometimes in oral speech, arises in inner speech always. Predication is the natural form of inner speech; psychologically, it consists of predicates only. It is as much a law of inner speech to omit subjects as it is a law of written speech to contain both subjects and predicates.

There are two ways to study the specificity of predicative speech. One is to trace the dynamics of the buildup of predication; the other is to compare the phenomenon of predicative speech with tendencies toward abbreviation discovered in oral speech and written speech.

Those factors responsible for abbreviation in oral speech are inevitably present in inner speech. We know what we are thinking about; i.e., we always know the subject and the situation. And since the subject of our inner dialogue is already known, we may just imply it.

Piaget once mentioned that we trust ourselves without proof; the necessity to defend and articulate one's position appears only in conversation with others. Psychological contact between partners in a conversation may establish a mutual perception leading to the understanding of abbreviated speech. In inner speech, the "mutual" perception is always there, in absolute form; therefore, a practically wordless "communication" of even the most complicated thoughts is the rule.

The predominance of predication is a product of development. In the beginning, egocentric speech is identical in structure with social speech, but in the process of its transformation into inner speech, it gradually becomes less complete and coherent as it becomes governed by an almost entirely predicative syntax. Experiments show clearly how and why the new syntax takes hold. The child talks about the things he sees or hears or does at a given moment. As a result, he tends to leave out the subject and all words connected with it, condensing his speech more and more until only predicates are left. The more differentiated the specific function of egocentric speech becomes, the more pronounced are its syntactic peculiarities—simplification and predication. Hand in hand with this change goes decreasing vocalization. When we converse with ourselves, we need even fewer words than Kitty and Levin did. Inner speech is speech almost without words.

An interesting parallel to the conversation between Kitty and Levin was found by Lemaître in his study of the inner speech of adolescents. One of Lemaître's subjects, a twelve-year-old boy, thought of the phrase "Les montagnes de la Suisse sont belles" as a line of letters: *L,m, d,l,S,s,b*—representing a foggy mountain landscape (Lemaître, 1905, p. 5).

With syntax and sound reduced to a minimum, meaning is more than ever in the forefront. Inner speech works with semantics, not phonetics. The specific semantic structure of inner speech also contributes to abbreviation. The syntax of meanings in inner speech is no less original than its grammatical syntax. Our investigation established three main semantic peculiarities of inner speech.

The first and basic one is the preponderance of the *sense* [*smysl*] of a word over its *meaning* [*znachenie*]—a distinction we owe to Frederic Paulhan.[12] The sense of a word, according to him, is the sum of all the psychological events aroused in our consciousness by the word. It is a dynamic, fluid, complex whole, which has several zones of unequal stability. Meaning is only one of the zones of sense, the most stable and precise zone. A word acquires its sense from the context in which it appears; in different contexts, it changes its sense. Meaning remains stable throughout the changes of sense. The dictionary meaning of a word is no more than a stone in the edifice of sense, no more than a potentiality that finds diversified realization in speech.

The last words of the previously mentioned fable by Krylov, "The Dragonfly and the Ant," are a good illustration of the difference between sense and meaning. The words "Go and dance!" have a definite and constant meaning, but in the context of the fable they acquire a much broader intellectual and affective sense. They mean both "Enjoy yourself!" and "Perish!" This enrichment of words by the sense they gain from the context is the fundamental law of the dynamics of word meanings. A word in a context means both more and less than the same word in isolation: more, because it acquires new context; less, because its meaning is limited and narrowed by the context. The sense of a word, says Paulhan, is a complex, mobile, protean phenomenon; it changes in different minds and situations and is almost unlimited. A word derives its sense from the sentence, which, in turn, gets its sense from the paragraph, the paragraph from the book, the book from all the works of the author.

Paulhan rendered a further service to psychology by analyzing the relation between word and sense and showing that they are much more independent of each other than word and meaning. It has long been known that words can change their sense. Recently it was pointed out that sense can change words or, better, that ideas often change their names. Just as the sense of a word is connected with the whole word, and not with its single sounds, the sense of a sentence is connected with the

whole sentence, and not with its individual words. Therefore, a word may sometimes be replaced by another without any change in sense. Words and senses are relatively
independent of each other.

Here once again we shall turn to Paulhan's analysis in
order to show the existence of certain phenomena in oral
speech that can also be experimentally detected in inner
speech. In oral speech, we move from the central and
permanent meaning of the word to its soft fringes and
ultimately to its sense. In inner speech, this prevalence of
sense over meaning, of sentence over word, and of context over sentence is the rule.

This leads us to the other semantic peculiarities of inner speech. Both concern word combination. One of
them is rather like agglutination—a way of combining
words fairly frequent in some languages and compara-
tively rare in others. German often forms one noun out
of several words or phrases. In some primitive languages,
such adhesion of words is a general rule. When several
words are merged into one word, the new word not only
expresses a rather complex idea, but designates all the
separate elements contained in that idea. Because the
stress is always on the main root or idea, such languages
are easy to understand. The egocentric speech of the
child displays some analogous phenomena. As egocentric
speech approaches inner speech, the child uses agglutination more and more as a way of forming compound
words to express complex ideas.

The third basic semantic peculiarity of inner speech is
the way in which senses of words combine and unite—a
process governed by different laws from those governing
combinations of meanings. When we observed this singular way of uniting words in egocentric speech, we called it
"influx of sense." The senses of different words flow into
one another—literally "influence" one another—so that
the earlier ones are contained in, and modify, the later

ones. Thus, a word that keeps recurring in a book or a poem sometimes absorbs all the variety of sense contained in it and becomes, in a way, equivalent to the work itself. The title of a literary work expresses its content and completes its sense to a much greater degree than does the name of a painting or of a piece of music. Titles like *Don Quixote, Hamlet,* and *Anna Karenina* illustrate this very clearly; the whole sense of a work is contained in one name. Another excellent example is Gogol's *Dead Souls.* Originally, the title referred to dead serfs whose names had not yet been removed from the official lists and who could still be bought and sold as if they were alive. It is in this sense that the words are used throughout the book, which is built up around this traffic in the dead. But through their intimate relation with the work as a whole, these two words acquire a new significance, an infinitely broader sense. When we reach the end of the book, "dead souls" means to us not so much the defunct serfs as all the characters in the story who are alive physically but dead spiritually.

In inner speech, the phenomenon reaches its peak. A single word is so saturated with sense that, like the title *Dead Souls,* it becomes a concentrate of sense. To unfold it into overt speech, one would need a multitude of words.

No wonder that egocentric speech and inner speech are incomprehensible to others. To understand a child's egocentric utterance, one should know beforehand the subject of the child's speech and the circumstances of communication.

Watson says that inner speech would be incomprehensible even if fully recorded. We have already mentioned such factors contributing to the peculiarity of inner speech as reduced sound, and idiosyncratic syntax and semantics, but there is one more factor that further increases the opaqueness of inner speech. Tolstoy describes in *Childhood, Adolescence, and Youth* how, between people in close psychological contact, words acquire special meanings understood only by the initiated. Such a dialect was used by the brothers Ignatiev, characters in this book by Tolstoy. There is an argot used and understood only by street children. In inner speech, the same kind of idiom develops—the kind that is difficult to translate into the language of ordinary communicative speech.

Actually, any attempt to impose multifaceted sense on one word results in the creation of an original idiom. In inner speech, one word stands for a number of thoughts and feelings, and sometimes substitutes for a long and profound discourse. And naturally this unique inner sense of the chosen word cannot be translated into ordinary external speech. Inner sense turns out to be incommensurable with the external meaning of the same word.

With this we shall conclude our survey of the peculiarities of inner speech, which we first observed in our investigation of egocentric speech. In looking for comparisons in external speech, we found that the latter already contains, potentially at least, the traits typical of inner speech; predication, decrease of vocalization, preponderance of sense over meaning, agglutination, etc., appear under certain conditions also in external speech. This, we believe, is the best confirmation of our hypothesis that inner speech originates through the differentiation of egocentric speech from the child's primary social speech.

All our observations indicate that inner speech is an autonomous speech function. We can confidently regard it as a *distinct plane of verbal thought*. It is evident that the transition from inner speech to external speech is not a simple translation from one language into another. It cannot be achieved by merely vocalizing silent speech. It is a complex, dynamic process involving the transformation of the predicative, idiomatic structure of inner speech into syntactically articulated speech intelligible to others.

VI

We can now return to the definition of inner speech that we proposed before presenting our analysis. Inner speech is not the interior aspect of external speech—it is a function in itself. It still remains speech, i.e., thought connected with words. But while in external speech thought is embodied in words, in inner speech words die as they bring forth thought. Inner speech is to a large extent thinking in pure meanings. It is a dynamic, shifting, unstable thing, fluttering between word and thought, the two more or less stable, more or less firmly delineated components of verbal thought. Its true nature and place can be understood only after examining the next plane of verbal thought, the one still more inward than inner speech.

That plane is thought itself. As we have said, every thought creates a connection, fulfills a function, solves a problem. The flow of thought is not accompanied by a simultaneous unfolding of speech. The two processes are not identical, and there is no rigid correspondence between the units of thought and speech. This is especially obvious when a thought process miscarries—when, as Dostoevsky put it, a thought "will not enter words."

Here one literary example will be appropriate. Gleb Uspensky's character, a poor peasant, who must address an official with some life-important issue, cannot put his thoughts into words. Embarrassed by his failure, he retreats and prays, asking the Lord "to give him a concept." This scene leaves the reader disturbed and depressed. But in its essence, the problem facing this poor and illiterate peasant is of the same kind constantly hounding thinkers and writers: How to put thoughts into words. Sometimes even the speech of Uspensky's character starts to resemble that of a poet: "I would tell you all of this, my friend, concealing nothing . . . but, you know, folks of my kind cannot talk. . . . It is as if they are all here, in my head, but cannot slip from the tongue. That is our, fools', sorrow" (Gleb Uspensky, 1949, p. 184).

In this fragment the watershed between thoughts and words becomes highly visible. If thoughts were identical in structure and development with speech, the case described by Uspensky would be impossible.

Thought has its own structure, and the transition from it to speech is no easy matter. The theater faced the problem of the thought behind the words before psychology did. In teaching his system of acting, Konstantin Stanislavsky required the actors to uncover the "subtext" of their lines in a play.[13] In Griboedov's comedy *Woe from Wit,* the hero, Chatsky, says to the heroine, who maintains that she has never stopped thinking of him, "Thrice blessed who believes. Believing warms the heart." Stanislavsky interpreted this as "Let us stop this talk"; but it could just as well be interpreted as "I do not believe you. You say it to comfort me," or as "Don't you see how you torment me? I wish I could believe you. That would be bliss." Every sentence that we say in real life has some kind of subtext, a thought hidden behind it. In the examples we gave earlier of the lack of coincidence between grammatical and psychological subject and predicate, we did not pursue our analysis to the end. Just as one sentence may express different thoughts, one thought may be expressed in different sentences. For instance, "The clock fell," in answer to the question "Why did the clock stop?" could mean, "It is not my fault that the clock is out of order; it fell." The same thought, self-justification, could take, among others, the form "It is not my habit to touch other people's things. I was just dusting here."

Thought, unlike speech, does not consist of separate units. When I wish to communicate the thought that today I saw a barefoot boy in a blue shirt running down the street, I do not see every item separately: the boy, the shirt, its blue color, his running, the absence of shoes. I conceive of all this in one thought, but I put it into separate words. A speaker often takes several minutes to disclose one thought. In his mind the whole thought is present at once, but in speech it has to be developed successively. A thought may be compared to a cloud shedding a shower of words. Precisely because thought does not have its automatic counterpart in words, the transition from thought to word leads through meaning. In our speech, there is always the hidden thought, the subtext. Because a direct transition from thought to word is impossible, there have always been laments about the inexpressibility of thought:

How shall the heart express itself?
How shall another understand?
F. Tiutchev

or

If only soul might speak without words!
A. Fet

To overcome this problem, new paths from thought to word leading through new word meanings must be cut. Velemir Khlebnikov compared his futuristic poetry with the construction of roads connecting one valley to another.[14]

Experience teaches us that thought does not express itself in words, but rather realizes itself in them. Sometimes such realization cannot be accomplished, as in the case of Uspensky's character. We must ask, Does this character know what he is going to think about? Yes, but he does it as one who wants to remember something but is unable to. Does he start thinking? Yes, but again he does it as one who is absorbed by remembering. Does he succeed in turning his thought into a process? No. The problem is that thought is mediated by signs externally, but it also is mediated internally, this time by word meanings. Direct communication between minds is impossible, not only physically but psychologically. Communication can be achieved only in a roundabout way. Thought must first pass through meanings and only then through words.

We come now to the last step in our analysis of inner planes of verbal thought. Thought is not the superior authority in this process. Thought is not begotten by thought; it is engendered by motivation, i.e., by our desires and needs, our interests and emotions. Behind every thought there is an affective-volitional tendency, which holds the answer to the last "why" in the analysis of thinking. A true and full understanding of another's thought is possible only when we understand its affective-volitional basis. We shall illustrate this by an example already used: the interpretation of parts in a play. Stanislavsky, in his instructions to actors, listed the motives behind the words of their parts for A. Griboedov's *Woe from Wit,* act I:

Text of the Play	Parallel Motives
SOPHYA:	
O, Chatsky, but I am glad you've come	Tries to hide her confusion.
CHATSKY:	
You are glad, that's very nice; But gladness such as yours not easily one tells. It rather seems to me, all told,	Tries to make her feel guilty by teasing her. Aren't you ashamed of yourself! Tries to force her to be frank.

That making man and horse
  catch cold
I've pleased myself and no one
  else

LIZA:
There, sir, and if you'd stood   Tries to calm him. Tries to help
  on the same landing here   Sophya in a difficult situation.
Five minutes, no, not five ago
You'd heard your name clear
  as clear.
You say, Miss! Tell him it was
  so.

SOPHYA:
And always so, no less, no   Tries to reassure Chatsky. I am
  more.   not guilty of anything!
No, as to that, I'm sure you
  can't reproach me.

CHATSKY:
Well, let's suppose it's so.   Let us stop this conversation;
Thrice blessed who believes.   etc.
Believing warms the heart.

To understand another's speech, it is not sufficient to understand his words—we must understand his thought. But even that is not enough—we must also know its motivation. No psychological analysis of an utterance is complete until that plane is reached.

We have come to the end of our analysis; let us survey its results. Verbal thought appeared as a complex, dynamic entity, and the relation of thought and word within it as a movement through a series of planes. Our analysis followed the process from the outermost plane to the innermost plane. In reality, the development of verbal thought takes the opposite course: from the motive that engenders a thought to the shaping of the thought, first in inner speech, then in meanings of words, and finally in words. It would be a mistake, however, to imagine that this is the only road from thought to word. The development may stop at any point in its complicated course: an infinite variety of movements to and fro, of ways still unknown to us, is possible. A study of these manifold variations lies beyond the scope of our present task.

Our investigation followed a rather unusual path. We wished to study the inner workings of thought and speech, hidden from direct observation. Meaning and the whole inward aspect of language, the side turned toward the person, not toward the outer world, have been so far an almost unknown territory. No matter how they were interpreted, the relations between thought and word were always considered constant, established forever. Our investigation has shown that they are, on the contrary, delicate, changeable relations between processes, which arise during the development of verbal thought. We did not intend to, and could not, exhaust the subject of verbal thought. We tried only to give a general conception of the infinite complexity of this dynamic structure—a conception starting from experimentally documented facts.

To association psychology, thought and word were united by external bonds, similar to the bonds between two nonsense syllables. Gestalt psychology introduced the concept of structural bonds, but, like the older theory, did not account for the specific relations between thought and word. All the other theories grouped themselves around two poles—either the behaviorist concept of thought as speech minus sound or the idealistic view, held by the Würzburg school and Bergson, that thought could be "pure," unrelated to language, and that it was distorted by words. Tiutchev's "A thought once uttered is a lie" could well serve as an epigraph for the latter group. Whether inclining toward pure naturalism or extreme idealism, all these theories have one trait in common—

their antihistorical bias. They study thought and speech without any reference to their developmental history.

Only a historical theory of inner speech can deal with this immense and complex problem. The relation between thought and word is a living process; thought is born through words. A word devoid of thought is a dead thing:

. . . and like bees in the deserted hive
The dead words have a rotten smell.
N. Gumilev

But thought that fails to realize itself in words also remains a "Stygian shadow" [O. Mandelstam]. Hegel considered word as a Being animated by thought. This Being is absolutely essential for our thinking.

The connection between thought and word, however, is neither preformed nor constant. It emerges in the course of development, and itself evolves. To the biblical "In the beginning was the Word," Goethe makes Faust reply, "In the beginning was the deed." The intent here is to detract from the value of the word, but we can accept this version if we emphasize it differently: In the *beginning* was the deed. The word was not the beginning— action was there first; it is the end of development, crowning the deed.

We cannot close our study without mentioning the perspectives that our investigation opens up. This is even more momentous a problem than that of thinking; what I mean is the problem of consciousness. We studied the inward aspects of speech, which were as unknown to science as the other side of the moon. We tried to establish the connection between word and object, word and reality. We attempted to study experimentally the dialectics of transition from perception to thinking, and to show that a generalized reflection of reality is the basic characteristic of words. This aspect of the word brings us to the threshold of a wider and deeper subject, i.e., the problem of the relation between word and consciousness. If perceptive consciousness and intellectual consciousness reflect reality differently, then we have two different forms of consciousness. *Thought and speech turn out to be the key to the nature of human consciousness.*

If language is as old as consciousness itself, and if language is a practical consciousness-for-others and, consequently, consciousness-for-myself, then not only one particular thought but all consciousness is connected with the development of the word. The word is a thing in our consciousness, as Ludwig Feuerbach put it, that is absolutely impossible for one person, but that becomes a reality for two. The word is a direct expression of the historical nature of human consciousness.

Consciousness is reflected in a word as the sun in a drop of water. A word relates to consciousness as a living cell relates to a whole organism, as an atom relates to the universe. A word is a microcosm of human consciousness.

Notes

Vygotsky in Context

1. Semyon Dobkin, "Ages and Days," in K. Levitin, ed., *One Is Not Born Personality* [sic], Moscow: Progress, 1983, p. 26.

2. Lev Vygotsky, *Sobranie sochinenii* [*Collected Papers*], vol. 3, Moscow: Pedagogika, 1983, pp. 273–291.

3. Semyon Dobkin, "Ages and Days," p. 36.

4. Lev Vygotsky, *The Psychology of Art,* Cambridge, MA: MIT Press, 1971. In the second Russian edition (1968) an essay on *Hamlet* was published as supplement. Unfortunately, the English edition of *The Psychology of Art* corresponds to the first Russian edition, in which this essay was omitted.

5. Alexander Luria, *The Making of Mind,* Cambridge, MA: Harvard University Press, 1979, pp. 38–39.

6. Lev Vygotsky, *Istoricheskii smysl psikhologicheskogo krizisa* [*The Historical meaning of the crisis in psychology*], in Lev Vygotsky, *Sobranie sochinenii* [*Collected Papers*], vol. 1, Moscow: Pedagogika, 1982.

7. Ibid., p. 299.

8. Sigmund Koch, "The Nature and Limits of Psychological Knowledge: Lessons of a Century qua 'Science,' " *American Psychologist,* 1981, 36:257–269.

9. Lev Vygotsky, *Crisis,* p. 304.

10. Ibid., p. 384.

11. Ibid., p. 397.

12. Ibid., p. 419.

13. Ibid., p. 419.

14. Lev Vygotsky, "Consciousness as a Problem of Psychology of Behavior," *Soviet Psychology*, 1979, 17:29–30.

15. George H. Mead, *Mind, Self and Society* (1934), Chicago: University of Chicago Press, 1974, pp. 47–48.

16. Lev Vygotsky, "The Instrumental Method in Psychology," in J. Wertsch, ed., *The Concept of Activity in Soviet Psychology*, New York: Sharpe, 1981, p. 141.

17. Lev Vygotsky, *Mind in Society*, Cambridge, MA: Harvard University Press, 1978, p. 57.

18. Alexei N. Leontiev, "Studies on the Cultural Development of the Child," *Journal of Genetic Psychology*, 1932, 40:52–83.

19. Lev Vygotsky, in J. Wertsch, ed., *The Concept of Activity in Soviet Psychology*, p. 155.

20. Published in volume 3 of the *Collected Papers*. Portions of this work were translated into English and published under the title *Mind in Society*, Cambridge, MA: Harvard University Press, 1978.

21. *Myshlenie i rech* was published in Russian in 1934, a few months after Vygotsky's death, and was reprinted in 1956 and 1982. It appeared in English as *Thought and Language* (Cambridge, MA: MIT Press, 1962).

22. Lev Vygotsky, *O psikhologicheskikh sistemakh* [*On Psychological Systems*] (1930), in the *Collected Papers*, vol. 1, p. 110.

23. Eugenia Hanfmann and Jacob Kasanin, *Conceptual Thinking in Schizophrenia*, New York: NMDM, 1942.

24. Peter Galperin, "Stages in the Development of Mental Acts," in M. Cole and I. Maltzman, eds., *A Handbook of Contemporary Soviet Psychology*, New York: Basic Books, 1969; Vasili Davydov, "A Concept of Educational Activity in Schoolchildren," *Soviet Psychology*, 1983, 21:50–76.

25. Luria's work was published in English as *Cognitive Development: Its Cultural and Social Foundations*, Cambridge, MA: Harvard University Press, 1976.

26. See volume 6 of Vygotsky's *Collected Papers*.

27. See volume 4 of Vygotsky's *Collected Papers*.

28. Lev Vygotsky, "Thought in Schizophrenia," *Archives of Neurology and Psychiatry*, 1934, 31:1063–1077.

29. See Alex Kozulin, *Psychology in Utopia*, Cambridge, MA: MIT Press, 1984, pp. 18–22.

30. Alexander Luria, *The Making of Mind*, Cambridge, MA: Harvard University Press, 1979, pp. 208–205.

31. Alexei A. Leontiev, Jr., "Tvorcheskii put A. N. Leontieva" ["The Productive Career of A. N. Leontiev"], in A. Zaporozhets et al., eds., *A. N. Leontiev i sovremennaia psikhologiia* [*A. N. Leontiev and Contemporary Psychology*], Moscow: MGU, 1983, p. 11. See also Alexei A. Leontiev, "The Productive Career of A. N. Leontiev, *Soviet Psychology*, 1984, 23:6–56.

32. Alexei N. Leontiev, "Ovladenie uchaschimisia nauchnymi poniatiiami kak problema pedagogicheskoi psikhologii ["The Acquisition of Scientific Concepts by Schoolchildren as a Problem of Educational Psychology"] (1935), in *Khrestomatiia po vozrastnoi i pedagogicheskoi psikhologii* [*Handbook of Developmental and Pedagogical Psychology*], vol. 1, Moscow: MGU, 1980, p. 14.

33. Michael Cole, "The Kharkov School of Developmental Psychology," *Soviet Psychology*, 1980, 18:5.

34. Peter Zinchenko, "The Problem of Involuntary Memory" (1939), *Soviet Psychology*, 1984, 22(2):66–67.

35. Ibid., p. 67.

36. Ibid., p. 70.

37. Alexei N. Leontiev, *Activity, Consciousness, and Personality*, Englewood Cliffs, NJ: Prentice-Hall, 1978, p. 62.

38. Alexei N. Leontiev, *Problems of the Development of the Mind*, Moscow: Progress, 1981, p. 281.

39. Alexei N. Leontiev, *Activity, Consciousness, and Personality*, p. 63.

40. Ibid., p. 64.

41. Ibid., p. 64.

42. Sergei L. Rubinstein, "Problemy sposobnostei i voprosy psikhologicheskoi teorii" ["The Problem of Abilities and the Questions of Psychological Theory"], *Voprosy psikhologii*, 1960, 3:7.

43. Alexei N. Leontiev, *Problems of the Development of the Mind*, pp. 318–349.

44. Ksenia A. Abulkhanova, *O sub'ekte psikhicheskoi deiatelnosti* [*The Subject of Psychological Activity*], Moscow: Nauka, 1973, p. 157.

45. *Thought and Language*, together with some minor works, was reprinted in 1956 in the volume *Izbrannye psikhologicheskie issledovaniia* [*Selected Psychological Investigations*]. In 1960 earlier unpublished papers of Vygotsky appeared in *Razvitie vysshykh psikhocheskikh funkzii*

[*Development of Higher Mental Functions*]. *The Psychology of Art* was published in 1965.

46. See Alexei N. Leontiev and Alexander Luria, Psikhologicheskie vozzreniia L. S. Vygotskogo ["Psychological Views of L. S. Vygotsky"], in L. S. Vygotsky, *Izbrannye psikhologicheskie issledovaniia*, [*Selected Psychological Investigations*], Moscow: APN, 1956.

47. Eric Yudin, "Deiatel'nost kak ob'iasnitel'nyi printsyp i kak predmet nauchnogo issledovaniia" ["Activity as an Explanatory Principle and as a Subject of Scientific Study"], *Voprosy filosofii*, 1976, 5:65:78.

48. Tatiana V. Akhutina, "Teoriia rechevogo obscheniia v trudakh Bakhtina i Vygotsky" ["The Theory of Verbal Communication in the Works of Bakhtin and Vygotsky"], *Vestnik Moscovskogo universiteta: psikhologiia*, 1984, 3:3–12.

49. Alexei A. Leontiev, Jr., "Sign and Activity," in J. Wertsch, ed., *The Concept of Activity in Soviet Psychology*, New York: Sharpe, 1981.

50. Lev Vygotsky, "Thought and speech," *Psychiatry*, 1939, 2:29–54.

51. Jerry Fodor, "Some Reflections on L. S. Vygotsky's *Thought and Language*," *Cognition*, 1972, 1:84.

52. See Lev Vygotsky, *Mind in Society: The Development of Higher Psychological Processes*, Cambridge, MA: Harvard University Press, 1978. A number of Vygotsky's papers were translated in J. Wertsch, ed., *The Concept of Activity in Soviet Psychology*, New York: Sharpe, 1981.

53. James Wertsch, ed., *Culture, Communication, and Cognition*, New York: Cambridge University Press, 1985.

54. Material used in this introduction is, in part, based upon work supported by the NSF under grant SES-8318883.

Author's Preface

1. Some chapters of this book were published earlier as separate papers or delivered as lectures: chapter 2 was published as the introduction to the Russian edition of Piaget's *The Language and Thought of the Child*, Moscow: Gosizdat, 1932; chapter 4 was published in *Estestvoznanie i Marxism*, 1929, 1; chapter 5 is based on a course of lectures on the experimental study of concept formation delivered at the Extension Division of the Second Moscow State University.

2. Vygotsky's own assessment of the limitations of his study may be found in section V of chapter 6. On the evolution of Vygotsky's views see my introduction.

Chapter 1

1. Oswald Kulpe, Carl Marbe, and Narziss Ach were the leading figures at the Würzburg Institute of Psychology. For the selection of their writings see Jean and George Mandler, eds., *Thinking: From Association to Gestalt*, New York: Wiley, 1964.

2. Vygotsky refers to studies in structural phonology that originated in the works of Nikolai Trubetskoi, Roman Jakobson, and other members of the Prague Linguistic Circle in the 1920s. See Maurice Leroy, *The Main Trends in Modern Linguistics*, Oxford: Blackwell, 1967, p. 66.

3. The problem of the interrelation between affect and intellect became a subject of Vygotsky's last, unfinished work, *Uchenie ob emotsiiakh* [*A Study of Emotions*] (1933), published in volume 6 of *Sobranie sochinenii* [*Collected Papers*].

Chapter 2

1. Piaget's first two books, *Le Langage et la pensée chez l'enfant*, Neuchatel-Paris: Delachaux and Nestle, 1923, and *Le Jugement et le raisonnement chez l'enfant*, Neuchatel-Paris: Delachaux and Nestle, 1924, were published in Russian in one volume under the title *Rech i myshlenie rebenka*, Moscow: Gosizdat, 1932. These works appeared in English as, respectively, *The Language and Thought of the Child*, London: Routledge and Kegan Paul, 1959, and *Judgment and Reasoning in the Child*, London: Routledge and Kegan Paul, 1969.

2. Edouard Claparède (1850–1934), Swiss child psychologist. See his "The Psychology of the Child at Geneva and the J. J. Rousseau Institute," *Journal of Genetic Psychology*, 1925, 32:92–104. His introduction appeared, in French, in the 1923 edition of Piaget's *La Langage et la pensée chez l'enfant*.

3. Charles Blondel (1876–1939), French psychologist, specialist in social and clinical psychology; see his "The Morbid Mind," *Psyche*, 1926, 24:73–86, and *The Troubled Conscience and the Insane Mind*, London: Kegan Paul, 1928. Lucien Levy-Bruhl (1857–1939), French sociologist and author of the concept of "primitive, prelogical mentality"; his works on preconceptual forms of thinking had a great influence on Vygotsky; see L. Levy-Bruhl, *Primitive Mentality*, New York: Macmillan, 1922.

4. Franz Brentano (1838–1917), German philosopher and psychologist. See his *Psychology from the Empirical Point of View*, New York: Humanities Press, 1973.

5. Eugen Bleuler (1857–1939), Swiss psychiatrist, best known as the author of the modern concept of schizophrenia. His study of autistic thinking, *Das autistische Denken* [*Autistic Thinking*] (1912), was published in Russian as *Autisticheskoe myshlenie*, Odessa, 1927. See also his "Autistic Thinking," *American Journal of Psychiatry*, 1912/13, 69:873–886.

6. Hans Larsson (1862–1944), Swedish philosopher. Vygotsky and Piaget refer to his book *La Logique de la poesie*, Paris: Leroux, 1919.

7. Piaget comments (supplement to L. Vygotsky, *Thought and Language*, Cambridge, MA: MIT Press, 1962, pp. 4–5):

I have used the term *egocentrism* to designate the initial inability to decenter, to shift the given cognitive perspective (*manque de décentration*). It might have been better to say simply "centrism," but since the initial centering of perspective is always relative to one's own position and action, I said "egocentrism" and pointed out that the unconscious egocentrism of thought to which I referred was quite unrelated to the common meaning of the term, hypertrophy of consciousness of self. Cognitive egocentrism, as I have tried to make clear, stems from a lack of differentiation between one's own point of view and the other possible ones, and not at all from an individualism that precedes relations with others (as in the conception of Rousseau, which has been occasionally imputed to me, a surprising misapprehension, which Vygotsky to be sure did not share).

Let us turn to what most troubles Vygotsky in my conception of egocentrism: its relationship to Bleuler's concept of autism and to Freud's "pleasure principle." On the first point, Vygotsky, who is a specialist on schizophrenia, does not deny, as some of my French critics do, that a certain amount of autism is normal for all people—which my teacher Bleuler also admitted. He finds only that I have overemphasized the resemblances between egocentrism and autism without bringing out the differences sufficiently—and in this he is certainly right. I emphasized the resemblances, whose existence Vygotsky does not deny, because they seemed to me to throw light on the genesis of symbolic games in children (see *Play, Dreams and Imitation in Childhood*). In them one can often see the "nondirected and autistic thought" which Bleuler speaks of and which I have tried to explain in terms of a predominance of assimilation over accommodation in the child's early play.

As for the "pleasure principle," which Freud sees as genetically prior to the "reality principle," Vygotsky is again right when he reproaches me for having accepted this oversimplified sequence too uncritically. The fact that all behavior is adaptive and that adaptation is always some form of equilibrium (stable or unstable) between assimilation and accommodation, permits us (1) to account for the early manifestation of the pleasure principle by the affective aspect of the frequently predominating assimilation, and (2) to agree with Vygotsky's point that adaptation to reality goes hand in hand with need and pleasure, because even when assimilation predominates it is always accompanied by some accommodation.

On the other hand, I cannot follow Vygotsky when he assumes that once having separated need and pleasure from their adaptive functions (which I do not believe I ever did, or at least if I did I quickly corrected this error: see *The Origins of Intelligence in Children*), I found myself obliged to conceive of realistic or objective thought as independent of concrete needs, as a kind of pure thought which looks for proof solely for its own satisfaction. On this point, all of my subsequent work on the development of intellectual operations out of action and on the development of logical structures from the co-ordination of actions shows that I do not separate thought from behavior. It took me some time to see, it is true, that the roots of logical operations lie deeper than the linguistic connections, and that my early study of thinking was centered too much on its linguistic aspects.

8. Pierre Janet (1859–1947), French psychologist and psychiatrist, best known for his studies in hysteria and the unconscious. Janet's works had a great influence on Vygotsky, who developed Janet's thesis that children begin to use the same forms of behavior in relation to themselves that others initially used in relation to them. See Lev Vygotsky, "The Genesis of Higher Mental Functions," in James Wertsch, ed., *The Concept of Activity in Soviet Psychology*, New York: Sharpe, 1981, p. 157. For a review of Janet's theories and a bibliography of his works, see Henri Ellenberg, *The Discovery of the Unconscious*, New York: Basic Books, 1970.

9. L.V.: Taking into account the complexity of processes involved, we would reject the idea of parallelism as incorrect.

10. L.V.: This study was undertaken in cooperation with Alexander Luria, Alexei Leontiev, Roza Levina, et al. See Vygotsky et al., "The Function and Fate of Egocentric Speech," in *Proceedings of the IX International Congress of Psychology* (New Haven, 1929), Princeton: Psychological Review Co., 1930.

11. Auguste Lemaître (1857–?), French psychologist. Vygotsky refers to his work "Observations sur le langage intérieur des enfants," *Archives de psychologie*, 1905, 4:1–43.

12. L.V.: In this respect certain remarks made by Bleuler in his discussion with C. G. Jung seem to be of a great importance (see Bleuler, 1912). Bleuler mentions that autistic thinking is possible in words as well as without them. We would like to add that some research has shown that a rapid development of the autistic type of thinking in children after the age of two is directly connected with the develop-

ment of speech. It might be also mentioned that the extraordinary development of imagination in puberty is connected with the radical development of concept formation that occurs in adolescents.

13. Narziss Ach (1871–1946), German psychologist, specialist in cognitive psychology. See his "Determining Tendencies" in Jean and George Mandler, eds., *Thinking: From Association to Gestalt*, New York: Wiley, 1964.

14. Wladimir Eliasberg (1887–?), German psychologist and psychiatrist. Vygotsky is probably referring to his work *Über die autonomische Kindersprache*, Berlin: Wein, 1928.

15. Emile Durkheim (1858–1917), French sociologist. Durkheim's concept of the social origin of the categories of human consciousness had a profound influence on Vygotsky. See E. Durkheim and M. Mauss, *Primitive Classification*, Chicago: University of Chicago Press, 1967; see also *The Elementary Forms of Religious Life*, New York: Macmillan, 1915. Alexander Bogdanov (1873–1928), Russian physician, philosopher, and writer, best known as a philosophical opponent of V. I. Lenin. See his *Essays in Tectology*, Seaside, CA: Intersystems, 1980.

16. Ernst Mach (1838–1916), Austrian-German physicist and philosopher. See his *The Analysis of Sensations*, Chicago: Open Court, 1959.

17. Marta Muchow (1892–1933), German child psychologist. Vygotsky is probably referring to her work *Psychologische Probleme der früheren Erziehung*, Erfurt: K. Stenger, 1929.

18. Maria Montessori (1870–1952), Italian educationalist. See her *The Montessori Method: Scientific Pedagogy as Applied to Child Education in "The Children Houses,"* New York: Stokes, 1964.

19. Hans Volkelt (1886–1964), German child psychologist. His work *Fortschritte der experimentellen Kinderpsychologie*, Jena: Fischer, 1926, was published in Russian as *Experimentalnaja psikhologija doshkolnika*, Moscow: Gosizdat, 1930.

20. Vygotsky is quoting here from Psalms 117 : 22.

Chapter 3

1. William Stern (1871–1938), German psychologist, specialist in child psychology, applied psychology, and personality theory. For his views on child development, see *Psychology of Early Childhood up to Six Years of Age*, New York: Holt, 1930. The Russian edition of this book was published in 1922.

2. Karl Bühler (1876–1963), Austrian psychologist, specialist in child psychology and language development. See his *The Mental Development of the Child*, New York: Harcourt, 1930. All attempts to identify Reimut have been unsuccessful.

3. Henri Wallon (1879–1962), French psychologist, specialist in child and medical psychology; see his *Les Origines de la pensée chez l'enfant*, Paris: PUF, 1963. Kurt Koffka (1886–1941), German-American Gestalt psychologist; see his *The Growth of the Mind*, London: Routledge and Kegan, 1928. Henri Delacroix (1873–1937), French psychologist; Vygotsky often quotes from his *La Langage et la pensée*, Paris: Alcan, 1924.

4. Wilheim Ament (1876–?), German psychologist; Vygotsky is most probably referring to his book *Die Entwicklung von Sprechen und Denken beim Kinde*, 1899. Heinreich Idelberger (1873–?), German child psychologist; Vygotsky is probably referring to his "Hauptprobleme der kindichen Sprachentwicklung," *Zeitschrift für pädagogische Psychologie*, 1903, 5:241–297, 425–456. Ernst Meumann (1856–1931), German psychologist, specialist in child and educational psychology; see his *The Psychology of Learning*, New York: Appleton, 1913.

Chapter 4

1. Vladimir Borovsky (1882–?), Russian zoopsychologist; see his "Psychology in the USSR," *Journal of Genetic Psychology*, 1929, 2:177–186. Vladmir Vagner (1849–1934), Russian biologist, specialist in comparative psychology and physiology. Johannes Lindworsky (1875–1939), German psychologist; see his *Theoretical Psychology*, St. Louis: Herder, 1932. Erich Jaensch (1883–1940), German psychologist; see his *Eidetic Imagery and Typological Methods of Investigation*, London: Paul, Trench and Traubner, 1927.

2. Leonard Hobhous (1864–1929), British zoologist and philosopher. Vygotsky is most probably referring to his book *Mind in Evolution*, New York: Macmillan, 1901.

3. Gustav Kafka (1883–1953), German psychologist.

4. L.V.: Hempelmann, while rejecting the possibility of any other function for animal speech beyond the expressive one, admits, nevertheless, that vocal warning signals produced by animals objectively play a communicative function. See F. Hempelmann, *Tierpsychologie vom Stundpunkte des Biologen*, Leipzig: Akademische Verlag, 1926, p. 530.

5. Karl von Frisch (1886–?), Austrian zoopsychologist, best known for his studies in the language of bees. See his *Bees: Their Vision, Chemical Senses, and Language,* Ithaca: Cornell University Press, 1950.

6. Charlotte Bühler (1893–1974), Austrian psychologist, wife and collaborator of Karl Bühler. Hildegard Hetzer and Beatrix Tudor-Hart belonged to Ch. Bühler's research group; see their book *The First Year of Life,* New york: Day, 1930.

7. Kurt Koffka (1886–1941), German-American Gestalt psychologist. See his *The Growth of the Mind,* London: Routledge and Kegan Paul, 1928.

8. Vygotsky refers here to his studies in the development of higher mental functions. See his *Mind in Society,* Cambridge, MA: Harvard University Press, 1978; see also section II of my introduction.

9. George Plekhanov (1856–1918), Russian philosopher-Marxist. See his *Essays in the History of Materialism,* London: Lane, 1934.

L.V.: Apparently what we see in the chimpanzee is not an instinctive use of objects, but some primordial intellectual operations with them. Plekhanov mentions that the very fact of the use of tools presupposes highly developed intelligence (Plekhanov, 1922, p. 138).

10. L.V.: Engels also mention that "we are not going to deny the ability of animals to carry out purposive actions." From Engels's point of view, the elementary forms of purposeful activity are present where there is a protoplasm, where proteins act and react. But this purposeful activity reaches its highest point of development in mammals" (Engels, 1925, p. 101).

11. L.V.: In another place Engels remarks that content of animal communication is such that it can be transmitted without words. At the same time pets, according to Engels, may have a *need* to speak. Their articulatory apparatus, however, in most cases, except in the case of parrots, precludes the realization of this need.

12. L.V.: The status of speech in animals, remarks Bastian Schmid, cannot be used as a measure of their behavior or intelligence. With respect to speech, chickens and pigs are more *advanced* animals than horses or elephants. See B. Schmid, *Die Sprache und andere Ansdrucksformen der Tiere,* Munich: Rösl, 1923, p. 46.

13. The cultural-historical approach to human thought and speech was in part carried out in studies described in chapters 5–7 of this book. See also Vygotsky's *Mind in Society,* Cambridge, MA: Harvard University Press, 1978.

Chapter 5

1. Dmitri Uznadze (1886–1950), founder of the Georgian school of psychology, best known as the author of psychological "set theory." Vygotsky refers to his work "Vyrabotka poniatii v doshkolnom vozraste" ["Concept Formation in Pre-School Children"], which was first published in German translation as "Die Begriffsbildung im vorschulpfischtigen Alter," *Zeitschrift für angewandte Psychologie*, 1929, 34:138–212, and later in the original language in 1966.

2. Since Vygotsky does not describe the test in detail, referring instead to Lev Sakharov's work, I take the liberty of inserting here the description given in E. Hanfmann and J. Kasanin (1942, pp. 9–10).

3. Sir Francis Galton's (1822–1911) "composite photographs" were intended to present the image of the statistically average person. Pictures of a number of people were taken with the help of one and the same photographic plate. As a result, divergent features mutually eliminated each other, while common features amplifying each other produced a composite portrait of the average man.

4. Pavel Blonsky (1884–1941), Russian philosopher, psychologist and educator. In the 1920s he was one of the leading Soviet child psychologists. On his career and views, see Alex Kozulin, *Psychology in Utopia*, Cambridge, MA: MIT Press, 1984, pp. 121–136.

5. Heinz Werner (1890–1964), German-American psychologist, specialist in developmental psychology. His views on mental development closely resembled those of Vygotsky. See his *Comparative Psychology of Mental Development*, New York: Science Editions, 1965.

6. The following elaboration of the experimental observations is taken from the study by E. Hanfmann and J. Kasanin (1942, pp. 30–31):

In many cases the group, or groups, created by the subject have quite the same appearance as in a consistent classification, and the lack of a true conceptual foundation is not revealed until the subject is required to put in operation the ideas that underlie this grouping. This happens at the moment of correction when the examiner turns one of the wrongly selected blocks and shows that the word written on it is different from the one on the sample block, e.g., that it is not *mur*. This is one of the critical points of the experiment. . . .

Subjects who have approached the task as a classification problem respond to correction immediately in a perfectly specific way. This response is adequately expressed in the statement, "Aha! Then it is not color" (or shape, etc). . . . The subject removes all the blocks he had placed with the sample one, and starts looking for another possible classification.

On the other hand, the outward behavior of the subject at the beginning of the experiment may have been that of attempting a classification. He may have placed all red blocks with the sample, proceeding quite consistently . . . and declared that he thinks those red blocks are the *murs*. Now the examiner turns up one of the chosen blocks and shows that it has a different name. . . . The subject sees it removed or even obediently removes it himself, but that is all he does; he makes no attempt to remove the other red blocks from the sample *mur*. To the examiner's question if he still thinks that those blocks belong together, and are *mur*, he answers definitely, "Yes, they still belong together because they are red." This striking reply betrays an attitude totally incompatible with a true classification approach and proves that the groups he had formed were actually pseudo-classes.

7. Vygotsky's discussion of the phenomenon of pseudoconcepts has far-reaching philosophical implications. First of all, if the conscious awareness of one's own intellectual operations ("concept-for-me") is only a secondary achievement, which follows the practical use of these operations, then the individual cannot be considered a self-conscious center of activity. The individual appears rather as a "construction" built at the crossroads of the inner and outer realities. Second, the phenomenon of functional equivalence between real and pseudoconcepts warns us against taking the functional appearance of communication for its ultimate content. The usage of "one and the same" words and subsequent "understanding" may be illusory. Such illusion of understanding, based on the confusion between functional and essential characteristics, constantly emerges in child-adult communication, in the dialogue between different social groups, and in contacts between different cultures. For further discussion of this point, see Alex Kozulin, "Psychology and Philosophical Anthropology: The Problem of Their Interaction," *The Philosophical Forum*, 1984, 15(4):443–458.

8. Alfred Storch (1888–?), German psychiatrist who elaborated parallels in the thinking of schizophrenics and primitive peoples. See his *The Primitive Archaic Forms of Inner Experience and Thought in Schizophrenia*, New York: NMDP, 1924.

9. Karl von Steinen (1855–1929), German explorer and anthropologist. See his *Unter den Naturvölkern Zentral-Brasiliens*, Berlin: Reimer, 1894.

10. A study of preconceptual thinking in traditional society was undertaken by Vygotsky's follower Alexander Luria. See his *Cognitive Development*, Cambridge, MA: Harvard University Press, 1976.

11. For a study of preconceptual thought in schizophrenics carried out from a point of view very close to that of Vygotsky, see H. Werner and B. Kaplan, *Symbol Formation*, New York: Wiley, 1963, chapter 18.

12. Richard Thurnwald (1869–1954), British anthropologist.

13. Alexander Potebnja (1835–1891), Russian linguist, follower of Humboldt. Potebnja's ideas, particularly the concept of "inner form of the word," seriously influenced Vygotsky. Even the title of Vygotsky's book echoes that of Potebnja's: *Mysl' i iazyk* [*Thought and Language*], 1862.

14. Ernst Kretschmer (1888–1964), German psychiatrist and psychologist. See his *Text-book of Medical Psychology*, London: Hogarth, 1952.

15. Karl Groos (1861–1946), German psychologist, specialist in child psychology. See his *The Play of Man*, New York: Appleton, 1901.

16. Oswald Kroh (1887–1955), German child psychologist. Vygotsky is probably referring to his paper "Intellektualnoe razvitie v period sozrevaniia" ["Intellectual Development in Adolescence"], in I. Ariamov, ed., *Pedologiia Junosti* [*Pedology of Youth*], Moscow, 1931.

17. August Messer (1867–1937), German psychologist. Vygotsky is probably referring to either "Experimentell-psychologische Untersuchungen über das Denken," *Arch. ges. Psychol*, 1906, 8:1–224, or *Empfindung und Denken,* Leipzig: Quelle and Meyer, 1908.

18. L.V.: Kretschmer mentions that those forms of primitive thinking are called complex, because they consist of conglomerates of images that are easily mutually replaceable. All of the above-mentioned authors perceive complex reasoning as a "primitive imagery stage in the development of concepts."

19. Peter Vogel (1887–?), German psychologist. Vygotsky is probably referring to his dissertation "Untersuchungen über die Denkbeziehungen in den Urteilen des Schulkindes," Giessen, 1911.

Chapter 6

1. Zhozephina Shif (1905–1977), Soviet psychologist, student and collaborator of Vygotsky. See her *Razvitie zhiteiskikh i nauchnykh poniatii* [*Development of Spontaneous and Scientific Concepts*], Moscow, 1935.

2. Piaget comments (supplement to L. Vygotsky, *Thought and Language,* Cambridge, MA: MIT Press, 1962, p. 9):

It was a real joy to me to discover from Vygotsky's book the way in which he approves of my having distinguished, for study purposes, between spontaneous and nonspontaneous concepts: one could have feared that a psychologist intent on the problems of school learning much more than we are might have tended to underestimate the part of the continuous structuring processes in the child's developing mental activity. It is true that when Vygotsky later charges me with having overstressed this distinction, I said to myself at first that he was taking away from me what he had just granted. But when he states his criticism more explicitly, saying that nonspontaneous concepts, too, receive an "imprint" of the child's mentality in the process of their acquisition and that an "interaction" of spontaneous and learned concepts must therefore be admitted, I once more felt in complete accord with him. Vygotsky in fact misunderstands me when he thinks that from my point of view the child's spontaneous thought must be known by educators only as an enemy must be known to be fought successfully. In all of my pedagogical writings, old [*Encyclopédie française,* article "*Education nouvelle*"] or recent [*"Le Droit à l'éducation,"* in *Droits de l'homme* (UNESCO)], I have, on the contrary, insisted that formal education could gain a great deal, much more than ordinary methods do at present, from a systematic utilization of the child's spontaneous mental development.

3. In his paper "On Psychological Systems" (1930), Vygotsky explained that "studying the development of thought and speech in childhood, we found that the process of their development depends not so much on the changes within these two functions, but rather on changes in the primary relations between them. . . . Their relations and connections do not remain constant. That is why the leading idea is that there is no constant formula of relation between thought and speech that would be applicable to all stages and forms of development or involution. Each of these stages has its own characteristic form of relation between these two functions" (Vygotsky, *Collected Papers,* vol. 1, 1980, p. 110). See also *Pedologiia podrostka* [*Pedology of the Adolescent*], in volume 4 of the *Collected Papers,* pp. 111–199.

4. Johannes Herbart (1776–1841), German philosopher, psychologist, and educationalist. See his *Outlines of Educational Doctrine,* New York: Macmillan, 1901.

5. L.V.: See the M.A. theses of these students of the Leningrad Herzen Teachers College: Arsenieva, Zabolotnova, Kanushina, Chanturia, Efes, Neifets, et al.

6. John Hulings Jackson (1835–1911), British neuropsychologist, the author of the concept of "vertical organization" of brain functions. Henry Head (1861–1940), British neuropsychologist who developed Jackson's ideas, particularly in their application to aphasia; see his *Aphasia and Kindred Disorders of Speech,* Cambridge: Cambridge University Press, 1926.

7. The concept of "zone of proximal development" was successfully adopted by some American psychologists. See B. Rogoff and J. Wertsch eds., *Children's Learning in the Zone of Proximal Development,* San Francisco: Jossey Bass, 1984.

8. Piaget comments (supplement to L. Vygotsky, *Thought and Language*, Cambridge, MA: MIT Press, 1962, pp. 11–12):

All this raises at least two problems, which Vygotsky formulates, but in the solution of which we differ somewhat. The first concerns the "interaction of spontaneous and nonspontaneous concepts." This interaction is more complex than Vygotsky believes. In some cases, what is transmitted by instruction is well assimilated by the child because it represents in fact an extension of some spontaneous constructions of his own. In such cases, his development is accelerated. But in other cases, the gifts of instruction are presented too soon or too late, or in a manner that precludes assimilation because it does not fit in with the child's spontaneous constructions. Then the child's development is impeded, or even deflected into barrenness, as so often happens in the teaching of the exact sciences. Therefore I do not believe, as Vygotsky seems to do, that new concepts, even at school level, are always acquired through adult didactic intervention. This may occur, but there is a much more productive form of instruction: the so-called "active" schools endeavor to create situations that, while not "spontaneous" in themselves, evoke spontaneous elaboration on the part of the child, if one manages both to spark his interest and to present the problem in such a way that it corresponds to the structures he had already formed himself.

The second problem, which is really an extension of the first on a more general level, is the relation between spontaneous concepts and scientific notions as such. In Vygotsky's system, the "key" to this problem is that "scientific and spontaneous concepts start from different points but eventually meet." On this point we are in complete accord, if he means that a true meeting takes place between the sociogenesis of scientific notions (in the history of science and in the transmission of knowledge from one generation to the next) and the psychogenesis of "spontaneous" structures (influenced, to be sure, by interaction with the social, familial, scholastic, etc., milieu), and not simply that psychogenesis is entirely determined by the historical and the ambient culture. I think that in putting it thus I am not making Vygotsky say more than he did, since he admits the part of spontaneity in development. It remains to determine wherein that part consists.

9. L.V.: In our studies, we observed this phenomenon in the development of historical concepts from the elementary generalization "now and then," and also as the development of sociological notions from the elementary generalization "ours and theirs."

10. Max Wertheimer (1880–1943), German-American Gestalt psychologist. See his *Productive Thinking*, New York: Harper, 1945.

11. Piaget comments (supplement to L. Vygotsky, *Thought and Language*, Cambridge, MA: MIT Press, 1962, pp. 12–14):

It is on this question of the nature of spontaneous activities that there still remains, perhaps, some divergence between Vygotsky and myself, but this difference is merely an extension of the one we noted concerning egocentrism and the role of decentering in the progress of mental development.

With respect to time lag in the emergence of conscious awareness we are pretty much in agreement, except that Vygotsky does not believe that lack of awareness is a residue of egocentrism. Let us look at the solution he proposes: (1) the late development of awareness must be simply the result of the well-known "law" according to which awareness and control appear only at the end point of the development of a function; (2) awareness at first is limited to the results of actions and only later extends to the "how," i.e., the operation itself. Both assertions are correct, but they merely state the facts without explaining them. The explanation begins when one understands that a subject whose perspective is determined by his action has no reason for becoming aware of anything except its results; decentering, on the other hand, i.e., shifting one's focus and comparing one action with other possible ones, particularly with the actions of other people, leads to an awareness of "how" and to true operations.

This difference in perspective between a simple linear schema like Vygotsky's and a schema of decentering is even more evident in the question of the principal motor of intellectual development. It would seem that, according to Vygotsky (though of course I do not know the rest of his work), the principal factor is to be sought in the "generalization of perceptions," the process of generalization being sufficient in itself to bring mental operations into consciousness. We, on the other hand, in studying the spontaneous development of scientific notions, have come to view as the central factor the very process of constructing operations, which consists in interiorized actions becoming reversible and co-ordinating themselves into patterns of structures subject to well-defined laws. The progress of generalization is only the result of this elaboration of operational structures, and these structures derive not from perception but from the total action.

Vygotsky himself was close to such a solution when he held that syncretism, juxtaposition, insensibility to contradiction, and other characteristics of the developmental level which we call today *preoperational* (in preference to *prelogical*), were all due to the lack of a system; for the organization of systems is in fact the most essential achievement marking the child's transition to the level of logical reasoning. But these systems are not simply the product of generalization: they are multiple and differentiated operational structures, whose gradual elaboration by the child we have learned to follow step by step.

A small example of this difference in our points of view is provided by Vygotsky's comment on class inclusion. In reading it, one gets the impression that the child discovers inclusion by a combination of generalization and learning: in learning to use the words *rose* and then *flower*, he first juxtaposes them, but as soon as he makes the generalization "all roses are flowers" and discovers that the converse is not true, he realizes that the class of roses is included in the class of flowers. Having studied such problems at first hand [Piaget and Szeminska,

The Child's Conception of Number, chapter VIII, and Inhelder and Piaget, *La Genèse des opérations logiques élémentaires,* Delachaux et Niestlé], we know how much more complex the question is. Even if he asserts that all roses are flowers and that not all flowers are roses, a child at first is unable to conclude that there are more flowers than roses. To achieve the inclusion, he has to organize an operational system such that A (roses) + A' (flowers other than roses) = B (flowers) and that A = B − A', consequently A < B; the reversibility of this system is a prerequisite for inclusion.

I have not discussed in this commentary the question of socialization as a condition of intellectual development, although Vygotsky raises it several times. From my present point of view, my earlier formulations are less relevant because the consideration of the operations and of the decentering involved in the organization of operational structures makes the issue appear in a new light. All logical thought is socialized because it implies the possibility of communication between individuals. But such interpersonal exchange proceeds through correspondences, reunions, intersections, and reciprocities, i.e., through operations. Thus there is identity between intra individual operations and the inter individual operations which constitute *co-operation* in the proper and quasi-etymological sense of the word. Actions, whether individual or interpersonal, are in essence co-ordinated and organized by the operational structures which are spontaneously constructed in the course of mental development.

Chapter 7

1. Osip Mandelstam (1891–1938), Russian poet. Vygotsky used as epigraph one of the early versions of Mandelstam's poem "Swallow." Some other images from the same poem, like "Stygian shadow," appear, quoted as well as unquoted, in Vygotsky's text. One may also find in Vygotsky's work some ideas developed by Mandelstam in his paper "On the Nature of Word"—see O. Mandelstam, *Selected Essays,* Austin: University of Texas Press, 1977.

2. The problem of analysis into elements versus analysis into units is the subject of Vladimir Zinchenko, "Vygotsky's Ideas about Units for the Analysis of Mind," in J. Wertsch, ed., *Culture, Communication, and Cognition: Vygotskian Perspectives,* New York: Cambridge University Press, 1985.

3. Otto Selz (1881–1943), German psychologist. See Nico Frijda and Adrian de Groot, eds., *Otto Selz: His Contribution to Psychology,* The Hague: Mouton, 1982.

4. Hermann Paul (1846–1921), German linguist. See his *Principles of the History of Language,* College Park, MD: McGrath, 1970.

5. Ivan Sechenov (1829–1905), Russian physiologist, the founder of

Russian reflexology; see his *Reflexes of the Brain,* Cambridge, MA: MIT Press, 1965. Vladimir Bekhterev (1857–1927), Russian physiologist and psychiatrist, pioneer in the study of associative reflexes in men; see his *General Principles of Human Reflexology,* New York: International Publishers, 1932.

6. Kurt Goldstein (1878–1965), German-American neuropsychologist. Vygotsky is most probably referring to his work *Über Aphasie,* Zurich: Orell Füssli, 1927, and "Die patologischen Tatsachen in ihrer Bedeutung für das Problem der Sprache," *Deutsche Gesellschaft für Psychologie, Kongress,* 1932, 12:145–164; see also his *Language and Language Disturbances,* New York: Grune and Stratton, 1947.

7. Abraham Anton Grünbaum (1885–1932), German psychologist. Vygotsky is probably referring to his work "Die Struktur der Kinderpsyche," *Zeitschrift für padagogische Psychologie,* 1927, 28:446–463.

8. L.V.: These findings were reported by L. Vygotsky et al., "The Function and Fate of Egocentric Speech," *Proceedings of the Ninth International Congress of Psychology* (New Haven, 1929), Princeton: Psychological Review Co., 1930.

9. Piaget comments (supplement to L. Vygotsky, *Thought and Language,* Cambridge, MA: MIT Press, 1962, pp. 6–8):

Before returning to Vygotsky, I should like to set forth myself what seems to me to remain significant in the positive and negative evidence gathered by my few followers and my many opponents.

1. The measurement of egocentric speech has shown that there are very great environmental and situational variations, so that contrary to my initial hopes we do not possess in these measures a valid gauge of intellectual egocentrism or even of verbal egocentrism.

2. The phenomenon itself, whose relative frequency at different developmental levels we had wanted to test, as well as its decline with age, has never been disputed because it has seldom been understood. When viewed in terms of a distorting centering on one's own action and of subsequent decentering, this phenomenon proved much more significant in the study of actions themselves and of their interiorization in the form of mental operations than in the field of language. It still remains possible, however, that a more systematic study of children's discussions, and especially of behavior directed at verification and proof (and accompanied by speech), may furnish valid metric indices.

This long preamble has seemed necessary to bring out how much I respect Vygotsky's position on the issue of egocentric speech, even though I cannot agree with him on all points. First, Vygotsky did realize that a real problem was involved, and not merely a question of statistics. Second, he himself verified the facts in question, instead of suppressing them through the artifices of measuring; and his observations on the frequency of egocentric speech in children when their activity is blocked and on the decrease of such speech during the period when inner speech begins to form are of very great interest. In the third place, he proposed a new hypothesis: that egocentric speech is the point of departure for the development of inner speech, which is found at a later stage of development, and that this interiorized language can serve both autistic ends and logical thinking. I find myself in complete agreement with these hypotheses.

On the other hand, what I think Vygotsky still failed to appreciate fully is egocentrism itself as the main obstacle to the co-ordination of viewpoints and to co-operation. Vygotsky reproaches me correctly for not emphasizing sufficiently from the start the functional aspect of these questions. Granted, but I did emphasize it later on. In *The Moral Judgment of the Child*, I studied children's group games (marbles, etc.) and noted that before the age of seven they do not know how to co-ordinate the rules during a game, so that each one plays for himself, and all win, without understanding that the point is competition. R. F. Nielsen, who has studied collaborative activities (building together, etc.) found *in the field of action itself* all the characteristics which I have emphasized with respect to speech. [R. F. Nielsen, *La Sociabilité chez l'enfant*, Delachaux et Niestlé]. Thus there exists a general phenomenon which it seems to me Vygotsky has neglected.

In brief, when Vygotsky concludes that the early function of language must be that of global communication and that later speech becomes differentiated into egocentric and communicative proper, I believe I agree with him. But when he maintains that these two linguistic forms are equally socialized and differ only in function, I cannot go along with him because the word *socialization* becomes ambiguous in this context: if an individual A mistakenly believes that an individual B thinks the way A does, and if he does not manage to understand the difference between the two points of view, this is, to be sure, social behavior in the sense that there is contact between the two, but I call such behavior unadapted from the point of view of intellectual co-operation. This point of view is the only aspect of the problem which has concerned me but which does not seem to have interested Vygotsky.

In his excellent work on twins, R. Zazzo formulates the problem clearly [R. Zazzo, *Les Jumeaux, le couple et la personne*, vol. II, p. 399]. According to him, the difficulty in the notion of egocentric speech arises from a confusion of two meanings which he feels I should have separated: (*a*) speech incapable of rational reciprocity, and (*b*) speech that is "not meant for others." But the fact is that from the standpoint of intellectual co-operation, which alone interested me, these two amount to the same thing. As far as I know I have never spoken of speech "not meant for others"; this would have been misleading, for I have always recognized that the child thinks he is talking to others and is making himself understood. My view is simply that in egocentric speech the child talks *for* himself (in the sense in which a lecturer may speak "for himself" alone, even though he naturally intends his words for the audience). Zazzo, citing a passage of mine which is actually quite clear, answers me seriously that the child does not speak "for himself" but "according to himself," (*selon lui*). . . . Granted! Let us replace "for himself" by "according to himself" in all of my writings. I still think this would change nothing in the only valid meaning of egocentrism: the lack of decentering, of the ability to shift mental perspective, in social relationships as well as in others. Moreover, I think that it is precisely co-operation with others (on the cognitive plane) that teaches us to speak "according" to others and not simply from our own point of view.

10. Evgeni Polivanov (1891–1938), Russian linguist; see his *Selected Works*, The Hague: Mouton, 1974. Lev Jakubinsky (1892–1945), Russian linguist; Vygotsky is most probably referring to his "O dialogicheskoi rechi" ["On Verbal Dialogue"], *Russkaia rech*, no. 1, Petrograd, 1923; this paper was translated by Jane Knox and published in the November issue of *Dispositio*, Ann Arbor: University of Michigan Press, 1979.

11. Wilhelm von Humboldt (1767–1835), German linguist, the author of the concept of the "inner form of speech." See *Humanist without Portfolio: An Anthology of the Writings of Wilhelm von Humboldt*, Detroit: Wayne State University Press, 1963.

12. Frederic Paulhan (1856–1931), French psychologist. Vygotsky is most probably referring to his paper "Qu'est-ce le sens des mots?" *Journal de psychologie*, 1928, 25:289–329.

13. Konstantin Stanislavsky (1863–1938), Russian stage director and theoretician of the theater. His notes for actors connected with the production of *Woe from Wit* are published in *Creating a Role*, New York: Theater Art Books, 1961.

14. Velemir Khlebnikov (1885–1922), Russian poet-futurist, innovator of language. See his *Snake Train: Poetry and Prose*, Ann Arbor: Ardis, 1976.

References

Ach, N., *Ueber die Begriffsbildung,* Bamberg: Buhner, 1921.

Bleuler, E., "Autistische Denken," *Jahrbuch fur psychoanalytische und psychopatologische Forschung,* 1912. Russian: *Autisticheskoe myshlenie,* Odessa, 1927.

Borovsky, V., *Vvedenie v sravnitelnuiu psikhologiiu* [*Introduction to Comparative Psychology*], Moscow: Gosizdat, 1927.

Bühler, Ch., Hetzer, H., and Tudor-Hart, B., *Sociologische und psychologische Studien über das erste Lebensjahr,* Jena: Fischer, 1927.

Bühler, K., *Abriss der geistigen Entwicklung des Kindes,* Leipzig: Quelle and Meyer, 1919.

Bühler, K., *The Mental Development of the Child,* New York: Harcourt Brace, 1930.

Claparède, E., "Introduction" to J. Piaget, *The Language and Thought of the Child,* London: Routledge and Kegan Paul, 1959.

Delacroix, H., *La Langage et la pensée,* Paris: Alcan, 1924.

Engels, F., *Dialektika prirody* [*Dialectics of Nature*], Moscow, 1925.

Frisch, K. von, "Über die 'Sprache' der Bieren," *Zoologische Jahrbuch* (Physiologie), 1923, no. 40.

Gesell, A., *Infancy and Human Growth,* New York: Macmillian, 1929.

Groos, K., *Das Seeleleben des Kindes,* Berlin: Reuther and Reichard, 1913.

Hanfmann, E., and Kasanin, J., *Conceptual Thinking in Schizophrenia,* New York: NMDM, 1942.

Kafka, G., *Handbuch der vergleichenden Psychologie,* vol. I, part 1, Munchen: Reinhardt, 1922.

Koffka, K., *Grundlagen der psychischen Entwicklung*, Osterwieck am Harz: Zickfeld, 1925.

Köhler, W., *Intelligenzpruefungen au Menschenaffen*, Berlin: Springer, 1921.

Köhler, W., *The Mentality of Apes*, London: Routledge and Kegen Paul, 1973.

Kulpe, O., "Sovremennaia psikhologiia myshleniia" ["Contemporary Psychology of Thinking"], in *Novye idei v filosofii*, 1914, no. 16.

Lemaître, A., "Observations sur le langage intericur des enfants," *Archives de psychologie*, 1905, no. 4, 1–43.

Lenin, V. I., *Philosophical Notebooks*, Moscow: Progress, 1961.

Levy-Bruhl, L., *Les Fonctions mentales dans les sociétés inférieures*, Paris: Alcan, 1918.

Marx, K., *Kapital [Capital]*, vol. 1, Moscow, 1920.

Meumann, E., "Die Entstehung der ersten Wortbedeutungen deim Kinde," in *Philosophische Studien*, 1902, 20.

Piaget, J., *La Causalité physique chez l'enfant*, Paris: Alcan, 1927.

Piaget, J., *Rech in myshlenie rebenka [The Language and Thought of the Child]*, Moscow: Gosizdat, 1932.

Piaget, J., "Psychologie de l'enfant et l'enseignement de l'histoire," *Bulletin trimestriel de la Conférence internationale pour l'enseignement de l'histoire*, 1933, no. 2.

Piaget, J., *The Language and Thought of the Child*, London: Routledge and Kegan Paul, 1959.

Piaget, J., *Judgment and Reasoning in the Child*, London: Routledge and Kegan Paul, 1969.

Plekhanov, G., *Ocherki po istorii materializama [Essays in the History of Materialism]*, Moscow, 1922.

Rimat, F., *Intelligenzunterersuchungen anschliessend an die Ach'sche Suchmethode*, Göttingen: Calvoer, 1925.

Sakharov, L., "O metodakh issledovaniia poniatii" ["Methods of Studying Concepts"], *Psikhologiia*, vol. 3, no. 1, 1930.

Sapir, E., *Language*, London: Ruppert Hart Davis, 1971.

Stern, C. and W., *Die Kindersprache*, Leipzig: Barth, 1928.

Stern, W., *Person und Sache*, vol. I, Leipzig: Barth, 1905.

Stern, W., *Psychologie der fruehen Kindheit*, Leipzig: Quelle and Meyer, 1914.

Storch, A., *The Primitive Archaic Forms of Inner Experience and Thought in Schizophrenia,* New York: NMDP, 1924.

Thorndike, E., *The Mental Life of the Monkeys,* New York: Macmillan, 1901.

Tolstoy, L., *Pedagogicheskie statli [Pedagogical Writings],* Moscow: Kushnerev, 1903.

Uspensky, G., *Izbrannye proizvedeniia [Collected Works],* Moscow, 1949.

Uznadze, D., "Vyrabotka poniatii v doshkolnom vozraste" [Concept Formation in Pre-School Children"], in D. Uznadze, *Psikhologicheskie issledovaniia [Psychological Investigations],* Moscow: Nauka, 1966.

Volkelt, H., *Fortschritte der experimentallen Kinderpsychologie,* 1926. Russian: *Eksperimentalnaia psikhologiia doshkolnika,* Moscow: Gosizdat, 1930.

Watson, J. B., *Psychology from the Standpoint of a Behaviorist,* Philadelphia: Lippincott, 1919.

Werner, H., *Einfuehrung in die Entwicklungspsychologie,* Leipzig: Barth, 1926.

Wundt, W., *Volkerpsychologie,* vol. I: *Die Sprache,* Leipzig: Engelmann, 1900.

Yerkes, R., "The Mental Life of Monkeys and Apes," in *Behavioral Monographs,* vol. 3, no. 1, 1916.

Yerkes, R., and Learned, B. W., *Chimpanzee Intelligence and Its Vocal Expression,* Baltimore: Williams and Wilkins, 1925.

Index